Making Up Society

Making Up Society
The Novels
of
George Eliot

Philip Fisher

UNIVERSITY OF PITTSBURGH PRESS

Published by the University of Pittsburgh Press, Pittsburgh, Pa. 15260
Copyright © 1981, University of Pittsburgh Press
Feffer and Simons, Inc., London
Manufactured in the United States of America

Library of Congress Cataloging in Publication Data

Fisher, Philip
  Making up society.

  Includes index.
    1. Eliot, George, 1819–1880—Criticism and interpretation. 2. Eliot,
George, 1819–1880—Political and social views. 3. Literature and society.
I. Title.
PR4688.F5   823'.8   81-4909
ISBN 0-8229-3800-6   AACR2

Excerpts from "Esthetique du Mal" by Wallace Stevens, from *The Collected
Poems of Wallace Stevens*, copyright © 1954, are quoted by permission of
Alfred A. Knopf, Inc.

To my parents,
Anna Walker Fisher and Leo Fisher

Contents

All references to Eliot's work are to the Personal Edition (New York: Doubleday, 1901) and will be indicated by volume and page after the quotation.

Making Up Society

1

George Eliot and
the Social Novel

Not every writer sets out to imagine society. Every work does imply a society, even in the limiting case where what it implies is that the public life is irrelevant, but to have the social component of reality as a goal, particularly in the novel, commits a writer to problems of both craft and thought. To imagine society implies that the public plane of our experience is in itself coherent, or, if obscure in part, at least legible on the whole. We read it as we read a handwriting where many letters cannot be deciphered, yet every sentence and, particularly, the drift of the whole can be understood. At the limit, society imposes the obligation on even the most interior or recalcitrant of events to take place in the terms of the community, to translate themselves, as passion does into marriage, into public forms to which the self feels as loyal as, or even more loyal than, it does to the source in private need and satisfaction. To imagine society is to imagine the possibility of this translation. Equally, it is to imagine that the moral life, with its vocabulary, can be viably interpreted by institutions, preserved in those impersonal forms of behavior we call customs, and made visible in the social drama of ceremony. Finally, it is to believe, or at least to hope, that the public judgments of criminal and hero, good man or pariah, stand close on the whole to the moral truth. Where this is possible we know that the truth about life must be consensual and not the reward of unique, personal quests; not the property of genius or of those who have lived in extremity, but close at hand, visible in the central relations and frictions of the everyday community.

This book is a study of the loss of society as a premise for the social novel. Consequently, it is also a study of the strategies for retaining the shaping effects of social demands in individual moral life once society itself has been lost as a moral term. By loss of society is meant the loss of faith in the way public life, the life of the community, registers, embodies, and interprets moral history. As the trust in community as a base of moral life weakens, decisive changes occur in the form of the social novel as it accommodates itself to the disappearance of society and to the change from the representation of individuals within a community to the description of selves surrounded by collections of unrelated others.

Many individual moments in the history of the social novel are decisive, but the novels of George Eliot restate the earlier terms of the problem, then risk a crucial experimentation with novelistic form that points toward the work of the modern writers who follow her. Eliot developed from a writer of social novels to a writer of social fictions. In her first triumphant phase she wrote, in rapid succession, three classic social novels: an epic and panoramic novel of society in *Adam Bede*, a social novel in the biographical form in *The Mill On the Floss*, and a mythic parable of society in *Silas Marner*. In each work, society is tested and affirmed in spite of its more and more puzzling and oblique distortions of individual moral histories. In her later works, Eliot no longer saw the community as a homeland chosen in those absolute moral situations where the only alternatives are, on the one hand, exile and isolation, and, on the other, full membership. Instead, she came to picture the social world as an ongoing invention, as, in many ways, science is—a collective, imaginative act that is proposed and tested piecemeal, defeated or established much as hypotheses are, maintained and revised continually by the common force of individual acts of choice and judgment.

5
George Eliot and the Social Novel

In two of her late novels, *Romola* and *Daniel Deronda*, she created heroic figures. Savonarola and Daniel Deronda individually make up society, as utopian thinkers do, or—a far more important parallel—as authors do. In both novels, Eliot herself is making up an entire world: that of Florence in the 1490s and that of the Jews in Europe and London. Savonarola attempts to revive his society by recalling Florence and Christianity to its authentic past just as Eliot, by writing the novel, is recalling her own countrymen to the Renaissance roots of their own civilization. Deronda, as an early Zionist beginning to create the concrete national world for Jews, repeats Eliot's own act as an author who writes of Jewish life in order to create, for the first time, a representational space for Jews like the one created in America for blacks by Mrs. Stowe's *Uncle Tom's Cabin*.

However, since the essence of even hypothetical societies rests on their being collective rather than individual, it is in *Middlemarch* that Eliot wrote her single great social fiction. Here the fictions, reputations, and possibilities are a shared invention. In *Middlemarch*, society is a hypothetical reality that is the responsibility and trust of every individual. Just as medicine is only the inventions, theories of disease, common beliefs (many of them incorrect), practices, and instruments of the present living set of doctors, so too the social fabric is made up both of and by individuals. Individuals author one another and authorize one another's acts. In *Middlemarch*, the characters make of living a social art because in living together they literally make one another up.

Throughout Eliot's later work, she alternated between a heroic, even apocalyptic, version of social fiction and a patient, collective version for which science and not art is the central parallel. The heroic and individual invention of fictions has as its models the artist and, more decisively, the liar. The morally troubling place of art in all of Eliot's works does not come simply from a moralizing fear of beauty. Rather, it has its source in the deep link she had created between the everyday acts of authorship and authority, by

Making Up Society

means of which social reality and personal identity are invented and then maintained, and the single-handed generation of the whole world of meaning for which the author of a novel is the central model, but for which, in actual life, the demagogue, the liar, the prophet, the madman, and the isolated scholar with his Key To All Mythologies are the telling instances.

In the titles of Eliot's novels lies a statement of one feature of the problem of the social novel. Five novels are named for the hero: *Adam Bede, Silas Marner, Romola, Felix Holt,* and *Daniel Deronda.* The two greatest novels are named for the community: *The Mill on the Floss* and *Middlemarch.* What is at stake is the way in which the public and private honor or ironize each other and the extent to which inner experience repeats the forms stabilized within social life. In each of Eliot's novels, one motif for the growing difficulty of accommodation between private moral histories and community forms is the relation between individual transgression and the subsequent trials and judgments the community imposes as it discovers and then mobilizes itself in the face of the transgression. All of Eliot's novels include trials, but only *Adam Bede* and *Felix Holt* conclude with formal court procedures, and, even in these two cases, an intervention by magic prevents the court from acting as we know it would. The whole of *Silas Marner* occurs as the life of a man after an unjust trial and banishment. Both *The Mill on the Floss* and *Middlemarch* conclude with the more devastating informal trials by rumor and community shunning. At the climax of *Romola,* Savonarola is tried as a heretic and burned at the stake, and in *Daniel Deronda* the moral circumstances in which Gwendolyn withholds rescue from her drowning husband are so complex that only the private trial before the moral authority of Deronda can occur. With the exception of *Felix Holt,* the trials become increasingly mysterious and inadequate to the issues of truth, responsibility, and atonement. The private moral fact eludes the social form and is ironized or betrayed by it.

7
George Eliot and the Social Novel

For Eliot, her experiments with different forms of the novel—
and from *Adam Bede* to *Daniel Deronda* she shows an almost
restless unwillingness to repeat the social form—amount to an
exploration using different lenses for the representation of society
and a search for a form loyal to both behavior and experience.
She sought a way of imagining the legitimate pressure of public
meanings that she could neither defy through rebellion nor disown
through anonymity. Maggie, in *The Mill on the Floss*, could
move to London, where she was unknown. The novel insists that
living with one's reputation, the public account and judgment of
one's acts, is essential not only to living in a community but also
to self-intelligibility. The novel *Silas Marner* immediately follows
The Mill on the Floss with a deep study of how far the loss of
self-intelligibility can go once the choice of anonymity has been
made or imposed. In a sense, *Silas Marner* is the alternative ending
to the death by water that has always left critics unhappy with
The Mill on the Floss. Community involves a visibility of acts
even where only misinterpretations remain. Being misread is one
cost of legibility. The alternative that Eliot represents in Marner
and Baldassare is an inner blank in which the self cannot any
longer remember how to read itself. The alternative is not solitude
but self-absence.

Ideally, in a society there would be a harmony between an act
good for the self and one good for the community; each benefit
would give health on each of the many levels between the self and
the society. An act would be tempered by the many levels on
which it has to give an account of itself. Maggie Tulliver's relationship with Philip Wakem is an example of an experience im-
peded by the irreconcilable claims of different levels of loyalty.
The love is, first, a tangled set of feelings that we understand
through our sense of Maggie's psychology. Second, the affair has
a completely different set of meanings as one further element of
the family ties between the Tullivers and Wakems. Third, since
the families themselves embody the historical tensions of two

Making Up Society

stages of the development of British industrialization, the love between the children is the possible token of a compromise that allows quiet transition. An act is even the sum of the possible misunderstandings that it lends itself to in different contexts, and it is partly through misinterpretation that the meaning of Maggie's day on the water with Stephen Guest has its value in her life.

To imagine society is also, in part, to represent the public reality itself with its institutions. These include the life of work and ambition, the life of human relationships not chosen for their own sake: doctor to patient, employer to worker, the relations of neighbors as well as of those who pass one another in the streets. Along with these relationships are the formal settings and cere-monial patterns of church and services, law courts and trials, schools or workshops. Within this sector of life arises an element of the self that is structured by professional demands and tempered by impersonal moods and formulas of behavior. The life of a doctor or a weaver, a clergyman or a carpenter, prints itself across the individual details of personal history and character.

Such relations and patterns are completely absent in a writer like Henry James. The public, formal details of life are never represented because the complex, interior relations that he does depict exist with a subtlety that the gross, absolute public life of funerals and weddings, legal judgments and professions, would totally obscure. Even the one undeniable social symbol that ap-pears everywhere in James—money—is never present in fact, only as psychology. Money is felt as power or freedom or corrup-tion. It does not exist in quantities but in those ways that we have of speaking of someone having "too much money for his own good," or "not enough to do the things he would like to do." Money is seen relative to desire or to one's ability to imagine uses. Throughout Eliot's work, but especially in *Middlemarch*, money, in its hundreds of concrete manifestations, stands as one of the key elements of social bonding, an element as important as love or family.

George Eliot and the Social Novel

Both public time and public space are further elements of the imagination of society. Time, whether the Christian year or the rural cycle of seasons, imposes a set of impersonal moods and anticipations that overlay private rhythms. The happiness of a holiday creates experience in a different way from personal accomplishment or pleasure. By public space is meant practically the entire world of *Adam Bede* or Joyce's *Ulysses*, that communal space of church, jail, hospital, school, library, restaurant, street, and brothel. This world, again, is almost completely absent from a novelist of the private life like James. The paradox of *Ulysses*, that public space is available only as a component of an utterly private monologue, or, to put it in reverse, that a book concerned with the self at its most intimate and invisible should take place so completely in the public streets—this paradox points to the extent to which *Ulysses* is about the failure of community and of continuity between public and personal. The failure is marked in the choice of an outsider, a Jew, as everyman. The outsider, by his incomprehension, makes the symbols of public life, like the mass interpreted by Bloom, glaringly absurd. The device of an outsider narrator, popular during the French Enlightenment, amounts to a protest against the peculiarities of any concrete society in the name of an abstract brotherhood of man; a universality, that, as Bloom illustrates it, is ideal in the negative sense—without content. A further example of the lack of content is the abstractness or impersonality of the public events. Bloom goes to the hospital to check on the birth of another child to Mina Purefoy, "just anybody," a person with whom he has no particular relationship. At the funeral of Dignam, the mourners seem to consist of men who hardly knew him at all.

A brief comparison of three events—the funeral of *Adam Bede*, Dignam's funeral in *Ulysses*, and the death of Milly Theale in James's *The Wings of the Dove*—will illustrate the contrast between the harmony of public and private so urgent in Eliot's work and the two defective halves of the lost harmony: the completely private and the blankly public. The private becomes all-meaning, and the feeling of concrete life has evaporated to the point where it is merely a symbol, while the public involves an objectivity and concreteness secured by draining the event, in advance, of any personal relation to the person through whom it is imagined.

Paddy Dignam was, in the only sentence spoken about him by those with Bloom at the funeral, "as decent a little man as ever wore a hat." None of the mourners recalls a single detail of Dignam's life, nor does Bloom in his stream of thoughts mention one of Dignam's qualities or experiences. No one seems to have known him at all. The immediate family are not seen by Bloom, and no sound of mourning or emotion is recorded. When Bloom thinks of him, it is the corpse he is curious about, not the man. Bloom is at any funeral; anyone is dead. The chapter, in its encyclopedic manner, is about death and only incidentally about Dignam. These mourners have come, as they would say, to pay their respects. The procedure is automatic at the grave: Bloom knows that the priest says the same consoling words, "Today in Paradise," over saint and sinner alike.

The importance of the outer event rests on its blankness of emotion. Bloom's thoughts are not taken back to the particulars of Dignam's life. Abstract as it is, the funeral can therefore more completely be ideal. It represents death itself. Bloom's experience can create itself around, but remain independent of, the details in front of him. Death calls up his father's suicide and the death of his son Rudy. But equally, the abstractness lets the mind play, in reverie, over death itself: burial customs, murder, suicide, the death of Parnell, decay, and transformation. The two poles of private memory and free speculative play are both linked to the event in front of him by analogue. In psychological terms, analogue—resemblance by detail or structure—is the key to association. As a result, what is essential appears through analogue, a secondary reality in the memory or imagination, and this analogue has force because of the emotional emptiness of the world of fact, a world

George Eliot and the Social Novel

unable to compel attention. The world of events and behavior appears as chatter and observed detail, running parallel to a world of reverie made up of memory and speculation. The two worlds interrupt each other and relate through accidental details that resemble, often by peculiar matches between incidental aspects, a kind of continuous punning. At bottom, the two streams are split.

Thus Joyce finds normal the division that, in the famous county fair scene in *Madame Bovary*, Flaubert presents as an ironic and desperate breakdown. The public life Flaubert gives through the fatuous oratory and then the almost comic awards for prize pigs and long service to the republic. Here is a public life that has no relation even to its own truth and needs, let alone to the inner life. The private worlds of Madame Bovary and Rodolphe present themselves in equally cliched and rhetorical trivializations about the world of feeling. On the pages of the novel the two alternate, and the technique of juxtaposition creates a shock. By Joyce's time, this synchronization is a normal technique, and in its own way it yields effects of pathos and beauty. But in Flaubert the stark drama includes an awareness of the loss that underlies the trivialization of both worlds in isolation. The irony is itself a form of protest that declares the split was not inevitable. In Joyce there is no such protest.

At the other extreme is the death of Milly Theale in *The Wings of the Dove*. The event exists only through the notice of it that reaches Kate and Densher, and it is given meaning by the twist that her final generosity in leaving her money to Densher creates in the plans of Kate and her lover. Milly's death, like the vague illness that preceded it, has a quality of choice and doom at the same time. In the terms of the book, it would be as accurate to say that she dies because she is too good for this world as it would be to say she dies of a heart condition. The metaphoric is real and the real mixes itself in symbol. The kind of equivocation found in a sentence like "she died of a broken heart" is the natural play between levels in the novel. But the reality of the death is not general, not public. The death *is* what it does in the lives of Densher, Kate, and Lord Mark. It *is* what it provokes in the dramas of others. The reality is like that of certain concepts in a dictionary where for the first term you are referred to a second, equally unknown, and, upon looking up the second, you are sent back to the first. You must know the whole before the meaning of the part exists, but the whole can only be grasped through the parts.

An event like the death of Milly Theale does not even aspire to a social form—the world of mourning and funerals, notices and condolences. The meaning is so private and *unique*, so intangible, that only in the world of art can it reach a statement equal in subtlety to its truth.

The unified experience of public and private, of behavior and experience—of funeral loss and death—can be illustrated in the funeral of Thias Bede in Eliot's first novel. The private fact of loss, the general one of death, and the public ceremony of funeral are are joined into a complex experience that, by its very nature, must be perceived from a number of points of view. Unlike Dignam's death, which was real but not (to anyone we can see in the Hades chapter) a loss, Thias Bede's is felt in relation to the past (the oppression of his family that is ended by his death) and the future (in the marriage and independence it makes possible for Adam). It is at once a moral example and a private grief. For the wife it seems to end her usefulness, but it also provides an opportunity to fulfill a set of customs that show respect for the dead. Patterns of customs and superstition take over and give grief an outlet in action. The dream that tells Lisbeth that Thias must be buried under the white thorn absorbs the final choice into a necessity dictated from without. Everywhere are imperatives: the correct linen, the exact burial spot, the watch over the dead, the words that must be said as the coffin is lowered. But alongside the drama of grief continues the public life to which it is incidental and the private lives we see in the Poysers' happy walk to church and Hetty's hope and disappointment about Arthur's absence from church.

George Eliot and the Social Novel

This scene from *Adam Bede* is not to be taken as a standard from which the similar ones in James or Joyce have fallen away. The intentions are clearly different in the three cases. The ambition in Eliot to represent a public life that supplies the materials for confronting, understanding, and, finally, giving voice to personal experience, is not urgent in James and Joyce. Still, a valid question exists of how far the novel, in the end, must be committed to Eliot's ambitions. To reach the implications of the loss of legibility that this book will study, a closer look at both terms, *society* and *self*, is necessary.

LEGIBILITY AND THE CONTINUITY OF EXPERIENCE

If we compare the conservative image of society we find in Eliot with the equally conservative one found in Shakespeare, we can see that the claims of society in Eliot's novels will always be precarious. The problematic side of the image is so prominent that the notion is in doubt from the start. It is both proposed and questioned in the same act of description.

For Eliot, it is always a local, miniature fragment of the overall order that is seen and examined. Never do we see beyond Hayslope or Raveloe or Middlemarch out to the more inclusive system of which local politics or religious controversy is only a weak reflection. We see only the local gentry, never the queen or king; only the present, particular clergy, never the church. Her skepticism of abstractions is at work here, as well as her faith in persons rather than ideas. But when only the local embodiments of power are visible, they can no longer be justified by the abstract arguments used, for example, by Shakespeare to defend the power itself. Because the social order stands between, and reflects, the order in the individual self and the order of the natural world, it draws upon our loyalty to both other orders and is defended by that loyalty. Society becomes sacred as well as personal. Whoever strikes the king strikes the same principles that, in another moment, he must rely on to save the harmony of his own soul. It is not only by metaphor that the Elizabethans could speak of the tyranny of a passion over the soul as well as of a ruler over the state.

For Eliot, this continuity of orders is no longer true. Order in the self, the struggle between duty and pleasure, or, to use the key Victorian phrase, the question of self-control, is independent of the problem of society. Society, in the notion of "my station and its duties," that combination of military and domestic service imagery, offers one form of self-imposed restraint that can be freely chosen. Although given, it must be self-imposed to be valid. It must be one determination of the self by the self, one way of willing to be oneself. In other words, to be valid, it too must be conscious and internalized and, in another key word, *willed*.

Outside the self, the social order itself has become autonomous. In a review, Eliot spoke of society as "incarnate history" (*Essays*, p. 182). Thus it is not a timeless reflection of the laws of order, as in Shakespeare, but a residue of accidents. A metaphor for this notion of society would be a cityscape that the eye can comprehend in an instant of time, a scene every detail of which results from independent decisions taken at different moments in the past, often under conditions that no longer exist. The decisions and accidents that lie behind every detail were part of every imaginable purpose but one: no one had in mind the scene, the cityscape before the eye. If society is incarnate history, then it is a texture of the arbitrary. Romantic history arises out of the antiquarian spirit of the late eighteenth century with its stress on curious dialects, beliefs, and customs, on anachronisms and ceremonies that refer to conditions that no longer exist. History of the kind important in Scott and the early works of Eliot centers on temporal decor, the lore of the past as it has been preserved. The past that no longer embodies the true relations among men, when emphasized, testifies to the inaccuracy in detail of the social surface to the truth of human lives as they are felt and lived. Such history is followed with an indulgent curiosity, an amusement about what bits of life, what decisions, do get incarnated, preserved, and incorporated

George Eliot and the Social Novel

into the structure of society.

But a deeper, a more Burkean meaning remains in the phrase "society is incarnate history." For if history remembers, it also forgets. To Burke, only the essential is finally preserved. Only that which suits and sustains many kinds of men in many circumstances will endure. For Burke, the trust in history joins to a belief that the institutions that endure refine themselves, lose what is local or accidental in their nature, and eventually achieve a more and more and more complex alignment with human needs. In the same essay, Eliot repeats the Burkean faith that what endures resembles the deeper currents of human nature. These deeper currents are not seen or articulated by the conscious mind at any one period. Certainly no man, setting out to write a constitution, would ever give more than a partial and distorted account of those needs. The wisdom incarnated in society would be—and this is most important—perhaps untrue to the experience of any one man, but true to that of mankind; untrue even to the consensus of what men at a given moment think they want, but true finally to what man is, not what he knows. Society is suprarational, more inclusive than what can be identified as the human condition by any mind at any moment. The almost religious importance of society in this formulation is captured by the word Eliot used, *incarnate*.

Loyalty to society in this case takes on the qualities of faith. It is not possible to comprehend that any individual is only a fragment of the truth mistaking itself for the whole. The theory rules out any moment of recognition like those possible in Shakespeare where, for example, Macbeth can see the chaos he has created, in the state and in himself. When the same forces guide particle and planet and both are comprehensible, the question of loyalty is one of reason. In Plato's theory, every moral error is a mistake of reasoning: no man can intelligently do wrong. But for Eliot, loyalty to society is a product of loyalty to the history it embodies. In other words, it is a product of loyalty to one's own past, a form of the natural piety celebrated by Wordsworth:

16
Making Up Society

The Child is father of the Man;
And I could wish my days to be
Bound each to each by natural piety.

The form of this loyalty makes it one with nostalgia, but, more important, it is one with a peremptory demand for continuity, a fervent belief that development, not succession, is the law of moral life. "The Child is father of the Man" means, in the sense important to Eliot, that a man is a visible, a legible product of what he was, and that the moral decisions of his life arrange themselves in a route that amounts to degeneration or growth, a route that is visible and comprehensible. In the pastoral metaphor commonplace in her novels, life is harvest. The confidence she shows that her understanding of moral process is adequate amounts to moral rationalism. Nemesis is of such importance in her moral vocabulary that the essential motive often seems to be to create a proof of responsibility, a responsibility dependent on strength or weakness of the will.

Moral legibility, the visible explanation a life carries with it, is the product of continuity. A unique kind of knowledge of one another is possible for people who pass the whole of their lives together in the same place, subject to the same public events, visible to one another automatically and with less of the secrecy and deception that are encouraged by life lived from place to place amid a constantly changing set of conditions and people. The journey from the self as a member of a continuous community, a society, to the self surrounded by unrelated others is only a pro-visional one. For the others quickly become the enigmatic set of impressions we see recorded in Proust and Conrad and Faulkner, or the ambiguous and sinister mysteries we see in James. The others are in league or hiding something, they are exploiting the half-lights of moral life in a discontinuous society. They are pass-ing themselves off as they choose and erasing any part of the past that has become inconvenient. The nineteenth century with its

George Eliot and the Social Novel

massive migrations created the possibility, on a general scale, of starting all over again, whether in another city or in America.

What is the distance from Madame Merle to Albertine to Lord Jim to Sutpen; from a deception that can, at last, be discovered, to a mystery of which no one person can ever have more than a part of the truth, to an enigma in which the moral truth can only be created by a chemistry between the observer and the actor, or, finally, to a moral life that can only exist by being imagined, as the truth about Sutpen is imagined in the excited meditation of Shreve and Quentin? The key factor in this sequence is that the conditions of social life have made the moral truth about others more and more precarious. The weight of discontinuity can be seen in the importance of the fact that all four characters—Mme. Merle, Albertine, Lord Jim, and Sutpen—are seen only in glimpses. All four exploit discontinuity by disappearing, by lying, by creating versions of their experience, by suppressing the past, in order to create the moral ambiguity and finally the enigmatic personal existence central to our sense of modern experience.

Discontinuity and its resultant condition, the self among inscrutable others, have widely affected the novel that follows Eliot. This can be indicated by mentioning several components of that novel. First is the importance of point of view, with its implication that the truth of moral life is not general, but created in someone's experience of the events, often a partial or even eccentric experience. The process of creating a version of an experience—the main process for Strether or Marlowe or Shreve and Quentin, and the all-important one for Marcel—underlines the resemblance of the novel of society to the detective novel. The others are mysterious, working, perhaps in concert, toward invisible goals. When questioned, they are as likely to lie or, as in James, answer with equivocation and vague ambiguity. The world of *The Castle* is not as far from that of *The Ambassadors* as we commonly think. The ambassador and the surveyor are both types of the puzzled *raisonneur* among the devious and enigmatic surfaces of modern public life. Both are detectives, both come from elsewhere, and both will be lucky to lose only what they thought they came to get.

Beyond the detective form, the importance of point of view, and the tendency of the surface of the novel to become a complex meditation that attempts to imagine the truth it can no longer know directly, the novel of society, once continuity has been lost, is marked by the loss of middle distance. Here Joyce is the best example. Between Stephen Dedalus, whom we cannot escape, and the numerous minor characters, who appear for a page or two, there is no middle distance of importance or interest. Only the father, Simon Dedalus, is an exception, and his steady decline is perhaps the one reminder of the type of moral process that is central to any of Eliot's novels. In *Ulysses*, the distinction is absolute. A character is either an appearance—just what he looks to be, now, to a given mind; the total of his behavior—or he is a self, a consciousness with responses, history, projection, and explanation. One effect of the span of a single day is that the characters who are appearances have no moral lives. Simon Dedalus, through his dozen or so moments in *A Portrait of the Artist as a Young Man*, creates a trajectory, a doom, a ten-year set of intervals that, in the reader's mind, lies plotted like a curve in analytic geometry. In *Ulysses*, instead of trajectories there are only situations, and the four or five appearances of Dedalus add up to elements of that static situation. Even Bloom, Stephen, and Molly, the characters for whom the past is given, have no history, only repetitions. One situation is an image of another, and the few combinations of betrayal or generosity repeat and reconstruct themselves through time. In Nietzsche's aphorism, "A man who has his character has one experience that occurs to him again and again." The notion of a timeless self, constant, unaffected by experience, leads to a final quality in the novel after the loss of continuity: the stress on experience rather than character. Experience is timeless but momentary, the experience of epiphany. The time span is that of revelation rather than development.

George Eliot and the Social Novel

These features, which, I believe, are direct consequences of the loss of continuity and with it the disappearance of society in which action and motive are legible, can be seen in the two short stories Eliot wrote during her earlier period. One, "The Lifted Veil," tells a parable of isolation through its use of and stress on point of view. The other, "Brother Jacob," is a study of the reverse, a study of the deceptiveness, secrecy, and change of identity possible when community is gone.

Parables of Social Loss

"The Lifted Veil" is, as her publisher, Blackwood, described it, a morbid tale. Almost an exercise in the macabre, the story calls to mind Edgar Allan Poe with his gothic melodrama, his abnormal psychology translated into the concrete materials of romance. The story is a nightmare of the social life in which all relations exist in extreme form. It is a fable of public life after the disappearance of society. The only one of Eliot's works narrated in the first person, it is also the work written before *Daniel Deronda* that is set closest to the present. The story was written in 1860, and the events take place up to 1850. The veil is knowledge of others. True to the melodrama of the story, the hero, Latimer, occupies both poles of knowledge and ignorance. Isolated, unable, as he says, "ever to unbosom myself to any human being," he is surrounded by mysterious, opaque others. Never is he as much alone as when in society. The thoughts and motives of others are incalculable, and their behavior dissembles or denies whatever it is they are truly feeling. Alone and surrounded by misleading clues, engulfed in social behavior that is more likely to work by contraries (be especially nice to those you are poisoning, show contempt for what you secretly love), Latimer, like those Jamesian heroes and heroines he so much resembles, is at the center of intrigues and complex intentions he can only half recognize, let alone understand.

True to the romance nature of the fable, Latimer also experiences the opposite—total knowledge. Given a mysterious power that might, like so many powers of knowledge in the modern novel, be a function of his disease, he finds at moments that he can read the minds of others, know their thoughts and feelings, their intentions and even the future. He feels only repulsion at the pettiness and banality he discovers. Only one person baffles him by remaining, for some reason, immune to his powers. Latimer falls in love with her. Or rather, for her he feels fascination. The enigmatic otherness, the unpredictability and unknowableness, act as intoxicants. Her exotic blankness, the supremely perverse relationship of what she does to what she feels: these are the sources of the fascination. The two poles of feeling, contemptuous repulsion and fascination, match the poles of total familiarity and total otherness.

The premise behind both contraries is the collapse of the truth of behavior, the truth of visible life. Here, as in the basic situation of the James novel, the situation is dominated by those who exploit the secrecy and inscrutability of social life to appear as what they are not or to hide what they are. But the key loss is of moral life that no longer records itself publicly, or feeling that never becomes behavior, and behavior that deliberately creates a false implication of feeling. When the unity is destroyed, the opposition of innocence moving within a social conspiracy (Latimer's position of ignorance, the situation of Isabel Archer and the heroes of *The Trial* and *The Castle*) and total knowledge in a moment of revelation (Latimer's other pole, the notion of epiphany, the moment of vision in James) divide the ground that remains. The defective pair of emotions, fascination and repulsion, follows. The way of seeing love as fascination haunted by the mysterious otherness of someone points to the connection between Latimer and Proust's Marcel. The other is an enigma, and therefore desired. When known, the other becomes a banality for which Stendhal's question is the summary: *N'est-ce que ça?*

Latimer marries the Bertha who remains the one mystery in his life, a life destroyed by too much or too little knowledge. At first she ignores him, and only later, after she has begun to poison him,

George Eliot and the Social Novel

does she begin showing solicitous concern for him, spending her evenings at home. The poison is given by a maid with whom Bertha shares that guilty, conspiratorial closeness that is the highest form of intimacy (it is that of Kate Croy and Densher in *The Wings of the Dove*) in this sinister world.

In an ending reminiscent of Poe with its peculiar use of science, the veil is lifted, and Latimer learns about his wife. The maid is on her deathbed. A scientist friend of Latimer's wants to experiment with bringing a corpse back to life by joining his own veins to those of the corpse for a moment. The story enters this fantastic realm to create the symbols it wants to underline. In her instant of regained life, the maid tells Latimer his wife has been slowly poisoning him. The scene calls up one final pair of defective poles of contact where there are no longer any relationships: through a common bloodstream, man is joined to woman, but to a stranger, and only to lift the veil that shows the marriage between Bertha and Latimer to be a slow destruction by poison.

Schematic as the story is, it fails mainly by not having the audacity to seize its unreality more openly in the manner of Poe, to become even more completely the parable it suggests. The scientist who experiments with others, like the artists or schemers who use others in James, expresses one extreme image of relations in public life. The great story of Dr. Frankenstein, who created another self—a self-made man—only to have it die of loneliness and incomprehension, begins, even before Poe and Hawthorne, the important heritage of the image.

"The Lifted Veil," as has been stressed, was Eliot's only attempt at first person narration. No one can doubt the extent to which the mystery and sinister collusiveness of social life is one of the principal undercurrents of the popularity of point of view in novels after Eliot's. Technique and result are interdependent. The power of vision that Latimer is cursed with is nothing but a variation on that essential Jamesian concept, experience, a power he defined in an unusual, socially charged way: "The power to guess the unseen

Making Up Society

from the seen, to trace the implication of things, to judge the whole piece by the pattern, the condition of feeling life in general so completely that you are well on your way to knowing any particular corner of it—this cluster of gifts may almost be said to constitute experience."[1] The words James uses assume the continuity, the legibility of public life, the absence of the very ambiguity and deception that are the major currents of the public life in his novels.

As the life around Latimer is cryptic and mute, so too is his own life in the eyes of others. Latimer writes the story at the moment of his death. "I wish to use my last hours of ease and strength in telling the strange story of my experience. I have never fully unbosomed myself to any human being" (*Essays*, p. 428). Only the privileged relationship of art, the community of narrator and reader, is exempt from the treacheries of social life. Only here are the life of trust and knowledge, the society of belief in the spoken word, the trust in fact and the explanation of fact, still in existence. Here alone, in the reader's community with Latimer, are the self and the complete presentation of the self one. The pseudosociety of art is the one point at which the public and private are seen in continuity and connection. To that extent, art provides, dependent on the true desire of the narrator to speak out and to make public the complete moral truth of his life, a reminder of the social community, the loss of which is the subject of the narration.

The part of Latimer's life that alternates between fascination and repulsion, between the silence of the mysterious others and the complete chatter of their inner lives, accounts for only one of the three states, the central one, of his life. Before the first development of his telepathic powers, he had, as he describes himself, "the poet's sensibility without the poet's voice" (p. 432). A love for nature and a rich, almost oversensitive inner life make up his quali-

---

1. Henry James, *The Future of the Novel*, ed. Leon Edel (New York: Vintage Books, 1956), p. 13.

George Eliot and the Social Novel

ties. Like Rousseau, he was happiest when he had blotted out the earth entirely, lying on his back in a boat, drifting in the middle of a lake. His was a life of reverie without motion, feeling without object, sensitivities with no technique for expressing the results: a life of, in the literal sense, detachment. Equally, in the third phase, people play less and less a part in his visions, and he becomes alive to the inanimate. Terrible landscapes, sublime scenes, ruins, visions of strange cities begin to haunt him. Every image has behind it some "unknown and pitiless presence" (p. 464) that he feels is demoniac, a negative form of the religious presence he can no longer feel or believe in. As he says: "To the utterly miserable—the unloving and the unloved—there is no religion possible, no worship but the worship of devils" (p. 460). Even more ominously present is the image of his own death.

The landscape seen in the boat, with its serene face, an innocence to be used as a refuge from society, turns, after the middle period of vision, into a final element of vision itself. Inscrutable but pitiless, it gives way in reverie to death, and to the final act before death: the confession of his life to the reader. The community of nature, where Latimer spent "my least solitary moments," gives way to the community of art, which requires the impending death that alone lifts the veil and allows the full truth to come to light. The death of the maid created the moment of first truth. Latimer's own death creates the second, public, moment of truth. The society of reader and narrator—the latter has died by the time the story is read—is only a figurative one, and that in itself is a mark of the extremity.

"The Lifted Veil" is the parable of this disintegration of self and society told in the tone of nightmare from one side of the equation, the side of the self. "Brother Jacob," the only other story Eliot wrote and a product of the same period, enters the problem from the opposite side, the point of view of society. The tone is that of farce, and the central problem involves exposing the impostor, the self-made man. The first thing the self-made man makes is his identity, the fiction of his origins and past, often of his name. Josiah Bounderby of Coketown, unveiled at last in Dickens's *Hard Times*, is the most striking example, the most profound is Bulstrode in *Middlemarch*, but the elements of the character are all present in comic form in Mr. David Faux of "Brother Jacob." Faux, whose name neatly combines "fox" and "false," is in every way a counterfeit, passing himself off as Mr. David Freely, a name that implies the negative freedom of a social situation where identity is free, as it is in the picaresque, where the freedom to adopt disguises or pseudonyms and to invent false accounts of oneself and one's past amounts to an inversion of society. Inversion in the world of "Brother Jacob" has become the norm. The free social identity of the road has become the rule within the society itself. Or, rather, this freedom is one sign of the new order that can still, in the comic situation of the story, be routed through exposure by the forces of the older system. David's youth is that mixture of dissatisfaction and personal complacency that creates free identity. "His soul swelled with the impatient sense that he ought to become something quite remarkable—that it was quite out of the question to put up with a narrow lot as other men did: he scorned the idea that he could accept an average. He was sure there was nothing average about him" (p. 476).

He runs away with his mother's savings, abandoning his family which includes an idiot brother, the brother Jacob of the title. Appearing years later, after a try at making his fortune in the West Indies—one of those several-year lacunae so common in the lives of the heroes that follow—Faux passes himself off as David Freely in the town of Grimworth and sets up a bake shop. His bakery gains business and profits by breaking down the household patterns of the town, replacing the often imperfect baking of its individual kitchens with products of the specialist: products sold for cash. The results are prosperity for Freely, better baked goods, and an increase in idle time for the housewives along with a need for more money to pay for what was once baked at home.

George Eliot and the Social Novel

His growing wealth leads David to decide to marry into the society he entered as a stranger only a few years before. At that moment an announcement seen by accident calls up the possibility of an inheritance left by the parents he robbed and deserted. Since any identity is only a way of exploiting a position relative to others, he sneaks home, gets the inheritance, and returns to Grimworth, where the marriage will signify his "arrival" in society. But, followed by his idiot brother Jacob, he is unmasked, and, in the common phrase, "put in his place." The idiot brother, like Bounderby's old mother in *Hard Times*, represents a simplicity and directness, a presocial innocence that lives only in the truth of natural bonds: brother to brother or mother to son. Like the uncorrupted part of the soul of Scrooge, this presocial image is part of the magic of the Victorian analysis of social and moral events. Unaffected by all the pretense and complexity of social deception simply because they are not sophisticated enough to be aware it exists, these creatures unmask by accident and preserve society from having the lie became permanent, as it would have, for example, in David's marriage.

The recourse to this element of social magic makes visible, as does the appeal to an uncorrupted nucleus in Scrooge or Silas Marner, the lack of any real safeguards, or, in the case of Scrooge or Marner, any real psychological route back to health. In the act of celebrating the triumph, the magical quality of the means reminds us that we are only pretending. The story of society successfully defended only makes us more aware that it is vulnerable. The element of dark fable underneath the story of regeneration and cure will be more fully analyzed in the discussion of *Silas Marner*. For now it is enough to say that the anxiety underneath a farce like "Brother Jacob" comes from the contrast of a literal predicament with a figurative solution. The chain of events that created the danger is historically and psychologically literal, while the deliverance, the redemption of the self in *Silas Marner* or of society in "Brother Jacob," is accurate only symbolically.

26
Making Up Society

The step from the farce of "Brother Jacob" to the tragedy of James's *Portrait of a Lady* is a very short one in terms of candor. The helplessness of society and its innocent heroine in the face of deceptions and the false mirrors of social behavior involves only a conscious recognition of what is unconsciously present in the comic victory by magic of "Brother Jacob." Even *The Portrait of a Lady* involves an unmasking, however late. The truth of all the relations becomes known to the victim as well as to the reader. In plot, the tragedy or farce depends on those notions of time: *just in time* or that final *too late* of *Othello* or *The Portrait of a Lady*. The final word *never* or *impossible* appears in the novel of society only with Proust and Kafka. The mystery of Albertine is final, absolute. Nor does it depend on secrets, on facts that can be withheld or revealed. The enigma is one that cannot lift, like fog or like veils, but something that recedes with the same speed as our pursuit.

The extreme case of Albertine reminds us through the contrast with "Brother Jacob" and "The Lifted Veil" how provisional is Eliot's statement of the two sides of the disintegration. For her, the division, with its attendant mystery, is not a starting point but a projected vision that she announces with an urgency arising from her confidence that something can still be done. The note of warning or premonition is sounded in these parables. The forces that Eliot calls on to counter the drift, both in her novelistic techniques and in her analysis of moral life, are the clearest sign that in her own strenuous way she believed the golden bowl of social life could still be held together.

VOCABULARY OF SELF: VOCABULARY OF SOCIETY

We would expect that an age dominated by the philosophy of self-interest, an age of individualism, the age of Bentham and expansive capitalism, would struggle with the question of society and the relations of self to society in a unique way and with a particular urgency. An important twist is given to the problem by the

George Eliot and the Social Novel

moral and social vocabularies in which it was stated. What is the relationship between self-interest and selfishness, between the economic unit, the individual, and the moral one, the solitary? A character praised for "industry, sobriety, and peace" in *Silas Marner* is in fact seen as a worker, not a man. At the same time, the language is anachronistic. The dichotomies so important to Eliot: duty and pleasure, desire and renunciation, or the odd associations of beauty with languor and sin, of manliness with stern, almost inhuman, uprightness—these alternatives demand a choice between an indulgence and an asceticism both equally unreal.

One sign of anachronism in the moral vocabulary was the Christian importance placed on charity. The criticism of false charity and the symbolism of the true act were meant to argue against the iron law of self-interest, but from a reference point already destroyed by the successes of the new society. While Dickens is the key to the misuse of charity, traces of it occur throughout Eliot as well. In Dickens's *Christmas Carol*, the fully stated problem of the relations of generosity and selfishness, isolation and society, exploiter and benefactor, is resolved by magic, or to use the Christian phrase, by conversion. The conversion is based on the comforting myth of the particle of uncorrupted humanity in the blackest villain, a remnant of innocence that can, at any moment, become the central point of a renewed self. At bottom this kind of magic amounts more to a refusal to believe in self-interest than a refutation of it. It amounts to a claim that this selfishness has only usurped temporarily, and it claims that at a certain level the self can never be corrupted by the forces that seem to dominate it. Under every bitter, aging Scrooge there remains a hidden, kindly grandfather. As in the fairy tales, the prince turned into a frog remains somewhere within, waiting for the spell to be broken.

Separate from the power to formulate or describe is the power to imagine. However delusory their moral vocabularies, the Victorian novelists created images of the results of individualism that were often profound. In the chapter on *Silas Marner*, we will face the problem of extracting the images from the framework of hopes and interpretations. Here it is enough to remember the ingredients of Marner's life at its low point. In him are visible the combinations of avarice and solitude, the sensuality of money, the endless work without goal other than the moments of displaced pleasure the money can give, the destruction of time, the near-empty but highly reasonable world he interposes between himself and the mysterious world he can no longer understand, the nearsightedness, the quantified, repetitive life, the secretiveness and the mysterious presence he has become to others. Believing in nothing and attached to no one, he is without family or connection to his own past. He endlessly turns his wheel to get gold, which he buries in the ground as though to complete the natural cycle and return to earth the metal for which, in his case, possession is the only use. Camus, like Eliot, reached back to the myth of Sisyphus for an analogue to the modern condition.

Alongside the miser, the second important character invented by the period is the self-made man, a man whose new, inverted snobbishness takes to boasting, like Dickens's Bounderby, of the depths of the ditch out of which he has climbed. Even this boast is hypocrisy, an inverted affectation. The words *self-made man*, a phrase that applies to Adam Bede as well as Bounderby, are almost an ontology for an age of individualism. Under Christianity men are created or made things, made by God. The claim of the post-Christian age does not go back to earlier notions, Greek for example, but extends the Christian words: man is self-made. In this there is continuity from the Victorians to Sartre, who means in his famous phrase "existence precedes essence" that man is creating the definition of man, men are creating man.

In social rather than religious terms, the self-made man is an orphan, that key character in the nineteenth-century novel, the one who must find what he is, where he belongs, the man who must make himself socially. Most of Eliot's young characters are without parents and often without homes as well. The orphan

George Eliot and the Social Novel

creates his own place; he does not take his father's. He is a free particle that will finally, through marriage and occupation, take a place, take on a fixed social meaning. In this career the orphan is a temporary outsider, unlike those two typical figures of the novel that follows in the late nineteenth and early twentieth centuries — the artist and the exile, both of whom permanently reject society and take on, as did James in England or Joyce in Paris, only a setting or an abstract community of artists. In that sense Stephen Dedalus, who discovers he must become an exile as soon as he feels himself an artist, is the twentieth century Pip or Jane Eyre.

No description of the social meaning of individualism, as it was felt in the context in which George Eliot faced it, is more profound than the two pages given to the subject in the second part of de Tocqueville's *Democracy in America*. The second book of part two is called "The Influence of Democracy on the Feelings of the Americans." The whole of the section is, then, a psychology of individualism. The second chapter, only a page and a half in length, is on individualism itself, a new concept in de Tocqueville's time. Individualism is a novel concept, he points out, different from *egoisme* or selfishness. The latter is a passionate and exaggerated love of the self that leads a man to see and value all things only in their relation to himself. Individualism begins with self-reliance, the search for one's opinions within the self, and turns in time into a considered and mature withdrawal from the larger given society in order to create a self-chosen circle of family and friends. In that, it is related to the way the mind retreats, in "common sense," to what it can "see the point of." Emerson's notion of self-reliance reflects the crucial elements of individualism. The relaxation, from without, of the claims upon the self increases the power of this movement toward self-determination, self-creation of as many of the conditions of one's life as is possible.

Like Burke, de Tocqueville stresses the claims of past and future, forefathers and descendants, as well as those of patronage and co-operation — the claims of those immediately above and below one in the feudal system. He does not weaken his picture by mentioning the claims of that new character of democratic social life, the "neighbor." "The woof of time is every instant broken and the track of the generations effaced. Those who went before are soon forgotten; of those who will come after, no one has any idea: the interest of man is confined to those in close propinquity to himself." Man lives in the city man has made, and everywhere he sees only his own power and the conditions he has set for his own life. In particular, de Tocqueville singles out those, an increasing class, who would be called self-made men. "They owe nothing to any man, they expect nothing from any man; they acquire the habit of always considering themselves as standing alone, and they are apt to imagine that their whole destiny is in their own hands."[2]

The image he calls up is, for all the criticism, a heroic one, and an allied problem in the period is that of the hero. Included here are the many novels "without a hero," as Thackeray subtitled *Vanity Fair,* and also the truly heroic lives the novelists never represented—those almost military, Napoleonic careers of the major capitalists with their campaigns and enemies, even their Darwinian self-image as the fittest. But to de Tocqueville, the final depth is the psychology of these men. "Thus not only does democracy make every man forget his ancestors, but it hides his descendants and separates his contemporaries from him; it throws him back forever upon himself alone, and threatens in the end to confine him within the solitude of his own heart."[3] The result, we would expect, would be an increase of intensity there, within the "solitude of his own heart." We would expect a headiness, a more complex analysis of the movements of the heart, as we get in Eliot or later in Proust, where the solitude described by de Tocqueville is the starting point—the very particular solitude born of the

---

2. Alexis de Tocqueville, *Democracy in America,* ed. Phillips Bradley (New York: Vintage Books, 1960), pp. 141, 142.

3. Ibid., p. 143.

George Eliot and the Social Novel

collapse of society. Out of that solitude we would also expect a lyricism, a beauty like that of impressionism and the art novels of Proust and Joyce.

De Tocqueville's characterization of individualism reflects almost exactly Eliot's language in describing another new social character, for whom she uses the German word *Philister*. More than a decade before Arnold gave the sarcastic description in *Culture and Anarchy* that made the word *philistine* a permanent social category in England, Eliot, in an important review of Riehl's *Natural History of German Life*, singles out the German type, the "Philister."

> The Philister is one who is indifferent to all social interests, all public life, as distinguished from selfish and private interests; he has no sympathy with political and social events except as they affect his own comfort and prosperity, as they offer him material for amusement or opportunity for gratifying his vanity. He has no social or political creed, but is always of the opinion which is most convenient for the moment. He is always in the majority. (*Essays*, p. 190)

Eliot elaborates the character by continuing beyond Riehl.

> We imagine the Philister is the personification of the spirit which judges everything from a lower point of view than the subject demands—. . . the affairs of the parish from the egoistic . . . the merits of the universe from the human point of view. (*Essays*, p. 191)

Since the essay on Riehl is her most important, and the one directly concerned with the question of society, several of its formulations deserve attention. The key is the reversal of the Enlightenment and romantic myth of the history of self and society.

For Rousseau, as for Locke and Hobbes, society appears historically after the self and is nothing but a contract among autonomous individuals who merge their individual wills into a general will. They surrender part of their freedom for the safety only the group can provide. Men enter society. Man (and each individual recapitulates the history) creates society. What is essential in this myth is the appeal to a human nature, a selfhood, that is totally *there* before men enter society, before men impose society, Rousseau's chains, on themselves. This selfhood is distorted by society, which passes out of the control of those who fashioned it, usurping more and more powers that were never foreseen in the original contract. To revolt, for both Rousseau and Shelley, is to regain freedom, to recover the self that in Rousseau's phrase is "born free but everywhere in chains."

As the nineteenth century progressed, sociology, natural history, and anthropology—of which Riehl's books, like those of Frazer, are eminent examples—began to develop a countermyth. The historical model they developed is the orthodox version today. Society *precedes* the individual self in this myth. It is false to picture separate individuals with feelings, sensations, sensibilities, projects, and opinions, who through a calculation of private advantage come to decide to band together for their self-interests. The group mind with its collective will, the hoard, the tribe, the community with its customs and common beliefs, is prior. The rigid practices, structures, and opinions imply that at first man had only a generic existence, like bees. Each man was "anyone," and that poignant modern wish, the desire to "be someone," was unthinkable. Out of the collective, the individual, the self, at last appears, like a precipitate in chemistry. Only after a long history of withdrawal, not recovery, do we reach the state described by de Tocqueville: the man whose opinions and feelings are his own, the man who has created the conditions of his life out of his own will, the man who owes nothing to nature, over which he has triumphed, and nothing to others, who are in fact in competition with him for the raw materials of the life structure he has imagined and created.

33
George Eliot and the Social Novel

Both Eliot and Riehl believed that what remained of the collective condition could still be seen in the peasantry. "In the cultivated world each individual has his style of speaking and writing; but among the peasantry it is the race, the district, the province, that has the style,—namely its dialect, its phraseology, its proverbs, and its songs, which belong alike to the entire body of the people" (*Essays*, p. 165). Even physique is not personal appearance but a mark of place and occupation, a general set of features shared with many others. In the one sentence italicized in the article, Eliot extends the claim to the extreme point: "*Custom with him holds the place of sentiment, of theory, and, in many cases, of affection*" (*Essays*, p. 170, Eliot's emphasis). In other words, the question would always be, What is done? and never What do I want to do? Never What do I want? and never What do I feel? but What is done? Or rather, because action is habitual, the question is unnecessary, and the whole questioning mode is unimportant.

In the mythic history that Eliot and Riehl present, the collective differentiates itself into three classes: aristocrats who own land, citizens who control commerce, and peasants who work the land. At this point the reasoning is deceptive, for there cannot be private ownership of land and a large landless peasantry unless in fact the collective has dissolved and the notion of property appeared. But Eliot claims this three-part structure is based on evolving function in historical time—the standard nineteenth-century conservative argument repeated by Burke, Coleridge, Carlyle, and Arnold, to name only a few.

With society in thirds, defectors begin to appear from all three social groups, and it is here and only here that the individual, in the full sense, begins to exist.

The fourth estate is a stratum produced by the perpetual abrasion of the other great social groups; it is the sign and result of the decomposition which is commencing in the organic constitution of society. Its elements are derived alike from the aristocracy, the bourgeoisie, and the peasantry. It assembles under its banner the deserters of historical society, and forms them into a terrible army, which is only just awakening to the consciousness of its corporate power. The tendency of this fourth estate, by the very process of its formation, is to do away with the distinctive historical character of the other estates, and to resolve their peculiar rank and vocation into a uniform social relation, founded on an abstract conception of society. (*Essays*, pp. 188–89)

When challenged, late in *Ulysses*, to define the word *nation*, Bloom gives the minimal reply: "A nation is the same people living in the same place." But as a result of the jokes of his audience, and to include the Jews, Bloom has to amend his definition to weaken it further: "Or else living in different places." It is this weakening that the figure of the exile, "those deserters," as Eliot calls them, implies in the history of society. After the period of decomposition she is describing, the exiles are everywhere: "someone living anywhere" has replaced that first stage of collective life where each one was "anyone living somewhere." Thus the conservative history reverses absolutely that of the Enlightenment: society and community precede the self, and in the end they create the self when they disappear.

A period of decomposition is one of twilight and transition. De Tocqueville stressed the temporary flash that individualism represented. It would be vigorous and coherent only in the period while public life was disappearing. Neither an alternative to historical society nor the stable form of life that would follow the society that has disintegrated, individualism and the prominence of the self that accompanies it were only a phase on the way to a more complete disintegration. The disappearance of society that provides, for a moment, the fuel for a vivid and robust private life will, in the stage that follows, destroy the coherence of the self.

George Eliot and the Social Novel

The man de Tocqueville describes as confined, at last, "entirely within the solitude of his own heart" soon finds that heart as enigmatic as the others surrounding him. A second reversal of myths is involved. In the romantic and traditional myth since Descartes, each individual, like Descartes in his experiment with doubt, is first of all certain of himself as a being. His own experience is what he knows and understands as a harmony—a self. He then constructs the selves of others by projection from what he knows of himself. Progress is outward from the self with more and more hypothetical conjecture entering at every stage as we move away from our own experience, of which we are certain.

Two elements that must be kept apart are mixed in this description: the self as a unity, and the wholeness of an individual experience. The second we know from ourselves first. The whole experience, with its behavior and feeling, the negative presence of what we wish we had done instead and what we are trying to do but falling short of doing—this completeness of experience we know from ourselves and imagine in others for whom we have evidence only of the fraction of the experience that reaches visible behavior. But the reverse is true for the idea of unity of the self, the notion in the novel of a "character" or in psychology of an "identity." Here, just as the child sees other bodies before he learns about his own, we see the unity in time and the continuity of others (the truth we now call identity, which literally means continuity, sameness in time) and only reflexively apply the category to ourselves. Even to speak of one's own identity is to adopt an external point of view, to see oneself, for a moment, as one more other.

I have stressed the enigmatic, fragmented nature of selfhood, the sinister and mysterious others in the major novels that follow Eliot's. Assumed was a central, confident self that had not yet come into doubt. But a trend visible in Proust is, I think, of primary importance. The stress has shifted, for Marcel, from having a character to having experiences. The loss of continuity in the others has turned them into apparitions that suddenly appear out of nowhere. The shocks of appearance are one of the repeated experiences of the book. Odette magically there on the street, Charlus in the brothel, Saint-Loup back in Paris; out of a void they appear, the conditions of their lives are unknown, and in a moment they recede again into the void. For Marcel, too, the critical element is not his character—what he is—but what moments of experience he has had. The notion of character is inseparable from the stern praise the nineteenth century gave those who "had character," which was close in meaning to "having backbone." One built character, constructed it by education and culture, and the result was the made man, the self-made man.

In a famous letter, Lawrence stated his lack of interest in portraying "characters" in the old meaning of that word. At the best moments in his writing, the people are acting out of parts of their being they have not made or willed. The extent to which we have to talk about moments, or perfectly realized experience, in Lawrence is important, for it is the structures that he could not discard except in the stories—those structures based on character and continuity, on dichotomy and dialectic of themes presented through dramas of contrasting characters—that account for the feeling that Lawrence often betrayed his material.

The importance of experience implies the last evaporation of coherence: the loss of continuity in time, the loss of self. The substance we are no longer aware of must underlie experience for there to be coherence. The epiphanies of Joyce are moments of time. Coherence through time counts less, and it is in fact hard to get a grip on the characters of *Ulysses* but very easy to enter any moment of experience. The effect of Freud on our language of the self is to stress further certain isolated moments, moments of trauma, as the key to a definition of what a self is.

Wordsworth, who also gave priority to moments of life, favored the two stages of life, childhood and extreme age, where character

George Eliot and the Social Novel

is least important, where man is least individual, least engaged in willing and fashioning life. The difficulty of finding a character in Wordsworth's *Prelude* gives a foretaste of the situation in the modern novel.

At the climactic moment of his most important chapter in *Ulysses*, his last stream of consciousness, Bloom picks up a stick to write a message on the beach. All the symbols of his solitude converge in this chapter. In the sand Bloom writes an "I" and then continues in the next space "AM A," but he cannot finish. It is hopeless. The sands will shift, the message can't last the tide. Even so, what is there to write? In the eighteenth century, it could have been L. Bloom, Esquire, "I am a gentleman"; the self identified as a place in a fixed system. In the nineteenth century, he could have imitated the title of that mock-realistic novel described in Gissing, a novel that would be called *Mr. Bailey, Grocer*. Bloom might have described himself by his function, "I am a salesman." But of course he isn't: the word tells nothing essential. He is the experiences he has, and in particular he is the sum of the three or four experiences that repeat again and again in his life. Is he even Leopold Bloom? Or is he Henry Flower, or really Leopold Virag, the name his father abandoned, or is he Poldy, or the L. Boom the newspaper mentions?

The unfinished sentence "I AM A . . ." Bloom tried to write is the fate of the self, and the fate of society with which the fate of the self is locked. This fate is the final stage of a history against which Eliot struggles. Her novels attempt to find a new expression for self and society. The experiment in social vocabulary is one with the problem of form in the social novel, the problem of artistic form as she faced it.

Eliot's own names amount to a miniature history of the problem and deserve to be recorded next to Bloom's. Born Mary Anne Evans, she changed her first name to Marian. She chose her own name. Then her name is Marian Lewes, a name again to which she has only a private claim. But Marian Lewes, her private self, is

Making Up Society

separated from her public self by another created identity, George Eliot. To write she must change even her sex. At last, in old age, she takes a final name, returning to Mary Ann and using her legal husband's last name, Cross. Mary Ann Cross.

Rilke's famous modern image sums up the history of the problem: "Oh quickly disappearing photograph in my more slowly disappearing hand." The coherence outside, the photograph, is the society, the continuity in time and place of a community. The hand is, of course, the self, temporarily the more vivid, the more fascinating when we first realize the photograph is fading, the public life is vanishing. But the self is only repeating, in a wider arc, the same curve.

2

Adam Bede

Few novels before Joyce's *Ulysses* have been centered so completely on the public spaces of society as *Adam Bede*. A catalogue of scenes testifies to the range and importance of the public world. From workshop to village green to rectory; from church to school to prison to court; road and inn, farm and forest: the drama of the book takes place within shared space that is a landscape of institutions. Even forest and road contain a negative social association that is part of the experience that is possible there. In these places social truths are vague and subject to concealment. In the forest Arthur seduces Hetty and is beaten by Adam. Every journey on the road is undertaken in illusory hope that gives way to despair. Places outside society are like the forest in Shakespeare where magic prevails: the laws suspended are felt in their absence. The meaning of experience there derives from the society to which the places are adjacent.

The homes that in our modern experience are divided physically from the public world to become the setting for personal experience are, in *Adam Bede*, part of a unity not yet divided in the facts of architecture. The Bede cottage includes the father's workshop; the rectory is both home and office. Bartle Massey lives and teaches in the same place. At the Hall Farm, the single most important place in the novel, every detail is at once economic and domestic. The man with two lives has not yet appeared. Dickens's Wemmick, who is the divided man, is one self in the city, at work, and a completely different self at home, in the castle surrounded by a moat. This typically modern man, suburban man with his divided self, does not exist in Hayslope. In his pair of lives, Wemmick has created two extremes that harden in the face of each other. His personal life is all whimsy and peculiarity, as though in defiance of the metallic calculation and uniformity of the world of business, his public world. Both mass man and eccentric individualist at once, Wemmick observes the strict rule that neither life can be mentioned in the territory of the other. Like the days and nights that spin away from each other in *Dr. Jekyll and Mr. Hyde*, the two worlds of Wemmick create two selves, and at last no self.

In *Adam Bede*, this division into private and public space has not occurred: all space is social. It is wrong to speak of the Bedes' cottage as though it were divided into a workshop and a living area: both are jointly places where work and human relationships happen interchangeably. Adam and Dinah recognize each other's love in the workshop. While carpentry goes on in the workshop, the whole of domestic economy defines the activity in the rest of the cottage. The rooms are not parlors where characters sit and talk as they do in Austen's novels. No scene takes place in the Bede cottage without a broom moving in the background. Domestic economy is not a special preserve, isolated from the real business of the society. The Hall Farm is the full expression of domestic economy: there is no other, no money economy in the novel.

Each space is experienced through use. The church is not described as though it were a stop on a tour—an empty building understood esthetically as an example of rural Gothic. It is not seen by an outsider but during a typical Sunday service—the moment when it is in meaningful relationship to the life of the community and the purposes that created it. It is thus presented on a particular Sunday in relation to the human fact that makes it most itself. The Sunday is that of the burial of Thias Bede. But no one use dominates a public space. The Sunday service is equally

Adam Bede

the scene of Hetty's anxiety about Arthur's absence from church. We will see later that experience in the process of use is utterly opposed to esthetic experience, and this opposition is one basis of the hostility to "beauty" apparent in Eliot's work. In the moment of use are joined memory and projection and the moment itself: what we have done here in the past, a past evoked by the details of the place that are continuous with the past; what we are doing now; and what we can allow ourselves to think of doing within the limits evoked by the place and the past.

Out of the junction of the three come the associations that make the place live in experience. To experience in use is to see church or school or prison alive. The physical details are interwoven with the events of life to the point that the material world becomes a physical memory in our selective experience of those details that call up experiences. This world is humanized through the public and private events with which it is entangled in memory, and it guarantees, in its own continuity, the continuity of experience.

The only cases in which Eliot represents something merely seen are those clumsy moments of narrative where a "stranger" is called up to provide a nominal point of view. More typically, the Hall Farm is introduced through the visit that the Reverend Irwine and Arthur pay, the minister to question Dinah about her preaching, Arthur to flirt with Hetty. Both characters and farm appear through function and activity. No overview of the farm is given, only the approach and the note that it is "Wittah" day. Mrs. Poyser is first seen ironing in a room where Dinah is mending linen. Behind the room where they are working is the dairy where Hetty is making butter.

This busyness, this constant scene of task and duty, is one mark of the social sense of character in the novel. Each one exists through his functions and is most alive (like the church on Sunday morning) when he is in use. We first see the schoolteacher when he is with his class. Dinah first appears in the act of preaching. Of course, the busy quality is also a close to comic example of the

importance of Work, that religious word for the Victorians.
Adam in the first chapter is "carving a shield in the centre of a
wooden mantelpiece" (p. 4). His first words are those of the copy-
book song.

> Awake, my soul, and with the sun
> Thy daily stage of duty run;
> Shake off dull sloth.   (P. 4)

Adam, who never seems far from his basket of tools, reminds us
with his humorlessness—even when about the "business" of courting—that the Victorian phrase for sex was "marital duties."

Those who are idle in the book are grotesque, like the sickly old
maids of Irwine's family, or, like Adam's mother, with her affecta-
tions and unreality. Even when walking through his fields to
church, Mr. Poyser feels his "fingers itch to be at the hay" (p.
199). Adam, walking out to bring Hetty back from Stoniton on a
beautiful day that gives him a sense of complete well-being, does
not delight in the view or luxuriate in his own feelings. "Adam was
intent on schemes by which the roads might be improved that
were so imperfect all through the country, and on picturing the
benefits that might come from the exertions of a single country
gentleman, if he would set his mind to getting the roads made good
in his own district" (p. 405). The word *industry* was both a public
and a private term, a social fact and a trait of character.

Each character registers through the array of tasks he is involved
in. Every social place, whether Adam's or Dinah's or Mr. Poyser's,
is less an honorific position than a round of chores. When the tasks
are visible, the place comes into view and is part of the identity of
the character. The ideal characters, Adam, Dinah, and the Poysers,
are always busy, always defined through what they are doing.
Another way of stating it is that they are always within society.

The danger of nature for those who cannot think of the roads
that might be improved can be seen in the following progression.

Adam Bede

The love scenes between Arthur and Hetty, the illicit affair, takes place in the forest, in nature; those between Adam and Hetty, the unwise courtship, take place in the garden at the Hall Farm, nature subdued and *industrialized* by man, but still nature. The scenes of recognition and declaration between Adam and Dinah take place indoors, and the most important happens in the workshop of the Bede cottage.

For even the most resolute, the most pure, nature is a danger. The contrast between Hetty and Dinah is most evident in the chapters that describe each in her bedroom at night. Hetty does not look out from her world of dreams and vanities. The scene beyond the window never attracts her attention. The little treasure box with which she is identified is a box of trinkets and gifts—a complete antithesis to Adam's toolbox—a box of fantasy materials and illusions. The candle and piece of mirror that complete the materials of vanity are the entire range of her vision. Her world is too small and unreal to include nature.

But in Dinah's room, nature is equally absent, as though selfishness and selflessness joined in resistance to the appeal.

And now the first thing she did on entering her room was to seat herself in this chair and look out on the peaceful fields beyond which the large moon was rising, just above the hedgerow elms. She liked the pasture best where the milch cows were lying, and next to that the meadow where the grass was half-mown, and lay in silvered sweeping lines. Her heart was very full, for there was to be only one more night on which she would look out on those fields for a long time to come; but she thought little of leaving the mere scene, for, to her, bleak Snowfield had just as many charms. She thought of all the dear people whom she had learned to care for among these peaceful fields, and who would now have a place in her loving remembrance forever. She thought of the struggles and the weariness that might lie before them in the rest of their life's journey, when she would be away from them, and know nothing of what was befalling them; and the pressure of this thought soon became too strong for her to enjoy the unresponding stillness of the moonlit fields. She closed her eyes that she might feel more intensely the presence of a Love and Sympathy deeper and more tender than was breathed from the earth and sky. (Pp. 161–62)

In the act of closing her eyes to fill herself with the miseries of others, alert to the call to sympathy, she only imposes a more extreme resistance to herself and the memories that are associated with the scene.

There is a negativity in both women. Dinah's eyes are closed to prevent a personal moment, and Hetty's are fixed on a mirror in which she sees the illusory self of her daydreams. The summary notes a flaw in Dinah alongside the more serious moral failure of Hetty. "What a strange contrast the two figures made, visible enough in that mingled twilight and moonlight! Hetty, her cheeks flushed and her eyes glistening from her imaginary drama, her beautiful arms and neck bare, her hair hanging in a curly tangle down her back, and the baubles in her ears. Dinah, covered with her long white dress, her pale face full of subdued emotion, almost like a lovely corpse into which the soul has returned charged with sublimer secrets and a sublimer love" (p. 164). The "lovely corpse" in which the human has died and been replaced by a "sublimer love" is a peculiar testimony against the natural humanity that must die to produce the sympathy of the sublimer love. This love assumes resistance to selfish impulse, not simply to the self—but no distinction is drawn.

There are moments when nature allies itself with the forces that transcend the self. It permits a moment of vision. More, it encourages that vision, as Adam points out. "I like to go to work by a road that'll take me up a bit of a hill, and see the fields for miles around me, and a bridge, or a town, or a bit of steeple here and there. It makes you feel the world's a big place, and there's other men working in it with their heads and hands besides yourself" (p. 123). The hill that brings him a sight of the complex human world of Hayslope's fields, bridges, and steeples—all signs of the conquest of nature by human purposes—encourages him to relate his own work to the wealth of projects around him.

Moments of this kind are rare in *Adam Bede*. Perhaps the moral point owes more to Adam's character than to the effects of wide views. In fact, as we might expect in a novel so centered on society, nature is the location of the dangers to social life. Nature is an alternative community. Since the selves of the young characters are not fixed but still in process of growth, nature and society are not alternative settings for a fixed self. Instead they are forces in dialogue with the self, forces that restrain or encourage aspects of the self. The pressures of nature are most visible in the relationship of Arthur and Hetty, which takes place in the Chase, the Donnithorne woods. Nature in extreme is a force in Hetty's flight and crime. The murder and the near-suicide take place under the almost hypnotic fascination of nature—nature not even adjacent to society, as the Chase was.

In the most important social act of the novel, Adam is appointed overseer of the woods by Arthur on the day of his coming of age. The act is the first of Arthur's majority, and it transfers power over the woods to the new forces of timber valuation and the industrialized use of nature. Adam is a carpenter, like Joseph. He transforms natural into social material, trees into tables and coffins. The woods over which Adam and the society he represents gain power are closely identified with sexual temptation, as in Arthur's affair with Hetty. Arthur, in fact, has a kind of headquarters in the wood, the hermitage. An alternative home, temporary to be sure, it brings him close to the divided life of Wemmick. The hermitage permits him a secret life alongside the public one he has in the Donnithorne mansion. The seduction of Hetty takes place at meetings in the woods, and their sexual encounters have the secret, socially exempt setting of the hermitage. The trees in the grove are described as "languid," a word often used for Arthur. The word calls up a physical and moral opposite, "uprightness," the word for Adam's almost rigid bearing.

The woods shelter the secret meetings that are unnatural. The book might seem guilty of a willfulness in symbolically equating a furtive relationship with a natural setting. In *Adam Bede*, a relationship that cannot give public voice to itself is marked with unreality and pretense that can be called unnatural. The seduction of a farm girl by the heir to the manor is, in this sense, unnatural.

For Rousseau, the social self is only the natural self hobbled by chains and turned artificial by an external set of public demands. Nothing could be further from the ideas Eliot held when she wrote *Adam Bede*. For Rousseau, the natural self can reappear and recover its freedom in nature. But in the grove, Arthur and Hetty are not free of their social selves, only free of the eyes of society. At their first meeting, Arthur "dared not look at the little buttermaker for the first minute or two" (p. 134). Hetty addresses him as "sir."

In all her dreams, Hetty thinks nothing of the sensations of passion, only of the social fiction that, because she is in love with a gentleman, she will soon be a lady. She is restless, withdrawn and discontented; she suffers from what we now call Bovaryism. She is impatient and indignant with her rounds of duties at the Poysers', because it is a life that defines her with too much concreteness. Hetty plans to become a lady's maid, a life more suited to her need for fantasy and a wealth of dreamlike possibilities, however remote. For her, Arthur's love is one gamble of this kind, a bartering of concrete reality, too crude for the self she would like to be, for a chance at a magical transformation into her fantasy self. In the woods we hear again and again the word *sir*. The woods permit a relaxation of the vigilance of society, a scrutiny represented as beneficial to the self. What is propriety but a constant reminder, through tokens of behavior, of what one, in fact, *is?* The bows and

Adam Bede

curtsies, the fact that Hetty is among those in church who must wait until the manorial family arrives and then stand while they enter: these are tokens of place and function. Hetty, even in the woods, is "the little butter-maker," but in the woods she is free to deceive herself about it.

Like the road in picaresque novels, the woods are outside society in a negative way, a way that encourages disguises and false identities as social as those left behind. Hetty can pretend she is close to becoming what she always fantasized being. Arthur, by encouraging the fantasy, can force her to trade on what she is: innocent and pretty. In bargaining with the little she does have, Hetty cuts off her retreat to "accepting what she is." After the crime she is uncommunicative and sullen, she is "dead." The fate that overtakes her in exile is the fulfillment of a process that was assured from the "killing" of the true self with which she began.

The choice Hetty makes to affirm a remotely possible fantasy self—the chance of a marriage with Arthur—by destroying her true self takes place in the woods, where the reminders of self— the acts of one's true life: minding children, making butter, cleaning the house—are absent. In the woods she is "someone" walking, she is her appearance, not her acts. Appearance and, in particular, beauty are dangerous, as the novel stresses again and again. In society one is always occupied, and, through the trappings and place of occupation, testifying to what one is. In the woods, just walking, the self can be what it looks like, or it can pretend to be what it wants. Only Arthur's memory places her as "the butter-maker." Otherwise she is a pretty girl walking, an esthetic rather than a social fact. But the memory holds, and it is only through deliberate unawareness on Hetty's part (a form of self-denial), and collusion in her fantasy on Arthur's, that the affair can exist.

The box of jewelry hidden in Hetty's drawer is a symbol of this. For jewelry has only a social meaning. Like a uniform, it has its being in the relation it creates to others. Jewelry that cannot be worn is a paradox of value. Of course, it is worn in those moments

Making Up Society

of impersonation before the mirror where, in another reversed symbol, Hetty sees not herself, but her possible self. She becomes that other she wants to be and is her own audience, her own society of admiring and envious commentators.

The narcissism and selfishness that seem to be defined by the symbols of the mirror and jewelry, the nightly ceremony with the secret hoard, are the opposite of the truth. These are signs of the most intense loss of self. It is a state of reverie and pretense in which the true self has been denied and bartered for the stage properties of a personal illusion. The two spaces that allow this killing of the self are the solitude of the bedroom, exempt as it is from the scrutiny of others, and the secrecy of the woods.

Adam, we are told, had not been in the woods of the Chase for years. His accidental walk there is a shortcut to return tools Seth had forgotten; he discovers the lovers. As always, Adam has with him his pet dog Gyp. Pets are everywhere in the novel: like gardens, they are portions of nature brought into the human order, tamed, and assigned a place. Nature becomes the servant or amusement of man. The woods placed under Adam's control will become part of the human system. When he discovers Arthur and Hetty in an embrace, he challenges Arthur. The fight between them is, along with the sexual relationship, the central break in the order and decorum of public life. Like the love affair, the fight happens in the woods. The challenge of the battle is not to the order and hierarchy, but to the disloyalty of Arthur to that system. The battle is to restore the importance of the social in all of their lives, and through that restoration to reach once again the respect for others that, from Adam's point of view, Arthur has denied. Adam accuses him of trifling both with Hetty and with Adam's own love for her. Trifling is the refusal to accept others as equivalent selves either by neglect—of the importance of Adam's feelings—or by complicity—in Hetty's illusions. In their encounter in the woods, Adam takes on the role of overseer of Arthur as well as of the woods. The letter he forces him to write breaking off the affair is the first mark of the moral husbandry Adam will assert for the rest of the novel.

Finally, it is important to note that Arthur's relationship to the woods is the best example of the very important relationship to nature of the aristocratic system he represents. The woods are annexed but not industrialized. They become the scene for the riding and hunting, for those stylized games that imitate the necessities of earlier life. The relationship of the "hermitage" to the real hut of a hermit, and even the pretense of hermit existence within the complex, socialized life of the aristocracy, point to the make-believe of that life. The riding and hunting, the play at being a soldier (before his exile and the beginning of his true military life), are all one with the make-believe little romance Arthur has with Hetty. It is nature in the annexed, make-believe wild sense of the Chase that is the scene of these games, whether hunt or love. The solid middle class that gains control with Adam's power over the woods will destroy the fiction and use the trees as raw material for its tables and coffins.

Beyond the preserves that have been maintained as imitations of wild nature is that true nature itself, truly beyond both society and identity, the scene of Hetty's murder of her child and flirtation with suicide—the two ultimate acts, the first against society, the second against self. That the second is not accomplished is more a sign that it was superfluous than that she shied away from it. In fact, Hetty does not kill the child so much as abandon it to nature. Without human care, without society, the child will die, as we say, "of exposure." Hetty buries the infant alive, returns it to the earth in a last hope for secrecy and unreality. With the truth of melodrama, one of the infant's hands appears above the ground to deny the pretense.

Hetty has run away to avoid the truth of what she has become. The pregnancy makes it impossible to marry Adam and conceal the extent of her affair with Arthur. She runs to Arthur, who isn't there, and then alternates between images of a return to Dinah and a final attempt at secrecy through suicide. "At last she was among the fields she had been dreaming of, on a long narrow pathway leading to a wood. If there should be a pool in that wood! . . . No, it was not a wood, only a wild brake, where there had once been gravel pits leaving mounds and hollows studded with brushwood and small trees" (p. 396). The nature she reaches is not primitive, nor prior to man, but nature from which man has withdrawn. The gravel pits, the sign of man's industry, are abandoned and overgrown. The scene is Hetty's emblem, for she is a person from whom the self is withdrawn, the social has been denied. The word *wood* that is repeated and rejected is used in the titles of the chapters in which her meetings with Arthur take place. The abandoned gravel pits are wilder, reclaimed by nature as the body is in suicide.

She finds the pool she imagined: "There it was black under the darkening sky: no motion, no sound near" (p. 396). The pool is cold. Gone are light, movement, sound, and heat. She falls asleep. The image of death, this little sleep, substitutes for the suicide. Hetty wakes feeling "dead already." In an important sense, of course, she *is* dead already, but she is denied the final concealment, that of disappearing without a trace from society. Could she vanish, she would keep part of her secret.

Dead as she is individually, she remains to carry out symbolically the public side of her life. Her willful silence in prison, her impassivity, is that of certain characters in dreams: they represent the dead. One sign of this death is that, after the moment at the pool, Hetty's point of view disappears from the novel. Her interior life no longer exists for the reader. She was, along with Arthur, the character whose states of mind dominated the interior sections of the book. From this point on, she exists only as an element in the dramas of others—Adam, Dinah, and the society that brings her to trial.

The trial that puts society and the reader in possession of the facts, destroying the last secrecy, leads to the sentence of death.

The sentence is not carried out by society. Hetty dies in exile, but death and exile are one and the same. The final death registers the truth of the death at the pond and the loss of self in the woods that preceded it. And it is in nature and solitude, the exile at home, that the self was first destroyed.

REFUSING SOCIETY

The other important death in the novel, that of Thias Bede, is also at the hands of nature, and that particularly important symbol of nature for Eliot, water. In Joyce, the identical symbolism occurs as a metaphor—on a verbal rather than a plot level—when Stephen thinks of the man drowned off Sandymount and then of his father, whose life has been destroyed by liquor. His father was drowned, he thinks, by a "high tide at a Dublin bar." The liquid that kills old Bede is only metaphorically water.

Death by water, sobriety, and drunkenness are motifs that recur throughout Eliot's novels. Here it is important, by way of an introduction to the notion of society in *Adam Bede*, to see the special way in which drunkenness, like Hetty's fantasy self, destroys both self and society. A drunken man is excused from responsibility: "He's not himself," we say. What we permit him are the antisocial forces; he can be violent or foolish, he can fight or stagger. He has no shame or self-respect. He can't walk a straight line.

In Adam's memory after his father's death, we see that once he began drinking, Thias was no longer himself. The family life turned to a burden, and Adam at one point ran away from home, only to return to take on the paternal role. Relationships in the family were inverted: the responsible son was forced to try to control the irresponsible father. Adam, who remembered saying with pride, "I'm Thias Bede's son," became "Adam Bede." Old Bede drinks at the Wagon Overthrown and takes on, in social terms, those two fatal qualities: secretiveness and unreliability.

The word *reliability* defines the way drunkenness destroys society. Thias, on the day of his final fling, leaves unfinished the coffin promised for the next day. Adam then must work all night to finish it so that they can "keep their word" and deliver it. The predictability that is essential for a social life based on industry is not different from that necessary for any community whatsoever. The cornerstones are two things: keeping one's word and being what one appears to be; reliability and visibility. The notion of reliability is, then, the social form of the idea of continuity that is the basis for wholeness in the self. The forces that destroy the legibility and reliability of the social life are imagined in the novel through the images of Arthur's sexual passion and Thias Bede's drunkenness. Again the Victorian word is vital: they spoke of "indulging" in liquor. Thias withdraws from community and family—deception and furtiveness are signs of that withdrawal—and indulges in a private set of moods. Drink replaces acts with states of being. Adam remembers his father as "wild and foolish, shouting out a song fitfully among his drunken companions at the Wagon Overthrown" (p. 49). The fitful song contrasts in Adam's memory with the skilled carpentry of his earlier days; the drunken companions replace the family.

In one of the comic moments of overexplicitness in the novel, Adam accepts a drink of whey from Mrs. Poyser and says: "Thank you, Mrs. Poyser . . . a drink of whey's allays a treat to me. I'd rather have it than beer anyday!" (p. 224). His comment proves the truth of one of the shrewdest comments ever made about Victorian realism. In an article about mid-nineteenth century painting, Jerrold Lanes has said: "The manner was realistic because it was intended to be persuasive; and it had to be persuasive because it was intended no longer merely to embody certain ideals, as Baroque history painting had done, but to *propagandize* on their behalf."[1] Adam, it is worth noting, is put in charge of overseeing

---

1. Jerrold Lanes, "Romantic Art in England," *Artforum* (Summer 1968): 31.

Adam Bede

the liquor on the day of celebration for Arthur's coming of age. Like the woods, the liquor is assigned to his rather stern control. Thias's actual death, as with Hetty's, only registers a destruction already complete. In particular, Thias lost his place as father, carpenter, and provider. At times wild and foolish, at others guilty and sullen, he was not dependable. At last he was a burden to his son. Once dead he is mourned, but it is what he once was that is missed. What drowned with him was the weight on others, and with his death freedom and a more natural life begin for Adam.

Hetty and Thias underline the social importance of visibility and reliable behavior. Equally, the community rests on a set of related projects that, for any one person, amounts to his identity. Hayslope differs from every later community drawn by Eliot in not having a money economy: the public life is one of services, not goods. Adam stays up to complete the coffin because it is needed for a funeral the next day, not to earn the pay. When he is appointed overseer of the woods, no salary is mentioned, only the social signs of the position such as his right to sit at the table of the main members of the community at the name-day dinner. When Adam accepts a job it is because it needs doing: we never hear of his pay. The concern with wills, bankruptcy, inheritance, avarice and debt, hoarding and generosity—the world of money so important in the rest of Eliot's work—is absent here. Work that is not pure service (as that of the minister or teacher is) produces goods so necessary (food, the products of carpentry) that no commerce is involved. Adam at one point intends to set up a business in fine furniture. His plan for a compact, movable, kitchen cupboard capable of "containing grocery, pickles, crockery, and house-linen in the utmost compactness without confusion" (p. 238) would introduce expensive items of convenience on a commercial basis. The idea is given up.

The services of Hayslope are stable. Adam follows his father into carpentry. Where a man's place is improved, it is on invitation. Adam is asked to take control over the woods because his ability matches the obvious need. He rises to become foreman and then owner of Burge's timberyard because he is the best man to fill an empty place. A social optimism at work in the novel assumes that in the long run rationality will rule. The one idea Adam has of making his own place, creating a place, is abandoned. The society is tolerant where its self-interest advises, and the one restriction on a man like Adam is the demand that he be patient and restrained in the use of his abilities. He must use his power within the order that exists and not introduce a new order of commerce that he can direct as he chooses.

Dinah, who has the possibility of being an even more direct challenge to the social order, abandons, like Adam, her independence for the place available within the community—she marries. Dinah's resistance, like that of Antigone, resulted from a call that questions community practices in the name of higher loyalties. Eliot carefully relates each of her actions to signs, dreams, or biblical forecasts. Inspiration guides every choice. She first preaches when unexpected circumstances and an inner call demand it. Of course, accidents and inner promptings also guided every step of Arthur and Hetty's affair. Dinah leaves the Poysers to return to Snowfield when a dream and a "casting" of the Bible direct her. It is even more important that Dinah has stepped out of her community role only to serve others more effectively. She is at the opposite pole from Hetty and Arthur, who deny society for indulgence and pleasure.

Underneath the apparently complete sacrifice of her ego, Dinah has made two choices. First, she takes upon herself the search for those who need her help the most. She might have stayed in Hayslope and responded when needs arose. She initiates, and, by leaving and deciding (even with the help of omens), she creates a role she must form herself, not one that is an existing place that she accepts. Like Adam when he plans to begin manufacturing cupboards for which he will have to convince housewives there is a need, Dinah, in the moment she gives up her actual community of

Hayslope, places herself in relation to an abstract role, that of nurse and comforter. Such a role can only arise as an occupation when community has, through specialization, disappeared. Dinah's second choice is a more obvious one. To follow this life of charity, she decides she must not marry. However different their reasons and moral levels, Dinah and Hetty are close in this choice. The crime Hetty commits in nature is the most unnatural crime: infanticide. In a society based on the family, or in any society where love rather than fear and authority binds men together, infanticide replaces parricide as the darkest social crime. Parricide and regicide are one, but, in a democracy, infanticide is the stroke that questions the bonds of society itself. To reach this point, Hetty must absolutely deny natural feeling in herself. The realm of natural feeling is in fact social feeling, and both are epitomized in the nineteenth century by the love of a mother for her child. That love is used in the period as a refutation of the iron law of self-interest and of the social contract theory of society. The general importance in the Victorian period of Renaissance paintings of the Madonna and Child is well known. George Eliot in Dresden was so overwhelmed by a Madonna and Child by Raphael that the hours she spent in the gallery count as one of the deepest experiences of her life. Hetty is beyond this inevitable claim of her nature, both social and human. What outweighs these claims is the need to deny reality of what she has become by destroying the evidence, the baby.

Dinah's choice not to marry reverses the social claims of her nature. Here it is for a moral purpose, not a selfish one. What she chooses is a life in abstract relation to mercy, instead of one where virtues answer to natural, immediate demands. Natural in this context means inevitable; given, not chosen. His father's drunkenness imposes responsibility on Adam, he does not seek it. Control over the woods is offered him, he does not compete for it.

The inspiration that guides Dinah is, however much the novel associates it with omens, hard to divide from will. A choice, personal or impersonal, is still an activity that radiates out from the self to determine the conditions of life. The alternative is a resignation to whatever is at hand. Dinah's entire life is a chosen role outside the given one of marriage and domesticity. However noble in moral terms that role might be, in social terms it is a more insidious danger to the community than Hetty's life. Morality and society join in condemning Hetty. By following a higher path, Dinah makes morally immune a social career that legitimates individuality—designing a life instead of accepting a place.

In de Tocqueville's terms, Dinah and Adam (in his project for the cupboards and in his self-reliance) are individualists, while Arthur and Hetty are egoists. In Dinah's Methodism, services are on the green. Feeling and conversion experiences replace the customs and ceremonies that take place in Irwine's church. Personal emotion substitutes for doctrine and democracy of sinners replaces the well-graduated pews, each assigned to a family, of the national church. Adam, too, embodies tendencies never developed in the novel. His is a world of expertise and technicians. In his area of knowledge, he gives way to no one who cannot demonstrate greater knowledge. This cuts across the respect by rank of the society of Hayslope. His promotion is held up by the old squire with whom he has quarreled over the price of a sewing box. When Adam beats Arthur in the woods, he demands a recognition of equality, a democracy of feeling where any man's desires are as important as any other's.

The marriage of Adam and Dinah, which so clearly breaks the logic of the book, forces each back into the place society has designed. Each retreats by choice, but the reasons are unconvincing. Historically, of course, the Adams and the Dinahs did not retreat. Goethe described romanticism as an acorn planted in the Greek vase of classicism, an acorn that in growth would destroy the vessel that fostered it. The individualism that was created out of a community like Hayslope had, by the date *Adam Bede* was written, destroyed that society. The novel takes place in 1799 and

Adam Bede

1800, the signature years of an old and a new century, an old and a new order. With the epilogue, the novel reaches to 1807, the years of Napoleon. In the imagination of the century, Napoleon reigned as the type of the man who rises to conquer the world. Any young man making his own place, even as a clerk in London, was setting out "to conquer the world." Even Henry James, in his final delirium, imagined himself Napoleon. The French Revolution is over when *Adam Bede*, begins, but the real fruit of the revolution is Napoleon, the self-made man.

To picture the Adams and Dinahs retiring early to modest lives in Hayslope is to turn the sociology of the book to idyll. Society is dependent on their willingness to abandon what they could achieve, because society must recognize in them its own highest virtues of industry and service raised to a way of life.

So far the society of *Adam Bede* has been seen mainly in re- action to the challenges it defeats or eludes: Thias Bede, Hetty, Arthur, Adam, and Dinah. Some of these challenges are self- destructive: old Bede's drinking finally leaves him too confused to cross the stream. Hetty, too, is self-destructive, but one com- ponent of the case demands a more active intervention by society. The two institutions called on to heal the social body do so with full success: religion and the law together intervene at the climax of the novel, and both are completely adequate to the jobs of dis- covering the truth, judging it, and recovering the harmony of society.

The adequacy of both institutions is, of course, in total contrast to the often ironic or painful relation of public to private truth in Eliot's later work. How thoroughly the society comes to terms with Arthur and Hetty can be seen by contrasting the three ideas of exposure, discovery, and confession. For the affair to exist, it must be secret, and each of Hetty's more horrible steps is taken to protect some part of the secret. But the pregnancy will expose the truth. The child's hand above the ground exposes the murder. Adam discovers the lovers in the wood. He learns of their relationship but not of its extent. He learns against their will. Hetty is discovered at the grave of her child, and, through the witness who tells of the discovery in court, the extent of the relationship becomes known. The society assembles the entire truth of what was concealed, but it does so without the aid of those who created the secrecy. In essence, a secret is only a split between experience and behavior.

Society's sovereignty is complete only when it can get the guilty one to acknowledge society by testifying against himself. In that act he disowns the self that did the crime in the name of his loyalty to society and his social self. For this reason most legal systems are lenient with the criminal who confesses. Iago's silence is so powerful in *Othello* because in the end he will not affirm the solidarity with others that his acts brought into question.

From Eliot's statement, we know that the scene of Hetty's confession to Dinah in the prison provided the starting point for *Adam Bede*.[2] This moment is the one that remained in her memory from the story told twenty-five years earlier by her aunt. The moment of confession goes beyond the thoroughness of exposure and discovery to make the success of society complete. The incident in the prison was the germ for the novel.

Through the Reverend Irwine, society avoids the incidental effects of the crime that threatened to destroy Hayslope. The Poysers do not uproot themselves in disgrace at the loss of their good name. Adam does not become what he is so close to in many ways—another wandering craftsman like Hardy's Jude. He even agrees to keep his job as overseer of the Donnithorne woods, conditioning his consent on Arthur's willingness to accept a punishment equal to Hetty's, a self-imposed exile that has no legal basis. Under the law, Arthur is not guilty. Like the retreats of Adam and Dinah, Arthur's exile keeps society stable through a private act.

---

2. John W. Cross, *The Life and Letters of George Eliot* (New York: Wanamaker, 1910), p. 281.

Adam Bede

The community that is renewed through Adam and Dinah's marriage and protected through the deaths of Hetty and Thias and the exile of Arthur has, as one of its images, those winter evenings at the Hall Farm, those evenings at the Poysers' "when the whole family, in patriarchal fashion, master and mistress, children and servants, were assembled in that glorious kitchen, at well-graduated distances from the blazing fire" (p. 100). The chairs differ in comfort and size; they seem fixed in their "well-graduated distances" forever. A stranger could decipher the social information in the seating arrangement. This is a world where every table has a "head," places of honor, and seats of lesser importance: no table has four equal sides. Space and direction are functions of meaning. In church, standing and sitting and elevated places or near and far pews mark out a little map of the society assembled there. Arthur rides whereas Adam walks. On meeting, people bow or rise, as the congregation does when the Donnithornes enter church.

Part of the intimism of Victorian realism, and a partial hint that the society of Hayslope is not viable, can be seen in the skepticism and irony that come into play whenever the novel deals with symbols of social order larger than the family. The winter evenings at the Poysers' are hierarchical, contented, and cheerful. Since the fire is blazing, all are, no doubt, warm. The slightly larger society at the church is described defensively through that irritating technique Eliot favored of imagining the comments of a sophisticated opponent and defeating his criticisms with sarcastic rebuttal. An indulgent nostalgia alone argue for the ritualized deference we see in the church.

Finally, the one ceremony of the society as a whole, Arthur's name day, is cut through with bitter sarcasm, and its images of order are parodied even by those present. Feasting, games, and dancing, the three symbolic acts of social harmony in the epic and the social novel, are the relaxations of the day. The diners eat at appropriate levels, some in the mansion, some on the lawn, the workers in town. The Donnithornes' social equals are absent: they will be feted separately on the next day. Those who are dining up-stairs cannot decide who will sit at the head of the table:

"It stands to sense," Mr. Casson was saying, "as old Mr. Poyser, as is th' oldest man i' the room, should sit at top o' the table. I wasn't butler fifteen year without learning the rights and wrongs about dinner."

"Nay, nay," said old Martin, "I'n gi'en up to my son; I'm no tenant now: let my son take my place. Th' ould folks ha' had their turn: they mun make way for the young uns."

"I should ha' thought the biggest tenant had the best rights more nor th' oldest," said Luke Britton, who was not fond of the critical Mr. Poyser; "there's Mr. Holdsworth has more land nor anybody else on th' estate."

"Well," said Mr. Poyser, "suppose we say the man wi' the foulest land shall sit at top; then whoever gets th' honour, there'll be no envying on him."

"Eh, there's Mester Massey," said Mr. Craig, who, being a neutral in the dispute, had no interest but in conciliation; "the schoolmaster ought to be able to tell you what's right. Who's to sit at top o' the table, Mr. Massey?"

"Why, the broadest man," said Bartle; "and then he won't take up other folk's room; and the next broadest must sit at the bottom."

This happy mode of settling the dispute produced much laughter. (P. 269)

Bartle's practical solution mocks the choices of oldest or richest suggested by the others, and it is adopted. When the games begin, the representatives of the upper class pass condescending comments on the prettiness of the "common" girls competing in the races. Arthur's aunt has chosen prizes of "grim-looking gowns" so as not to encourage "a love of finery among women of that class" (p. 285). When Bessy Cranage wins and is given the prize, "her

Adam Bede

lip fell," and she retreats to cry under a tree. The deliberately ugly prizes call up the great sophistication in England of the psychology of class. In the early nineteenth century, in many orphanages the children were permitted to sing only in chorus, never as soloists, so that they would not become "individuals."

At the dance that follows the games, the unreality reaches a peak: "Arthur entered in his regimentals, leading Mrs. Irwine to a carpet-covered dais ornamented with hot-house plants, where she and Miss Anne were to be seated with old Mr. Donnithorne, that they might look on at the dancing, like the kings and queens in the plays" (p. 292). Mrs. Irwine, the standard for affectation and harmless absurdity in the novel, refers to her son, the minister, as "Dauphin." They are only like kings and queens in the plays— apparently even the stage has more reality than the ceremony at Hayslope. The dance itself is not an occasion for grace and conversation, wit and polish; it is not a Mozartian moment in the style of Jane Austen. It is a rustic dance, filled with cruel deceptions. Adam holds Hetty for the first time, but, a moment before, Hetty's locket had been pulled out by the infant she was holding. It broke on the floor to show a lock of dark hair. Adam's day of triumph (he is named overseer of the woods and dances with Hetty) contains the first hint of the reality around him.

The bitter falsity or comic emptiness of the social forms at the name-day celebration show the skepticism that comes into play as the novel moves toward the larger, concentric circles of order in Hayslope. The one scene that would have reversed the trend is significantly absent. Eliot omits the formal and personal elements of the trial. It is not a legal system or a court of law before which we see Hetty, but Justice itself, abstract, ahistorical, depersonalized. By showing public functions without forms, Eliot underlines the point that the forms we do see are without function.

The chairs around the fire at the Hall Farm are celebrated, the benches at strategic distances in church are mentioned with quaint indulgence, but the Byzantine arrangements of the nameday are hollow and oppressive, fit only for jokes. Involved is the domesticity, the regional sense of social life. The forms are more valid the closer they are to persons. The Hall Farm is a more honorable institution than the whole manor of which it is a part, or the invisible "all England" of which the manor is in its turn a part. But the personal nature of structures is only a part of the answer.

When we move beyond the Hall Farm, it is not only structures that become brittle. The patriarchal authority and right to respect that Mr. Poyser enjoys in his family are not extended to old Squire Donnithorne's public reign. Living "beyond his time," the old squire weighs on Arthur and stands in his way as much as Thias Bede did for Adam. Wrong-headed and arbitrary, he is also weak, and in one of the scenes in the novel there for its own sake he is defeated by Mrs. Poyser. Arthur, who plans to replace the old squire's neglect and willfulness with a benevolent reign, is defeated by his own weakness. The respect and love he wants from his tenants are wiped away by his affair. If anyone comes to power on the name day it is Adam, but he must pretend to remain a subordinate in a system he is coming to control.

The life of the rich and idle is pictured with contempt. As in all of Eliot's novels, the aristocracy spends its time "riding," not in work but in aimless exercises to use up its energy. Irwine's sisters are pampered and make an occupation out of being sick. When the entire group is assembled for the games on name day, they are described with an acidity Eliot reserves for the idle rich:

Soon after four o'clock, splendid old Mrs. Irwine in her damask satin and jewels and black lace, was led out by Arthur, followed by the whole family party, to her raised seat under the striped marquee, where she was to give out the prizes to the victors. Staid, formal Miss Lydia had requested to resign this queenly office to the royal old lady, and Arthur was pleased with this opportunity of gratifying his godmother's taste for stateliness. Old Mr. Donnithorne, the deli-

Adam Bede

cately clean, finely scented withered old man, led out Miss Irwine with his air of punctillious, acid politeness; Mr. Gawaine brought Miss Lydia, looking neutral and stiff in an elegant peach-blossom silk; and Mr. Irwine came last with his pale sister Anne. (P. 281)

Without energy or even color, all bachelors or old maids, widows or widowers, sickly almost as a privilege of breeding, they are the image of a society too feeble to continue or reproduce. The only child is that conceived by Arthur and Hetty, the child Hetty murders.

If what we see in *Adam Bede* involves a withering at the extremes and a surge of new life from the center, the book could more confidently be taken as a version of the regeneration that is constant in social life. But when we reach back to the center, the family, the question is more puzzling. Although the Poysers are at the center of the social reality of the novel, they are peripheral characters. They have no "personal lives," and we are never given their feelings or private relationships. Like Bartle Massey or the Irwines, they are pure behavior, pure public life. They do not develop or decline; there is little variation in their moods, and we are not given their response to the one disturbing event in their lives—Hetty's crime. Even more, we never see them tested by crisis. The possibility that they might be forced to move away because of Hetty's disgrace is dealt with by others. The abstract danger that the old squire will cancel their lease, again the risk of uprooting, is dissolved by his death. Placid and unchanging, they seem untouched by the moral and psychological complexities of the lives we see around them. They seem to breathe another air entirely. Yet it is with them, through their point of view, that we approach both public scenes: church and name day. The ritual harvest feast that is the third social event celebrates the Poysers' harvest. Finally, the many scenes of proposal and recognition take place at the Hall Farm.

The Hall Farm is thus at the center and, at the same time, protected from the scrutiny and moral rigor applied in detail elsewhere. Around the Hall Farm accumulate the nostalgia and hazy charm that lead the narrative into idyll. The dairy is described with an intensity beyond realism. "Such coolness, such purity, such fresh fragrance of new pressed cheese, of firm butter, of wooden vessels perpetually bathed in pure water; such soft colouring of red-earthenware and creamy surfaces, brown wood and polished tin, grey limestone and rich orange rust on the tin weights and hooks and hinges" (p. 84). The details tumble forth, evoked and savored in a litany of nostalgia. Here is the idyllic view of the country Eliot spoke against in her essay on Riehl, the idyll based on distance, the country seen from the city. Idyll is country life, she wrote, seen in a vague abstract way. The rustic is the countryman seen from two hundred and twenty yards. Up close, the scene with its confusions and discordant details becomes once again a human one.

In Schiller's great essay *On Naive and Sentimental Poetry*, the poet must either be nature or seek her. He must be naive or sentimental. For those who have lost the country and lost the past, the sentimental is the last contact with nature. The sentimental mode has as its two form the idyll and the elegy, paradise and paradise lost. If the moods that make up the charm of the Hall Farm chapters are specified, they are the idyllic and the elegiac. One of those chapters ends with the apostrophe to Old Leisure. In one page the sentimentality, elegy, and idyll are all combined in tribute to a life that, as we see in the rest of the book, is anything but leisured; in fact, it is a life of bustle and unending work.

Finally, the family life of duties and work that is imposed and never chosen, the life of butter-making and fence-mending, the life of harvest and housecleaning, of a total harmony between economic and domestic life—this pattern is completely irrelevant to those characters whose moral lives are our concern in the book. The force of the family has vanished not only at the aristocratic level. Hetty and Dinah are orphans. Adam and Seth have no family, only a mother and father who burden them. Arthur has no family and lives with his grandfather. Bartle Massey, Adam's mentor, and the Reverend Irwine, who is Arthur's advisor, are both bachelors. From the younger generation only one marriage results, that of Adam and Dinah. This marriage is less a sign of renewal than of a concentration of the energies of the new society. They have renounced a break with Hayslope, but neither Adam nor Dinah has given up the habits of character that make that break, in the long run, inevitable. In their marriage lies the form of a patient new society that is content, at first, merely to administer the patterns of the old.

On the final page of the novel, the Poysers walk in at the gate of the lumberyard now owned by Adam, the Hall Farm paying its respects to the new center of power.

3

The Mill on the Floss

We can gauge the darkness and paradox that have entered into
the relation of public and private truth in *The Mill on the
Floss* by recalling the union of personal redemption and social
reconciliation in the trial of Hetty and contrasting it with the trial
by water Maggie points out in her picture book when she is nine
years old. " 'It's a dreadful picture isn't it? But I can't help looking
at it. That old woman in the water's a witch—they've put her in
to find out whether she's a witch or no, and if she swims she's a
witch, and if she's drowned—and killed, you know—she's innocent, and not a witch, but only a poor silly old woman. But what
good would it do her then, you know, when she was drowned?' "
(p. 15). To come under suspicion is to be lost. If she saves herself
by swimming, she is given to the fire as a witch. Only by sinking
can she clear her name. Like a test of substances in chemistry, the
trial by water proves and manifests the being of the old woman.
But the satisfactions are those of tragedy where innocence can only
be known in consenting to be sacrificed. In Hetty's trial, three aims
of justice met: the truth was established, the society torn by the
crime was mended and affirmed, and the criminal was brought to
renounce her crime and begin to earn her way back into the community. In the trial by water, only the first goal is met. The truth
is known, but only in a very dubious way. As justice, it is as wayward and mysterious as the supposed crimes of the witch herself.

The Mill on the Floss

Like the many medieval tests it resembles, the trial by water is a proof by ordeal.

Since the old woman is lost as soon as she must be tested, the human question becomes: how did she begin to be conspicuous? Once noticed, she was thought different; once different, her substance must be known. By the laws of the ordeal, she can be known only by being destroyed. The old woman is outside the community the moment she registers in its vision, the moment she is noticed. Unlike Hetty, who is exiled only to affirm through suffering her new self, the witch is in exile as soon as questions about her arise. From that point she is of no concern as a person. The trial satisfies the community's curiosity but does not rehabilitate the witch. Executed either way, she is unimportant, and the community is purified instead of healed.

The water in which the old woman is placed is more an acid that dissolves a surface that conceals her substance. Magic and chemistry at once, the water forces the truth out of the body at the moment of death. The normal medieval legal process was trial by torture. The water releases the truth because it is the executioner; the real magic is the magic of death.

The legend reported in the twelfth chapter shows that the water that tested the witch is the same water that works the Tulliver mill and flows past the town of St. Ogg's. Ogg, a boatman who lived by ferrying passengers across the Floss, was tested one stormy night by a woman, clad in rags and carrying a child, who wanted passage across the river. All other boatmen refused, but Ogg agreed. When they reached the other side, she revealed herself as the Virgin and gave Ogg the assurance that his boat would never be in peril. Both the Virgin and Ogg manifest themselves in this legend. As in magic, the gap between appearance and substance is extreme: the Virgin is in rags, and the heroic future saint is just another impoverished boatman. His ordeal over, Ogg is transformed into a magical figure over whom floods and currents have no power. At last he is St. Ogg and rules like a local divinity the town named after him.

Witch and saint are both exceptional. Both are outside humanity. The one saves the lives of men and beasts in time of flood, the other blights both with curses and potions. The water reveals substance only when the substance is miraculous. St. Ogg has the blessed Virgin in his boat. And, in Maggie's picture of the witch, there is one other figure she points out: " 'And this dreadful blacksmith with his arms akimbo, laughing—oh, isn't he ugly?—I'll tell you what he is. He's the devil *really*' " (p. 15).

Maggie Tulliver is tested twice by the river. In the final flood of the book, she is the image of St. Ogg, rescuing her brother Tom. Guided on in the darkness by a mysterious protective power, she saves Tom only to be killed by the one force St. Ogg never had to overcome—machinery broken loose from the wharf. In Tom's moment of recognition, he understands that Maggie's presence has behind it "a story of almost divinely protected effort" (p. 556). The other test is the boat ride with Stephen Guest, where Maggie faces the choice of the witch: to die socially, her reputation ruined, whether she returns or elopes. Doomed either way, she takes the choice of every hero and heroine in Hanry James—to pay for everything but to get nothing for herself. By a solitary integrity, an innocence that proves itself by its willingness to stand and pay for the crimes it didn't commit, Maggie, in the act of becoming isolated and visible, has lost any chance at more than a private vindication. She dies in the flood that arrives immediately after she has learned she must leave St. Ogg's. She must be " 'a lonely wanderer, cut off from her past' " (p. 530). An exile, she has broken the continuity of place and objects and people that guarantees the continuity of experience. The word *familiar* and the word *family* have the same root. The break in continuity is the death of what is meant by the self in *The Mill on the Floss*.

In spite of the many small jokes pointing out that the mill really isn't on the Floss, we can be glad that in her title Eliot accepted the literal inaccuracy to bring the two great symbols of her book into prominence. If we think of the flood, the Tulliver mill comes to be

The Mill on the Floss

on the Floss at last, and the title amounts to a stress on the final moment of homecoming and reconciliation, the moment, to use Proust's phrase, when the past is recaptured. Unlike Marcel, Maggie can recover the past only in the moment of losing it irrevocably. So too, Tom repays the debts and moves back to the mill, only to see the family life he has given everything to reestablish sliding away at an accelerating rate. Proust, who saw George Eliot as a forerunner, would have marked Tom's cry of "Maggsie" in the boat as one of those moments where time loops back upon itself. The past and present, pinned together by magic at certain rare moments, replace for Proust the continuity of living memory that is basic in Eliot. For Eliot, the moment of recaptured time is not made permanent by art but erased by death. The Proustian world of three experiences—in time, in memory, and in art—rests on an atomization of life into moments that could not be further from Eliot's world of permanent conditions. The moment when the mill is on the Floss is the catastrophe that joins for a moment the point from which life started and the current that carried life relentlessly away.

Speaking of Maggie late in the novel, Eliot says, "Maggie's destiny, then, is at present hidden, and we must wait for it to reveal itself like the course of an unmapped river: we only know the river is full and rapid, and that for all rivers there is the same final home" (p. 427). The image was a favorite elegiac one for Arnold, and he used it repeatedly, but its implication is obvious enough to be overlooked: the linear motion of the river is the image of a career or trajectory. Maggie's life is a sequence of acts that define and finally make visible a substance. At last there is an identity, like Tom's, that is created and willed into existence.

The river that tests substance and affirms, once the whole course is charted, the truth of a life is a metaphor of time that replaces those of space in *Adam Bede*. The arrangement of seats in the Hayslope church or around the Poyser fire embodies a truth of substance reflected everywhere in Hayslope life in modes of dress and, particularly, in the round of tasks that amounts to the occupation of one's place. To elude these marks of truth, Hetty must enter a world of fantasy and begin to seek out the solitude of bedroom or woods in order to carry out the fantasy away from the recognition that is continuous in the community life. Where everyone not only looks like but is doing "what he is," the self is legible to others and identified. The surrender to secrecy and fantasy involves shedding function, or performing it an a mechanical way that notifies those around that "this isn't really me."

When we move to the social being that opens up only in time, we reach the cluster of new images that are those of *The Mill on the Floss*. A man "on his way up" in the world, as Tom is, is not what he appears *now* to be. In fact, all men are falling, like Mr. Tulliver, or rising, like Mr. Deane. Or they are retired, like Mr. Glegg. Every man is "making his way." In the commerical language that dominates this world, life tests "what kind of stuff" you are made of. Mr. Deane is proud that Tom "appeared to be made out of such good commercial stuff" (p. 327). We speak of men "of Mr. Deane's stamp" (p. 457). And, as Mr. Deane tells Tom in his first interview, " 'If you want to slip into a round hole, you must make a ball of yourself' " (p. 245).

On the public surface of life, both place and self are made. They are the final product compared to which any other good one makes is incidental. In St. Ogg's they are the only products, since money there is made in commerce and speculation, not in manufacture. The product, the self, is willed through free choice. A man can be "anything he wants to be" if only he sets his mind to it.

Since Tom Tulliver is the self-made man of the book, the man who, by will and singlemindedness, sets out to project and become what he projects, his case is, as Eliot said, of equal importance with Maggie's. To stress at once the paradox of Tom and one of the telling points of the book, it is of value to look at the phrase "Tom is not what he appears now to be." Tom is not the young clerk at Guest and Company that the conditions of his life as a boarder at

The Mill on the Floss

Bob Jakin's imply. All men are found eventually to be men of "substance," like Mr. Deane, or "insubstantial," like Mr. Tulliver. A man like Tom, who is on his way, is nothing yet. Tom, like capitalism itself, stores up and invests. Both money and reputation are parts of the stock Tom is accumulating. Someday he will cash in by converting both money and reputation into position, and begin displaying that position through goods, through consumption. For the sake of this future of reality, the present is empty. " 'I want to have plenty of work'," Tom tells Mr. Deane. " 'There's nothing else I care about much' " (p. 424). Tom's life outside his work is described by Bob Jakin. " 'Mr. Tom 'ull sit by himself so glumpish, a-knitten his brow, an' a-lookin at the fire of a night. . . . My wife says when she goes in sometimes, an' he takes no notice of her, he sits lookin' into the fire, and frownin' as if he were watchin' folks at work in it' " (p. 414).

Prominent in Tom's small parlor is one possession from the past, the large old Bible in which Tom signed his father's curse on Wakem and on which he, in turn, forces Maggie to renounce Philip. As the Bible makes clear, the future toward which Tom sells off his present is nothing but the past. First to pay off his father's debts and then to recover the mill—he has no goals but the re-creation of a past that is slipping from him at an ever increasing rate. Each partial wiping of the slate is matched, in those sour co-incidences familiar from *Adam Bede*, with a resounding collapse that makes the loss of the past more definitive. When the debts are paid, Mr. Tulliver, on his way home from the celebration, strikes Wakem and dies. After Tom's three years of work, the family must leave the mill and separate. The father is dead, Maggie goes off to teach, Tom moves to lodgings, and Mrs. Tulliver circulates among her contemptuous sisters. Tom's efforts indirectly pro-duced, as well as coincided with, this disaster. After three more years, Tom has recovered the mill, but, on the day he moves back home, Maggie elopes with Stephen Guest, disgracing the family in a final way. And when Maggie at last returns in the flood to the mill and reconciliation with Tom, they are cut off by death.

Every paradise is a paradise lost, the maxim reminds us. The motives of Tom's life suspend him halfway between old and new orders. With the techniques of will and energy, he sets out not to construct an abstract self and position (as Mr. Deane had done, as Bounderby did in Dickens's *Hard Times*) but to re-create his past. Tom knows that what he proposes "might not be agreeable to his uncle" (p. 422). But in a profound sense that our time has made banal (in, for example, the end of the movie *Citizen Kane*), it is only a transformed past to which we can go forward once we have to "make up" a self to become.

It is easy to notice a fall into sentimental falsity in the lines that end the final chapter. "The boat reappeared—but brother and sister had gone down in an embrace never to be parted: living through again in one supreme moment, the days when they had clasped their little hands in love, and roamed the daisied fields together" (p. 557). Alarm bells go off for any reader of Victorian novels when the words *little* and *clasped* are near enough to be in the same sentence. And "daisied fields" we find difficult to remember from the early chapters, let alone the "love" that we recall as fights and sulking pride. But the words are close to those that ended the second book after the children learned "what their father was"—a failed man. "They had entered the thorny wilderness, and the golden gates of their childhood had for ever closed behind them" (p. 266). This ideality *is* the past created through the moment of loss.

Nostalgia is the inevitable product of the discontinuity that creates the rhythm of loss and recovery. In Novalis's great phrase, memory is the one paradise from which we can never be expelled. But memory is continuity of the inner life alone. It is in terms of the need for a wider continuity, public as well as internal, that *The Mill on the Floss* must be interpreted. The continuity of memory is the wholeness of the river once its course has been charted, the wholeness of the Floss. Beyond that is the greater continuity Eliot

The Mill on the Floss

saw as the ground of the first—and it is to this continuity that Tom sacrifices his present and future, Maggie her love for Stephen and Philip, and both their lives—the continuity of the mill.

THE CONTINUITY OF OBJECTS

To approach the continuity of the mill, the clearest path is to consider first the degraded nature of objects when they are "things." In *Adam Bede,* only Hetty is characterized by things— the box in which her treasures accumulate. Trinkets, lockets, and finally the letter from Arthur: these things were the treasures of her life. Other characters were embodied in the acts of their occupations. Even places, like the church, were defined through the use that was made of them, and they were seen in the novel only when alive through relationship to the meanings of the community life. Hetty, whose self was split into the round of life she only grudgingly carried out and the fantasy existence of her evenings alone, needed, for definition in the novel, the box of things that were the stage properties for those moments when, in front of the mirror, she came alive. Audience and actor, her two selves joined in the theater of display and appreciation. The things were tokens of a social reality not her own. In the mirror appeared the self she might someday be, and in that closed circle she was self and other—a new society.

The box with its secret society characterized the pathology of Hetty. But in *The Mill on the Floss*, the treasure chest is the hearth of every home. Hoarding replaces use as the symbolic value of "things" eclipse their actual values as "goods." The central absurdity of "things" is reached in Aunt Pullet who, in a ridiculous ceremony, tries on the hat she is afraid she will never be able to wear before Mrs. Tulliver. This little display takes place in the best room of the Pullet house, a room always kept dark and locked. "Aunt Pullet paused and unlocked a door which opened on something still more solemn than the passage: a darkened room, in which the outer light, entering feebly, showed what looked like the corpses

Making Up Society

of furniture in white shrouds. Everything that was not shrouded stood with its legs upward" (p. 94). The hat is wrapped in silver paper in a locked wardrobe in this graveyard of furniture. The things are being protected from people, particularly children. Instead of being items of comfort, they are tyrannical objects for which human beings are curators and guards. Upended they are of no use; covered they are of no decorative value. In a literal sense, they are dead to the human needs they were created for.

Symbolically they live, making up Aunt Pullet's hoard. The hat in the silver paper might stay there forever if relations keep dying so that Aunt Pullet is forced to stay in mourning. For one moment in the unlocked room, she is seen in it, and it is registered as part of her. "Then beginning to cry, she said, 'Sister if you should never see that bonnet again till I'm dead and gone, you'll remember I showed it to you this day' " (p. 96).

Mrs. Tulliver herself has an equal hoard at home. In the first chapter we learn of her sheets: " 'I've put out sheets for the best bed. . . . They aren't the best sheets, but they're good enough for anybody to sleep in, be he who he will; for as for them best Holland sheets, I should repent buyin' them, only they'll do to lay us out in. And if you was to die tomorrow, Mr. Tulliver, they're mangled beautiful, an' all ready, an' smell of lavender as it 'ud be a pleasure to lay 'em out' " (p. 8). Only the dead get the best sheets, but in Mrs. Tulliver's voice one can hear how they are savored and used by the living. When Mr. Tulliver fails and the family is to be "sold up," Mrs. Tulliver is found by Tom and Maggie in the storeroom where all the precious best things are kept. "Mrs. Tulliver was seated there with all her laid-up treasures. One of the linen-chests was open: the silver teapot was unwrapped from its many folds of paper, and the best china was laid out on the top of the closed linen chest; spoons and skewers and ladles were spread in rows on the shelves; and the poor woman was shaking her head and weeping" (p. 215).

Her things scattered by auction over the countryside, Mrs. Tulliver is a broken woman. Years later she speaks of the sale like a woman whose children have been lost. " 'I'm sure it was no wish o' mine, iver, as I should lie awake o' nights thinking of my best-bleached linen all over the country' " (p. 483). After the linen chests are gone, the family life revolves around a new box with its hoard: Mr. Tulliver's tin box, in which the money to pay off the debts is accumulating. The box was "the only sight that brought a faint beam of pleasure into the miller's eyes" (p. 295).

Aunt Glegg, like the Tullivers after their fall, dispenses with goods entirely since they are bulky and must be protected, like the chairs in Aunt Pullet's locked room. Aunt Glegg's ideal of life involves having her money "out working." She wants "to have sums of interest coming in more frequently and secrete it in various corners, baffling the most ingenious of thieves" (p. 136). Finally, money is best, not inconvenient things that have to be kept upside down or in locked rooms. Money is pure symbol. Ideally compact for hoarding, it is the final abstract reduction. Far beyond the degraded goods of Aunt Pullet's locked best room—her "things"—money has pure existence in the mind of the possessor. It doesn't even have to be hidden in corners like Mrs. Glegg's but can be out on speculation as Tom's always is.

The joke Tom plays on Maggie during his school days is a perfect parable of the social theater created by these secreted hoards. Tom bribes his drill teacher to leave him the sword the old soldier has brought. He hides it under his bed, and the sword is, like Hetty's earrings, the stage property of his fantasy existence. Tom brings Maggie to his room and has her close her eyes. He belts on the sword, blackens his face with cork, and reveals himself. Maggie looks, is bewildered, then laughs, but Tom, who wants to appear ferocious, draws the sword. Maggie begins to scream and Tom, unused to its weight, drops the sword, nearly laming himself.

Like all the Dodsons, Tom hoards to surprise. Tom and his father accumulate all the money and suddenly reveal themselves, free of the disgrace of bankruptcy. The Dodson badge was to be not only rich but "richer than was supposed." Like Mrs. Tulliver's sheets, all would come out at the funeral. Tom in his lodgings is more than he appears. No one climbs, but all store up and then leap, to the amazement of the others. This social magic is the game of understatement followed by triumphant display. To this sequence is opposed the life of the Stellings, who spend more than they have in order to make a show. Mr. Tulliver before his fall is insubstantial in this way. In either direction, one is playing with the fiction of appearance. Since one is what one has, not what one does—we never learn exactly what Tom or Guest and Company do—the social surface is full of hyperbole and understatement, both purely abstract. To use Wilde's epigram, the surface is abstract because it is based on price, not value. Things have price, goods have value.

What value remains is always mediated value. René Girard in his *Desire, Deceit, and the Novel* has examined the notion of mediated desire. By extension to things, we can speak of mediated value. Aunt Pullet's hat is a very uncertain thing in her own eyes. She knows it must be right: she has spent a lot of money for it and has had it made by the right milliner. But still she is anxious. She cannot look at the hat to calm her uncertainty. Only by looking into the eyes of Mrs. Tulliver, who is looking at the hat, can she be certain of its value. In another moment the certainty is lost again. Tom with his sword must also display it and see it in Maggie's eyes. When value is mediated, the community life resolves into a series of performances in which everyone takes turns being actor and audience. Surprise is everything, and in the eyes of the others each one is being marked and placed. The notion of reputation central to both crises of the book—Mr. Tulliver's bankruptcy and Maggie's elopement—depends in its waywardness on mediated value. In this it is unlike the "good name" of the Poysers in *Adam Bede*, which could be shaken only by an actual crime, and even then could reestablish itself at once.

After Maggie's return, she walks through the streets and sees in the silence and contempt of the townspeople her "social value":

> But she had no sooner passed beyond the narrower streets which she had to thread from Bob's dwelling, than she became aware of unusual glances cast at her; and this consciousness made her hurry along nervously, afraid to look to right or left. Presently, however, she came full on Mrs. and Miss Turnbull, old acquaintances of the family; they both looked at her strangely, and turned a little aside without speaking. . . . But now she knew that she was about to pass a group of gentlemen, who were standing at the door of the billiard-rooms and she could not help seeing young Torry step out a little with his glass at his eye, and bow to her with that air of nonchalance which he might have bestowed on a friendly barmaid. (P. 526)

And this scandal will not lift, even in the face of testimony from Stephen, Lucy, and Philip. Rather, it spreads and contaminates anyone who tries to help her. Finally, even Dr. Kenn cannot escape the grip of rumors over Maggie's name, and he tells her she must leave St. Ogg's. The notion of reputation, crucial as an element of continuity, will be treated in detail in a later section.

To the degraded objects that are hoarded, seen in mediated value, or replaced completely by money, Eliot does not contrast objects that are simply useful. If we think for a moment of Bob Jakin's penknife, an insignificant object that appears at several points in the book, and contrast it with Tom's sword, the other pole will become clear. The knife was not bought, or rented as Tom's sword was. It was a gift to Bob from Tom, a gift given out of simple gratitude and friendship. When the two boys fight, it is the penknife that Bob throws after Tom in a moment of pique, and it is thrown because it is the mark of the friendship. So as not to waste a good knife, Bob retrieves it after Tom leaves. After the Tullivers have fallen, Bob comes to offer his help, and, when Tom seems not to recognize him, he identifies himself: " 'Why you don't remember Bob, then, as you gen the pocketknife to, Mr.

Tom?' " (p. 254). And he pulls out the knife, which now has broken blades. He hasn't replaced them. " 'They might be cheatin' me an' givin' me another knife istid, for there isn't such a blade i' the country—it's got used to my hand, like. An' there was niver nobody else gen me nothin' " (p. 254). The knife is so familiar that, in Bob's striking words, "it's got used to my hand." It is not the best knife for use now that the blades are broken. But it is the only knife that is continous with Bob's own past and a concrete record of the friendship. Tom's sword, like Hetty's earrings, is part of what Eliot called the "theatre of the imagination," but Bob's knife is concrete memory, an object blessed not with symbolic fantasy meanings, like those of Tom's sword, but with the force to renew and preserve. To anyone who simply looks at it, the knife is nothing at all. For Bob himself it is not something to look at. Nor is he proud of the knife; he simply uses it.

At the other extreme, the pocketknife must be contrasted with those objects in Proust like the madeleine that, once dipped in tea, opens into the past with the suddenness of magic. In Proust, the tiny cake dipped in tea is the trigger of involuntary memory. Suddenly, an object releases the past, an object that was of no importance in itself in the past it recalls. What occurs is a moment of intense recovery, an experience of being flooded by the past called up by the object. The knife, however, is not important as a source of intense moments. Calm, continuous, living memory is held within it in a way that makes notice unnecessary. And the knife is not incidental; it is what we call a token of the intimacy. Last, it is a necessary object of use, a tool. In Proust, sensations rather than objects trigger the experience of memory; that is the key to the esthetic nature of memory in his work. Nothing could be less esthetic than the pocketknife.

Bob Jakin's knife, then, is different from the "best knife" for the job, the one he would choose if he were in a store looking over all possible knives. Equally, it is different from the knife Aunt Pullet would keep in a box and spend her time protecting and displaying.

The Mill on the Floss

This knife is one of the world of objects that in the book are crucial to the concrete sense of continuity of the self, to legibility, and central to the reasons why bankruptcy (being "sold up") and exile, both of which take away this world of familiar objects, are forms of death.

When Maggie realizes that even her books have been sold in the auction that follows the family's bankruptcy, she describes the weight of familiar things. " 'Our dear old Pilgrim's Progress that you coloured with your little paints; and that picture of Pilgrim with a mantle on, looking just like a turtle—oh dear!' Maggie went on, half sobbing as she turned over the few books. 'I thought we should never part with that while we lived—everything is going away from us—the end of our lives will have nothing in it like the beginning'! " (p. 246). As the auctioneer would say, these are items of "sentimental value only." Mrs. Tulliver tells time by "the year [she] bought the sugar tongs." In a limited way, even her linen chests record a continuity, although it is only a history of purchases.

The bankruptcy has two effects: one is on the name of the family, and this Tom sets out to repair; but the other is beyond repair, for the auction scatters their past and wipes out the chance to live continuously within the familiar. That failure kills Mr. Tulliver symbolically. He drops into a coma that is described as a "living death." He is "not himself," Maggie tells Tom. He recognizes nothing until an accident occurs that is meant to show the profound power of familiar objects. Mr. Tulliver is brought back from the dead. Tom and Mr. Glegg are searching for a note.

> Mr. Glegg had lifted out the parchments, and had fortunately drawn back a little when the iron holder gave way, and the heavy lid fell with a loud bang, that resounded over the house.
>
> Perhaps there was something in that sound more than the mere fact of the strong vibration that produced the instan-

taneous effect on the frame of the prostrate man, and for the time completely shook off the obstruction of paralysis. The chest had belonged to his father and his father's father, and it had always been rather a solemn business to visit it. All long-known objects, even a mere window fastening or a particular door-latch, have sounds which are a sort of recognized voice to us. . . . In the same moment when all the eyes in room were turned upon him, he started up and looked at the chest, the parchments in Mr. Glegg's hand, and Tom holding the tin box, with a glance of perfect consciousness and recognition. (P. 236)

Maggie comes and kisses him "as if her father were come back to her from the dead" (p. 237). And when Mr. Tulliver does at last revive, the family tries to explain what has taken place, but it is of no use. "The full sense of the present could only be imparted gradually by new experience—not by mere words, which must remain weaker than the impressions left by the old experiences" (p. 272).

The guarantee that radiates from these objects is the continuous presence of the past, and, further, a stability against which the changes of the present can register. In the background, it is clear that the involuntary memory so magical in Proust is in fact a kind of local reprieve to the general fate of the past—it is lost, temps perdu. The premise is that the discontinuity of memory can be overcome now and then. Like the magical reappearance of people who are lost to sight as a condition of their being, the local joy is bordered by a permanent despair.

What Eliot records with an urgent force is that it is the disappearance of the world we know, the familiar world, that precipitates us into a world we choose and create. This later world is ruled by esthetics, the preference for one thing over another by the sensations it gives us, by how it looks. In one of the most important statements of the novel, she equates the two worlds.

The Mill on the Floss

There is no sense of ease like the ease we felt in those scenes where we were born, where objects became dear to us before we had known the labour of choice, and where the outer world seemed only an extension of our own personality: we accepted and loved it as we accepted our own sense of existence and our own limbs. Very commonplace, even ugly that furniture of our early home might look if it were put up to auction: an improved taste in upholstery scorns it; and is not the striving after something better and better in our surroundings, the grand characteristic that distinguishes man from the brute. . . . But Heaven knows where that striving might lead us if our affections had not a trick of twining around those old inferior things—if the loves and sanctities of our life had no deep immovable roots in memory. One's delight in an elderberry bush, overhanging the confused leafage of a hedgerow bank, as a more gladdening sight than the finest cistus or fuchsia spreading itself on the softest undulating turf, is an entirely unjustifiable preference to a landscape gardener, or to any of those severely regulated minds who are free from the weakness of any attachment that does not rest on a demonstrable superiority of qualities. (P. 162)

The demonstrable superiority of qualities is the esthetic within the "labour of choice." This choice is, of course, not limited to things. The tourist relates to place in this contrast of qualities.

One key document for the generation that followed Eliot's was Pater's conclusion to *The Renaissance* with its idea of life as a continuous choice of experiences. "Our failure is to form habits: for after all habit is relative to a stereotyped world," Pater wrote.[1] Every moment some form is perfect, and by esthetic choice we select it to be our experience for that moment. We seize that per-

---

1. Walter Pater, *The Renaissance* (1873; reprint ed., New York: Mentor Books, 1960), p. 194.

fection, experience it, then discard it in favor of another form reaching perfection. Pater raises discontinuity to vision—the prose poem replaces the novel. Life is atomized and preserved in memory, experienced as are the discrete paintings on a museum wall. Man is a spectator, or, to speak economically, a shopper. In James's novels, he is that defective type: the collector.

The world we choose is what Maggie rejects when she leaves Stephen. When she elopes with him, she realizes "she had rent the ties that had given meaning to duty, and had made herself an outlawed soul, with no guide but the wayward choice of her own passion." (p. 504). The labor of choice that underlies estheticism sustains equally its opposite—the self-made man is one who projects what he chooses to be, then struggles to become what he has chosen. When Dr. Frankenstein creates, he first chooses every feature of the self he will make. Each feature will be the perfection of beauty. In the process of creation something goes wrong, and a monster is produced. The final thing chosen by the self-made man is the fiction of his own past. Bounderby takes that final step and chooses a new past that he, like Mr. Deane in his talks with Tom, gives out as an object lesson in social success.

Opposed to the labor of choice in Eliot's statement we find no permanent state, only the paradise of childhood. Then we did not look at the objects as one does at an auction, translating them into money, comparing them as better or worse examples of a style, or even, as with antiques, seeing those styles historically as an abstract past. They are there before we notice them. Like Bob Jakin's knife, they are "used to us"; and a diffuse memory is inseparable from the sensation we have of them, and feeling is joined to both sensation and memory. Because this is true only in childhood, the catastrophes of the novel—the auction and Maggie's exile—are melodramatic and superficially particular versions of the inevitable loss of the world of childhood and with it the world of continuity. Finally, Bob's knife will lose its blades and be replaced; finally, even the mill itself will be destroyed. The erosions of time, which we neither cause nor can prevent, are the universal part of the catastrophes of the novel.

But, in speaking of the habit of seeking for something better and better, Eliot includes the second, the willed destruction that both Maggie and Tom refuse. This destruction is at the hands of taste and mediated value. Unlike his uncle, Mr. Deane, Tom is not working for a better home in a better part of town. With prosperity, the Deanes change the things in their lives so that what they have can speak to others. These carriages and houses are those of "anyone" with so many thousands per year. They exist for envy and appreciation. Now and then they humble someone who didn't realize "who he was dealing with."

The mill that is Tom's goal is the epitome of the world of familiar objects. It is home. After his recovery, Mr. Tulliver takes the humiliating job with his enemy to keep his family in the mill he no longer owns.

> He couldn't bear to think of himself living on any other spot than this, where he knew the sound of every gate and door, and felt that the shape and colour of every roof and broken hillock was good, because his growing senses had been fed on them. Our instructed vagrancy, which has hardly time to linger by the hedgerows, but runs away early to the tropics, and is at home with palms and banyans—which is nourished on books of travel and stretches the *theatre of its imagination* to the Zambesi—can hardly get a dim notion of what an old-fashioned man like Tulliver felt for this spot, where all his memories centred, and where life seemed like a familiar smooth-handled tool that the fingers clutch with loving ease. (P. 282, emphasis added)

The novelty created through choice opposes the smooth-handled tool. In the phrase the "theatre of its imagination" Eliot describes the self-alienation into roles, the community split into audience and others that is the alternative to Mr. Tulliver's painful choice. The mill is not recovered. After Tulliver strikes Wakem and dies, the family must leave, and when later Wakem sells the mill, it is to Guest and Company, who will convert it to steam and operate it with Tom as manager. At the moment of even this partial victory for Tom, Maggie elopes. Her disgrace guarantees that the family will be split forever. Tom is alone in the mill when the flood comes; what he holds is the symbol of the past, not its substance.

Beyond the mill are the more abstract loyalties and ties of which it is the emblem. Bob's knife is not only an object of continuity in his life, a unity of self; equally it is a token of intimacy bound up with the fate of his relationship to Tom. Thrown after Tom in a quarrel, produced to remind Tom of the friendship, the knife is a public mark of bonds of concern. The words *ties* and *loyalties* appear again and again in the chapters centered on Maggie. Like familair objects, they are there before we notice them. Opposed are the ties of choice, love or friendship, where we see and compare and select. Tom is unified. He never rebels against the pattern of enemies and allies his father forces on him. The oath Tom writes in the Bible is internalized and natural to him. Maggie turns wayward and even willful in every case where she is exposed to what is fatal to her loyalties. The very qualities of impulsiveness and rebelliousness are absolutely destructive to the deeper loyalties, however delightful they appear when it is the superficial constraints of her early life she is defying. Of course, the restraints on her are unreasonable, but that means only that she wouldn't have chosen them herself. Her meetings with Philip Wakem in the Red Deeps, her equivocation with Stephen Guest that leads to the kiss in the conservatory or the walk at Aunt Moss's farm—all the breaches take place in nature, as does the most important breach of all, the flight with Guest on the river.

When Maggie begins to realize the implications of a marriage with Stephen, she thinks with a grim extremity that takes its tone from the fact that this is the first perception of what she has done.

The Mill on the Floss

Stripped of its frantic exaggeration, the analysis holds true. It was a "breach of faith and cruel selfishness: she had rent the ties that had given meaning to duty, and had made herself an outlawed soul, with no guide but the wayward choice of her own passion. . . . Her life with Stephen could have no sacredness: she must forever sink and wander vaguely driven by uncertain impulse" (p. 504). It must be remembered that, for the three years between her father's death and her return to St. Ogg's as a guest at Lucy's, Maggie was a schoolteacher. But on the plane of the novel she didn't exist any more than Mr. Tulliver did for the length of his coma. Those three years are never summarized or referred to in the novel. Maggie *is* only when she is within the loyalties and resonant realities of St. Ogg's. The exile she must go into at the end is the exact equal to the death the book concludes with. Maggie's word *wanderer* is the same used in *Adam Bede* for Hetty when she was on the road, her nightmare picaresque. The word is the title of a great Anglo-Saxon complaint cataloguing the miseries of the man with no home, the man outside the law. Maggie's is an outlawed soul because she cannot identify herself with the loyalties imposed on her. Equally, she cannot free herself from them and define herself through choices.

The permanence represented by the mill or Maggie's love for Tom in their childhood might be no more than sentimental bonds, important in memory but otherwise only symbolically important for the continuity of self and existence in society. The exact society represented in the novel has a bearing on the course of loyalty and the fate of continuity and society.

Judgment and Discontinuity

The action of the novel takes place over ten years; that of *Adam Bede* took a little more than a year—if we neglect the epilogue. In the childhood chapters, Maggie is nine, at the bankruptcy she is thirteen, the affair with Philip and her father's death happen when she is sixteen, and the final third of the novel finds her nineteen.

Making Up Society

Tom, who began at thirteen, is now twenty-three. The one year of *Adam Bede* encompasses a static world tested and healed through the period of attraction, mating, pregnancy, birth, and judgment: the rural year of sowing and harvest, cycles that end where they begin. The ten years of *The Mill on the Floss* are a span of development in a situation no longer based on place. The career of a life, the chart of a river in Eliot's image, takes time to reveal substance.

A reader's comprehension of the meaning of a choice or a turn in the novel is not limited to the ten-year span. If we ask how an action is visible, how it comes to be seen for what it is, we reach one of the most complex motives for continuity, one that is built into the narrative itself. Tom's violent repudiation of Maggie after her return, unmarried, from the flight with Guest is explained by Eliot.

> There had arisen in Tom a repulsion towards Maggie that derived its very intensity from their early childish love in the time when they had clasped tiny fingers together, and their later sense of nearness in a common duty and a common sorrow: the sight of her, as he has told her, was hateful to him. In this branch of the Dodson family Aunt Glegg found a stronger nature than her own—a nature in which family feeling had lost the character of clanship, in taking on a doubly deep dye of personal pride. (Pp. 533–34)

Tom's feeling is a trait transformed and inverted in time and by his circumstances, but it is continuous—as a diamond is to coal—with its source. Tom himself, we hear the aunts speculate earlier, must be either a Dodson or a Tulliver. Maggie's impetuousness is a version of her father's, and his is traced back to Ralph Tulliver, an ancestor who ruined himself. The important issue is not heredity or determination. Tom, after all, is an unpredictable variation, as different from the Dodson aunts as a lump of coal from oil. We comprehend by echoes in the novel: Tom scolding Maggie at nine, barring the gate at nineteen. The explanation of his act forces Eliot to recapitulate their entire past and allude beyond them to family traits. In heredity there is the vision of an impersonal factor in personality, a community of blood. Many of Maggie's acts are explained as well by saying "she's a Tulliver" as by any reference to her character or past. In the Tulliver blood are "elements of generous imprudence, warm affection, and hot-tempered rashness" (p. 291).

Occasionally the explanation refers to the society at large or the period. Of the Glegg's hoarding, we are told the sociology, not the source in personal history. "In old-fashioned times an independence was hardly ever made without a little miserliness as a condition and you would have found that quality in every provincial district combined with characters as various as the fruits from which we can extract acid" (p. 130). What is needed of sociology or family history is supplied by the author, but the chief need for comprehension is an accurate sense of the past. When Maggie reads Thomas à Kempis, she begins a new life of renunciation. "From what you know of her, you will not be surprised that she threw some exaggeration and wilfulness, some pride and impetuosity even into her self-renunciation: her own life was still a drama for her, in which she demanded of herself that her part should be played with intensity" (p. 311). Unlike those characters in Austen who are placed with a few phrases in the first chapter and remain in focus throughout, Eliot's important characters come only gradually into register. Mr. Tulliver is the greatest accomplishment of characterization in the novel; step by step he gathers weight. What increases is not so much his complexity as the complexity of our comprehension. When Tom stands at the gate of the mill his whole life has centered on recovering, he says to Maggie: "You don't belong to me. . . . You will find no home with me." The weight of the words is a sum of our familiarity with Tom. We understand him through our knowledge of the sequence of the book. The light on the moment is nine-tenths reflected light.

Making Up Society

One goal in Eliot continues directly the tradition of the novel of manners. It is a goal she shares with Jane Austen: the action creates situations in which we judge characters who are in the process of judging one another. Both reader and society share the same goal. Characters are exiled from the society as Lydia Bennett and Hetty Sorrel are, and the judgments of reader and society are based on the same comprehension and move in parallel.

One element of the tragedy in *The Mill on the Floss* arises from the fact that, under the new society, reputation—the judgment of society—will be as arbitrary as any mediated value, and it will no longer coincide with the judgment of art, the reader's judgment. Loss of continuity underlies the situation where only art can assemble the materials to comprehend. Only the reader is in a position to evaluate the key acts. The importance of judgment might seem weakened by the concern with sympathy. In fact, the harshness of Eliot's moral world depends on the loyalty to judgment and expiation in spite of her more prominent mentions of sympathy. She is as far as possible from that aphorism of Enlightenment psychology, *Tout comprendre, c'est tout pardonner.* Sympathy does not forgive, because that runs against the process of nemesis—Eliot's repeated assertion that evil acts have inevitable, destructive consequence both in the one who does the act and in the lives of the innocent around him. Her use of nemesis as an argument against wrongdoing amounts to an attempt to create a pragmatic, earthly replacement for the lost Christian idea of inevitable punishment after death. Where sympathy and nemesis clash, it is nemesis that is stronger. Dinah reaches a moment of perfect sympathy with Hetty in jail and then offers to ride with her to the gallows.

The divergence between the judgment of art made by the reader, with the materials assembled through the narrative, and that of society, which bases itself only on the way actions become visible, can be seen in two of the catastrophes of the book: Mr. Tulliver's fight with Wakem and Maggie's elopement. The fight never

The Mill on the Floss

reaches public knowledge; it exists only as rumor. It has been "hushed up" and deliberately erased by all who know of it. Yet it causes the death of Mr. Tulliver, the move from the mill, and the splitting up of the rest of the family—Tom into lodgings, Maggie to a teaching post, Mrs. Tulliver to her sisters. Once hushed up, the fight disappears from explanations and makes the acts that follow cryptic. For the reader, who does know, the essence of the act depends on Tulliver's impetuosity, the depth of helplessness into which the failure threw him, and the sudden pride he felt in paying off the debts. By accident he meets Wakem, who adopts a "haughtier tone than usual" to criticize a trivial point of Tulliver's work. On the one day of his life when Tulliver's pride has returned, Wakem calls up the humiliation from which he has just surfaced. Mistaking Tulliver's excitement for the flush of drink, Wakem insults him again, and the fight begins.

In the scene both men act out of mistaken or accidentally inappropriate ideas of the other. Even worse, both act out of unconscious resentment and pride. Only the reader has the knowledge of the feelings and circumstances that ignite through the characters to produce the fight. Neither man is in focus for the other, neither is completely aware of himself. After the event, the death of Tulliver and the silence of Wakem conspire to "hush it up." Lucy Deane, two years later, speaks of it only as "some dreadful quarrel" (p. 387).

The place of detail in moral judgment is argued by Eliot near the end of the novel.

The casuists have become a byword of reproach; but their perverted spirit of minute discrimination was the shadow of a truth to which eyes and hearts are too often fatally sealed: the truth, that moral judgments must remain false and hollow, unless they are checked and enlightened by a perpetual reference to the special circumstances that mark the individual lot.

All people of broad, strong sense have an instinctive re-

pugnance to the men of maxims; because such people early
discern that the mysterious complexity of our life is not to be
embraced by maxims. . . . And the man of maxims is the
popular representative of the minds that are guided in their
moral judgment solely by general rules, thinking that these
will lead them to justice by a ready-made patent method,
without the trouble of exerting patience, discrimination, impartiality—without any care to assure themselves whether
they have the insight that comes from a hardly-earned estimate of temptation, or from a life livid and intense enough
to have created a wide fellow-feeling with all that is human.
(Pp. 531–32)

Maggie's highly ambiguous elopement is the central test of the gap
of judgment. Those who are loyal to her are so without discrimination. Bob Jakin acts from sympathy, as does Mrs. Tulliver; both
are indifferent to what she has or has not done. Mrs. Glegg calls on
family loyalty in a way that makes us see it as an extended egoism
driving her to protect Maggie as "one of our own." Only Dr. Kenn
takes Maggie's side on the evidence of the story she tells and the
letter from Stephen. Lucy and Philip, who have known Maggie
longest, come closest to an intelligent judgment. At the extreme is
the town, the others for whom this is that great event—a scandal.
   Parallel to the magical rises and falls in economic life is the taste
for moral melodrama in St. Ogg's. Reputation is the equivalent of
social appearance, and both undergo the test for substance. The
bankruptcy that tears the veil of Mr. Tulliver's appearance as a
man of substance is one with the sudden destruction of Maggie's
reputation. She is a "fallen woman" just as her father is a man who
has taken a "fall." The drama of surprise and catastrophe that
occurs because of the gap between appearance and substance is a
drama manipulated and turned to theater on both sides. The alternative of "patience, discrimination, and impartiality" assumes a
contemplative objectivity that is an exact description of a possible

relationship between a reader and the characters in a novel, but a far from accurate account of social life.

Only Dr. Kenn, who is in the neutralized occupation of clergyman, acts with the objectivity Eliot describes. Behind his accuracy is a moment of intuitive understanding that marked their first meeting.

> "Oh, I *must* go," said Maggie, earnestly, looking at Dr. Kenn with an expression of reliance, as if she had told him her history in those three words. It was one of those moments of implicit revelation which will sometimes happen even between people who meet quite transiently—on a mile's journey, perhaps, or when resting by the wayside. There is always this possibility of a word or look from a stranger to keep alive the sense of human brotherhood. (P. 464)

This implicit revelation between strangers becomes a substitute release. Maggie's words intimate, they do not confess. Maggie is forced by Tom to confess to her meetings with Philip Wakem. Later she volunteers the story of the elopement to Dr. Kenn. But the burden of isolation is not a set of secrets like Hetty's, or like the fight between Tulliver and Wakem that has been deliberately concealed. The real burden is an invisible and, at the extreme, unconscious level of her experience that makes of her behavior alone —and even more of the appearance of her behavior in the distortions of scandal—a half truth reversed by the missing details.

The surface of behavior is confused by more than the intimations like those in Maggie's words "I *must* go." In fact, that surface, as we see it in the relations of Maggie, Lucy, Philip, and Stephen in the sixth book, is a treacherous mixture of clues and suspicions, transferred emotion, reversal, concealment, betrayal, and even unconscious purposes. When Philip chooses a song to sing, it is "an indirect expression to Maggie of what he could not prevail on himself to say directly" (p. 444). And when Stephen talks to Maggie, he begins to stroke the ears of the dog in her lap. "It seemed to Stephen like some action in a dream that he was obliged to do, and wonder at himself all the while—to go on stroking Minny's ear. Yet is was very pleasant: he only wished he dared look at Maggie, and that she would look at him. . . . She was unable to look up, and saw nothing but Minny's black wavy coat" (p. 431). The transfer to the dog is less visible than Philip's song because it was not intended as a sign. In compensation for his growing feeling for Maggie, Stephen becomes more attentive to Lucy. "It was a subtle act of conscience in Stephen that even he was not aware of." With his growing feeling for Maggie, "there had sprung up an apparent distance between them" (p. 428). When Lucy first introduced Maggie to Stephen, the abrasiveness between them worried her, but it was a sign of their great attraction to each other.

Most of what occurs is invisible, disguised, or concealed. Experience becomes tacit and complex until an entry into a room becomes a drama.

When Philip entered the room he was going merely to bow to Maggie, feeling that their acquaintance was a secret which he was bound not to betray; but when she advanced towards him and put out her hand, he guessed at once that Lucy had been taken into her confidence. It was a moment of some agitation to both, though Philip had spent many hours preparing it; but like all persons who have passed through life with little expectation of sympathy, he seldom lost his self-control, and shrank with the most sensitive pride from any noticeable betrayal of emotion. A little extra paleness, a little tension of the nostril when he spoke, and the voice pitched in a higher key, that to strangers would seem expressive of cold indifference, were all the signs Philip usually gave on an inward drama that was not without its fierceness. But Maggie, who had little more power of concealing the impressions made upon her than if she had been constructed of musical strings, felt her eyes getting larger with tears as they took one another's hands in silence. They were not painful tears: they had rather something of the same origin as the tears of women and children shed when they have found some protection to cling to, and look back on the threatened danger. For Philip, who a little while ago was associated continually in Maggie's mind with the sense that Tom might reproach her with some justice, had now, in this short space, become a sort of outward conscience to her that she might fly to for rescue and strength. Her tranquil, tender affection for Philip, with its root deep down in her childhood, and its memories of long quiet talk confirming by distinct successive impressions the first instinctive bias—the fact that in him the appeal was more strongly to her pity and womanly devotedness than to her vanity or other egoistic excitability of her nature, seemed now to make a sacred place, a sanctuary where she could find refuge from an alluring influence the best part of herself must resist. (P. 436–37)

The clues of paleness and tension are visible only to Maggie, and that Maggie now finds Philip a rescue only she and the reader understand. Maggie's new attraction to Stephen makes her display to Philip seem safe to her, but he will assume she is expressing a love we know is vanishing. Now Philip is a sanctuary. What each of the four knows and assumes about the others has passed into complete fragmentation. About himself, each stops short of the "less conscious purposes" (p. 491) that are vital in the mix of the action.

Paradoxically, the details that Eliot demonstrates to be essential for moral judgment she also demonstrates to be unavailable, even to oneself. Philip begins to suspect the feeling between Stephen and Maggie when he sees Stephen anticipate her need for a footstool. "This sudden eagerness in Stephen, and the change in Maggie's face, which was painfully reflecting a beam from his . . .

[was] charged with a painful meaning" (p. 446). But the attraction he sees is itself only half the truth. The mystery of this social world is one familiar from Proust and Henry James. In James or Proust, reader and character know only as much as each other. We learn of the parentage of Pansy at the same moment Isabel does. The truth she comes to learn about the circumstances of her marriage is revealed to the readers at the same time. In Proust, what is enigmatic to Marcel is equally so for us. But in *The Mill on the Floss*, it is otherwise. There is still a whole truth to which the partial versions are ironically or pathetically compared. The whole truth is that of the novel, the reader's experience. Even where unconscious motives operate, we know them, and we do not suspect others of which we have not been told. Moral judgment holds force because there is still one plane on which experience is legible, the plane of art. But within the plane of society, every self—in that terrible image used by Pater and then by T. S. Eliot in *The Waste Land*—confirms a prison. Each hears only rumors and sees only clues.

Mr. Tulliver's final word is "puzzling," and the phrase "it's a puzzling world" identifies him in a Dickensian way. The word applies with greater and greater force as we move out from the self in the novel. Unlike *Adam Bede*, *The Mill on the Floss* does not even register the life beyond the family except as a violent, inscrutable, and arbitrary set of events that can make family and personal life unstable. The two elements of that life are the law and financial speculation. Both are offstage. The verdicts that go against Tulliver bankrupt the family, but we never learn why, and the money Tom saves he makes in speculation, not from his small salary. The law is not that of *Adam Bede* but an arena for spite and foolish conflicts that get decided by craft. It is more important to have a better lawyer than a stronger case, and no one would mention the word *justice* in connection with these frivolous disputes. The social life has divided into allies and enemies, and problems of water rights that should be settled by private agreement are forced into a legal format that, with expense and hatred, can destroy all sides. Alone among the elements of public life, education is represented in the novel, and, far from bringing Tom Tulliver into life, it crushes and obscures his best traits and leads him to doubt the worth of what he can do and to respect a set of qualities that are of no point to his life.

The institutions of life have disappeared, and those that remain are dangerous and unpredictable. To the vanished society the novel can oppose only the one institution: the family. In the family itself, quarrels are the equivalent of the lawsuits of the wider life. The first book balances the quarrel with the Gleggs against the lawsuit over water rights. Both are dangerous for the same reason: Mrs. Glegg, by calling in her money, will endanger the family's financial position as much as the lawsuit will.

Family meetings are abrasive encounters where friction and resentment nearly split the group at every moment. Every encounter in the early books ends with someone walking out. Tom leaves Maggie to play with Bob Jakin, but the two quarrel and Tom walks away. Mrs. Glegg feels insulted and walks out of the Tulliver home. When Maggie, Tom, and Mrs. Tulliver visit the Pullets with Lucy Deane, Tom and Lucy abandon Maggie, who takes revenge by pushing Lucy into the mud. Then, in the most dramatic desertion, Maggie runs away to join the gypsies. In miniature, the first book acts out the destruction of every tie.

With the gypsies the novel creates the first of its symbols of those who live in the land but not in the society. Maggie runs to them because she has always been told she is like a gypsy. Everyone comments on her dark skin, and she goes to find out where she belongs. She finds she was wrong, but the gypsies represent a pole outside the social life, a pole of those who accept being outlaws and wanderers. Two of the stories mentioned in the novel suggest the extremes of those who renounce society—*Pilgrim's Progress* and the parable of prodigal son. The pilgrim and the prodigal son both renounce and depart. The novel, by balancing the one against the other, stresses the ambiguity of the act itself.

Making Up Society

More important than the gypsies or the images of pilgrim and prodigal son are the implications of the character of Philip Wakem. An outsider by accident of birth, he is a hunchback and therefore exempt, different, someone with whom all relationships take on a special tone and set of unwritten rules. Philip is also an artist. To measure the distance between the importance of society to Eliot and its unimportance for Joyce, there is the symbol for Joyce's artist, Icarus, who soars above humanity. For Eliot, at this point, the artist is the hunchback who has fallen beneath. The story associated with Philip Wakem is that painful Greek fable of the inconvenience and yet the necessity of heroes for society, the story of Philoctetes. With his festering foot—the equal of Philip's hump—Philoctetes offends his companions in the Greek camp at the siege of Troy and is sent off to an island to complain in solitude. An omen tells the Greeks that Troy cannot be taken without Philoctetes' bow, and Ulysses is sent to bring it from the island. If the bow is taken, Philoctetes will starve; if he returns with the bow, society will be cursed with his suffering; and if neither returns, the siege will not end.

Eliot is not alone in equating the artist in modern society with Philoctetes. The title of Edmund Wilson's book of essays, *The Wound and the Bow*, describes Philoctetes, but the wound is more the Freudian one that "hurts into song." Disqualified from the world, Philip develops a compensating sense of beauty, a sensitivity that Eliot implies is part of his illness. As an outsider, he can *see* life, but being a spectator is in an inferior, degraded relationship to the world. Neither Philip nor Philoctetes chose this role. Philip's was imposed by the accident, the catastrophe, of his birth; Philoctetes' wound came from a serpent's bite. Both are exiles on an island of pain even when at home.

At certain moments in the novel, the born otherness that Philip represents seems only a more visible statement of the general condition. When talking of the Dodsons and Tullivers, Eliot suggests the inevitability of conflict.

The Mill on the Floss

I share with you this sense of oppressive narrowness; but it is necessary that we should feel it, if we care to understand how it acted on the lives of Tom and Maggie—how it acted on young natures in many generations, that in the onward tendency of things have risen above the mental level of the generation before them, to which they have been nevertheless tied by the strongest fibres of their hearts. The suffering whether of martyr or victim, which belongs to every historical period, is represented in this way in every town, and by hundreds of obscure hearths. (P. 289)

Martyrs and victims are one with Philoctetes and the witch. The wound and the hump are finally, in this current of feeling in the novel, one's uniqueness, one's self. Maggie's impetuosity is her recourse when the arbitrary rules are irreconcilable with what she is. Since her hair never will curl the way the others insist it must, Maggie cuts it off. If she must be a failure by their standards—for reasons in the nature of things—she can at least grab the side of defiance and exaggerate the difference into a distinction. And it is there that we reach the case of the witch.

What is the most necessary is the most impossible. The details that alone make judgment rational are buried in privacy or even in the unconscious. The continuity that makes life legible, even to oneself, rests on loyalties that destroy the very self that continuity was to make legible. If each persons is different in substance, each is, like Philoctetes, on an island.

It is the intensity of perception on both sides of the impasse that creates the energy of the novel and creates, likewise, the stalemate. The choice is between a self more and more inscrutable within a mysterious social life of motives and concealments, or a self frustrated and resentful within an intolerable narrowness. With the loyalties and ties or without them, the novel probes to the point of impasse. None of Eliot's other novels radiates the energy of this attempt to face everything and give up nothing. The mill that

Making Up Society

cannot be lost and cannot be recovered is the emblem of the chance for continuous, visible life. Mr. Tulliver, Tom, and Maggie, the three whose interior lives dominate the book, the three who follow one another in giving direction and energy to the book—each fails to hold the mill and dies. The first third of the novel is Mr. Tulliver's; his bankruptcy is his death. Tom's energy nearly recovers the mill, but at the price of the family unity the mill stood for. And Maggie reaches the mill in the flood in a victory even more marked with defeat than Tom's. The deaths of all three are deaths of exhaustion, life wasted in an impasse it cannot leap beyond.

4

Silas Marner

Like the Book of Job, *Silas Marner* takes the form of a process of subtraction and loss that plunges to an absolute nadir, a just-above-zero of the human condition, and then recovers by a process of addition until the end restates the beginning. Whether Job or Marner, there is an unreality, a gratuitous quality about the "recovery" quite different from the equally arbitrary fall. The accident that brings the thief to Marner's door is of a different order from the one that brings the tiny infant crawling through the snow. Loss at an accelerating rate we can believe in, as we do in avalanches, but no one has seen the rocks rise back up the mountain. In certain moods everyone believes in a kind of law of gravity in life as well as stones; one of the motifs of *Ulysses* is the phrase "32 ft. per second per second," the law of falling bodies.

The optimism of Job or *Silas Marner* is of a kind in which we hope rather than believe. In reading either book, we are closer to those stories of subtraction without end, *King Lear* or Wordsworth's "The Ruined Cottage," than we are to genuinely confident works. We do not believe in the recovery because we know that a man never sits in his chair with the same ease after he has once been sold up. So much of happiness is the confidence that it will not disappear in the blink of an eye, and the man wasted once by arbitrary events will never live without the anxiety that what he has might be gone by morning. While the end of the Book of Job or *Silas*

Marner resembles the beginning, it does so only on the surface of events, in the numbers of friends and sheep. Job knows what no happy man ever considers: that the ground he walks on is thin paper over a gulf.

A look at the specific form of the recovery provides even more reason to place it in quotation marks. With a knot, it is true that to return to the beginning, you must exactly reverse the steps that led to the complexity. People after a disaster often fasten on the sequence and imagine that by repeating every step of it in reverse order, they will return from the predicament. This habit is pure fantasy in history or psychology. When thinkers realized in the nineteenth century how religion had taken on an economic vocabulary under the rise of capitalism, until it gave way to an economic image of man, many saw the antidote in attempts at religious revival. But sequences do not reverse in history.

To take the central example in *Silas Marner*, one of Eliot's absolutely correct insights was the growing importance of things, of hoarded goods in which one's value was recorded. In *Adam Bede* and *The Mill on the Floss,* these goods are a key to the new society, an intense center of life and self-recognition. The hoard of goods, along with reputation, states one's place and identity. It replaces the relations of station in the earlier society, relations to those above and beneath one, and equally it replaces the web of tasks that spoke one's place. When the community and round of duties no longer articulate the self, the relation to these gives way to a relation of things. And these things speak out in public to declare "what one is." The process is in one direction. But, like those who imagined religion as the cure for the condition it had been unable to prevent, Eliot pictures in *Silas Marner* the mirror image of the true history: she shows the gold hoard giving way to the child and, through the child, to the web of community.

In other words, the cure is only the catastrophe run backward; to imagine rescue is only to imagine the disaster in reverse. What offers itself as optimism is historically and psychologically the

Silas Marner

equivalent of a pessimism so hopelessly evocative of the problem that it can see no solution but the vanishing of the conditions that caused it.

For this reason, the story of Marner stands alongside that other fable of a weaver, Wordsworth's "Ruined Cottage." Both are tales of destruction, first of community, then of life itself. Weaving was the single most important English industry in the period of transition to capitalism. Just as Melville chose whaling, that first New England industry, so Wordsworth and Eliot chose weaving to create a generalized statement. When she wrote to her publisher about *Silas Marner*, Eliot mentioned Wordsworth and imagined her story was of a kind no one would like now that the old poet was dead. The poem offers its bleak images in simple chronicle without the surface of sentimental reassurance and facile hope. But *Silas Marner*, too, is made of these images and tells in parallel of a double destruction.

The community of the Lantern Yard is shattered by treachery that grows out of a sexual attraction. Marner's fiancée and his best friend fall secretly in love. Sarah cannot break the engagement. "Their engagement was known to the church, and had been recognized in the prayer-meetings; it could not be broken off without strict investigation, and Sarah could render no reason that would be sanctioned by the feeling of the community" (p. 222). In the control through the public notice that the community takes of private feeling lies the strict demand that all life be social life. Sarah and Vane conspire to disgrace Silas through an accusation of robbery: they accuse him of the crime they commit against him. The community never appears except in the tragic injustice of Silas's trial. From the trial of Hetty to that of the witch to that of Silas there is a direct line. Silas is tried by an appeal to chance, by the drawing of lots that declares him guilty.

Silas accuses his friend, breaks with him, finds his engagement ended, blasphemes against God, renounces his faith, and leaves the Lantern Yard to appear in Raveloe, a mysterious stranger. A weaver, he relates to others only through his industry; otherwise he is as unfathomable to them as a witch. He is credited with powers to cure or blight. Men like Marner "were to the last regarded as aliens by their rustic neighbors, and usually contracted the eccentric habits which belong to a state of loneliness" (p. 216). The neighbors' suspicion finally produces oddities that it can use to justify its originally groundless fear. In describing the effect on Silas himself, Eliot makes the most direct statement in all her work of the relationship of a sense of self to a sense of community and familiarity.

> Even people whose lives have been made various by learning, sometimes find it hard to keep a fast hold on their habitual views of life, on their faith in the Invisible, nay on the sense that their past joys and sorrows are a real experience, when they are suddenly transported to a new land, where the beings around them know nothing of their history, and share none of their ideas—where their mother earth shows another lap, and human life has other forms than those on which their souls have been nourished. Minds that have been unhinged from their old faith and love, have perhaps sought this Lethean influence of exile, in which the past becomes dreamy because its symbols have vanished, and the present too is dreamy because it is linked with no memories. (P. 226)

At last even the present is dreamy—a mere sensation—in the absence of echoing experience, the texture of memories and objects and known relationships in which every thread leads to another, every event defines itself against other events.

Marner in Raveloe is reduced to that position from which so many later novels begin. "In this strange world, made a hopeless riddle to him, he might, if he had had a less intense nature, have sat weaving—looking towards the end of his pattern, or towards the end of his web, till he forgot the riddle, and everything else but his immediate sensations" (p. 231). The words are similar to Pater's in the conclusion to *The Renaissance*. "Experience, already reduced to a swarm of impressions, is ringed round for each one of us by that thick wall of personality through which no real voice has ever pierced on its way to us, or from us to that which we can only conjecture to be without."[1] To try to untangle Marner's riddle, as so many novels of investigation do in the next generation; or to create a miniature rational world of work and patterns that, with our shortsightedness, we can contemplate instead of the riddle; or to begin to take pleasure in atomized, immediate sensation as those after Pater did—all three are in bondage to the same reading of life, the same incomprehensibility of social, and, in consequence, individual existence.

Marner's is the solution by work. Reducing life to a closed universe where one is absolutely in control—a self-made universe— he cannot see beyond the cycles of project and payment, work promised and work delivered, money owed and money paid. The world makes sense because it is empty. Only two elements exist, the loom and the hoard of gold. Like Hetty, Marner in the evening ritualizes his sensuality into a relationship with his hoard. He enjoys the "companionship" (p. 232) of his money, the society of inanimate things.

Three of the great mythic figures of the mid-nineteenth-century novel are misers: Dickens's Scrooge, Balzac's Grandet, and Eliot's Marner. Avarice is the essential deadly sin in an age of individualism. In de Tocqueville's description, the social energies are hoarded, and capitalism is a public form of hoarding, capital accumulation. Behind the self-made man stand two mythic figures: the monster and the miser, Frankenstein's creation and Scrooge.

Paradoxically, the miser, man totally in isolation, always hoards goods that have only social value—money, diamonds, jewelry. No

---

1. Walter Pater, *The Renaissance* (1873; reprint ed., New York: Mentor Books, 1960), p. 157.

miser hoards what he needs to live. Hetty, when most alone, was most intensely involved in social fantasies. The miser accumulates what a change of social forms can turn to junk, like those Indian graves filled with treasures of beads. The miser lives in a theater of the imagination, as Eliot called it, a make-believe society that seems solid and ultimate in its simplicity, but is as fragile as the society of riddles it has replaced.

Although everyone guesses Silas has gold hidden in his cottage, no one can steal it. Legibility and community create one another. "How could they have spent the money in their own village without betraying themselves? They would be obliged to 'run away'—a course as dark and dubious as a balloon journey" (p. 232). After the theft Marner accuses Jem Rodney, whose defense cannot be questioned. " 'What could I ha' done with his money? I could as easy steal the parson's surplice and wear it' " (p. 270). The money is stolen by those who could never be suspected of needing it, the rich, and Marner reaches the bottom. The theft proves that even a miser is still in society. The man most isolated remains part of the intentions of those around him, part of their imaginations if nothing else. In the Victorian novel, there is often a grim proof that society exists whether we will it or not. The agents of this proof are crime, illegitimacy, and contagious diseases. In *Bleak House*, the most distant corners of society are shown connected by their ability to ravage one another. Jo carries the disease; Esther's illegitimate parentage binds high and low; crime is woven through the whole. Society exists at least enough for everyone to stalemate one another at law while the inheritance that should be shared by all vanishes.

When Dunstan Cass enters Marner's cottage and when Godfrey's child crawls through the open door, society still exists in this minimal, negative sense. The opium addict dies in Marner's front yard on her way to disgrace Godfrey by revealing that she is his wife. The childlessness of Godfrey's marriage to Nancy is symbolically a result of the earlier marriage. Had the prudery of the time not enforced silence, Eliot might have openly stated that the childlessness was the result of venereal disease.

Only twice are high and low connected in the novel. The first time is when Dunstan Cass enters to steal the gold. It is a startling moment because only the rich can steal this money, since only they don't need it. The second event is the visit of Godfrey to steal Eppie, to reclaim her. United by catastrophe, by their ability to damage each other, the extremes of rich and poor never meet otherwise. No society includes them. The characters of the novel are individuals who enter relationships with one another, who make up their lives with one another; no network exists into which they find themselves integrated at birth.

Silas Marner is the first of Eliot's novels that critics speak of by parts, a Marner half connected only at flash points with a Cass half. Each novel that follows can be divided similarly. Nothing unites the parts but events. Yet nothing is more essential and at the same time more hopeless in Eliot's ambition than the demand that experience must have its meaning in terms of a wider frame than that of individual history. Biography seems the obvious form for her to work in, but it is the one form that is most untrue to what she knows as the truth of events. If experience is legible through the context of individual history—as it is for Freud, who finds the complete meaning of an event within the absolute vacuum of the patient's memory—then the self is the one reference point for motive and the one goal of action.

Looking back at Adam's life or Maggie's, we can see that the most important changes were not willed and could not be understood with only their lives as contexts. The love affair between Hetty and Arthur indirectly gives the critical turn to Adam's life. Her father's feud with Wakem and the family bankruptcy do the same for Maggie. Silas's whole life is altered by the love between his fiancée and his friend. None of these lives makes sense as a project; none can be talked of in the language of Mr. Deane, where a man can be anything he wants to be. Mr. Deane's is the language of the biographical form, the motto of which is "Be yourself." Dozens of later novels follow the pattern of Joyce's *Portrait of the Artist As a Young Man* and base themselves on the sensitive, isolated hero, often an artist, surrounded by others who are completely different from him and who affect him mainly by temporarily preventing him from "finding himself," and then from "being himself." This self is harmonious and complete; each part has meaning through the others; each is in focus when seen against the whole of the self. But this self that is like a work of art, because it has complete meaning in itself, is self-explanatory but not self-sufficient. It is in exile.

Where the biographical form is accepted, the values of will, energy, and the imagination to project the self in a daring and novel way follow. The form can be used against the grain: Dickens did so in *Great Expectations*. Pip's life is like that of a puppet at the end of strings so long that they pass out of sight. Practically without will, he is here, then moved there, claimed and reclaimed. But the use of a form against itself is like a temperance speech in a tavern. Eliot combines lives because she must, in order to keep the legibility of lives that, as she shows, only make sense in the wider context of other lives.

At the same time, she is detailing the disappearance of society, the natural context of wider meaning. Family and society, the Tullivers and the village of Hayslope, make the magic circle James spoke of. "Really, universally, relations stop nowhere, and the exquisite problem of the artist is eternally but to draw, by a geometry of his own, the circle within which they shall happily appear to do so."[2] James is wrong in assuming there is no natural circle; Hayslope and the family life of the Tullivers are natural circles, those of continuous existence: the same people in the same place through time. An image from Marner indicates the challenge

---

2. Henry James, *The Art of Fiction*, ed. R. P. Blackmur (New York: Scribner's, 1934), p. 5.

to the novel from the new society in which circles do only "appear" final. Marner, an outsider even after fifteen years in Raveloe, appears like a ghost at the Casses' New Year's Eve party. In his arms he holds an unknown child. He is an outsider holding a stranger. By the laws of melodrama, he has brought the child to its home and into the sight of its father, who is married secretly in another town. The secrecy of Godfrey's life carries further, by willing it, the type of discontinuity thrust on Marner. The natural circle does not exist. Only the circle of art makes sense of this moment in the doorway. Marner knows a fraction, Godfrey a little more, the rest of the party know nothing, and never will: the reader knows it all.

A more extreme example is the group that assembles in the first chapters of James's *Portrait of a Lady*: Daniel Touchett, Ralph, Mrs. Touchett, Isabel, Lord Warburton, and Mme. Merle. In life, as James knows it, in rootless life, real relations end nowhere. In Hayslope they do end; Raveloe is halfway between Hayslope and Gardencourt, between community and collection. Where art closes the circle, as it does in Raveloe, it stands as an illusory barrier to incomprehensibility. There is only a step between those circles closed by art and those closed by the imagination, whether sane or insane—between the circles in James's *Sacred Fount* or Faulkner's *Absalom, Absalom!*

The narratives we see divided in parts are only the first of the synthetic replacements Eliot found for the community she lost. The form of the social novel was lost along with the community. To the extent that family was at least a miniature community in *The Mill on the Floss*, the first two of her novels showed the disintegration in process. *Silas Marner* is the first of her works after the fall. The Cass half of the novel is the context for our comprehension—but not his own—of Marner's life. Like Maggie and Adam, he is shaped by life. The keys to his life are outside: the betrayal by his friend, the robbery, the appearance of the child. He responds but does not initiate. Passivity, resignation, and

Making Up Society

acceptance are the inversions of the initiative, imagination, and energy of the self-made man. The virtues are those of characters made by catastrophes they could not even foresee, let alone prevent.

Within the Cass chapters, the novel outlines a grammar of inverted appearances and truths. Three families exist: the squire and his sons; Godfrey's first marriage with Molly and the child that results; and Godfrey's second, childless marriage with Nancy. Each family is seen only in glimpses of moments when it is acting out the truth of the relationship, a truth that is always a savage reversal of the public meaning of the tie. Godfrey lies out of necessity, Dunstan for pleasure. In the first family, one brother is blackmailing the other, and both rob the father. When any two meet, they argue, and when Dunstan disappears no one misses him, no search is made. Godfrey would be pleased to learn of his brother's death.

The second family exists only in Molly's journey through the snow to disgrace her husband, the dishonor him at the party by revealing the marriage. She falls asleep from the opium and dies. Godfrey arrives only to make sure she is dead. Again bonds are inverted; twice Godfrey is best served by the deaths of those he is most closely related to.

The single great moment in the novel is the final reversal of what Eliot would call natural human bonds. The scene is the exact equivalent of Hetty's murder of her child. A contrast of the two scenes shows the extent to which psychology and internal action have replaced public events in Eliot's work. Melodrama gives way to the subtleties of the modern social novel where action is invisible or inscrutable or both. Godfrey stands in Marner's cottage after he has been assured that the woman to whom he is secretly married is dead. One danger remains: the child. If the child didn't exist, he would be free of the past—something he is forced, by inversion, to desire. Only one last detail to erase, and the previous years will be a blank. He looks at the child. "The wide-open blue eyes looked up at Godfrey's without any uneasiness or sign of recognition: the child could make no audible claim on its father; and the father felt a strange mixture of feelings, a conflict of regret and joy, that the pulse of that little heart had no response for the half-jealous yearning in his own, when the blue eyes turned away from him slowly and fixed themselves on the weaver's queer face" (p. 337). In the joy he feels that the child treats him as a stranger, he has reached a point equivalent to Hetty's.

Godfrey's third family is likewise in sight only at a moment of paradox. The fifteen years skipped pass over what happiness he and Nancy had. We see only his confession of his earlier marriage. The two try to recover Eppie and fail. The crisis of this part of the novel concerns Eppie's choice. Will she live with her legal father, her father in fact, or stay with Silas? Godfrey's claim would be recognized by society; any court would award him custody. But Silas is the father in supplying the recognition Godfrey denied her.

The ties are concealed or denied or perverted until they are unrecognizable. Brother, father, family—none has reality, all conceal the true bonds that are independent of the formal relationships. Before disappearing, the society is distorted into grotesque variants on what it was to be. It is the rich that rob the poor.

The harsh substance of the book provides the motive for the compensating surface of sentimentality. The marriage that concludes the book, the symbolic holy family (in which there is more of true family feeling than in any of the actual families of the novel) made up of Silas, Dolly Winthrop, and Eppie, does not weigh against the treachery and paradox that have destroyed both communities, that of the Lantern Yard and that of Raveloe. The neat satisfactions of justice in the novel are deceptive: the fog that allows the robbery conceals the stone pits that punish the thief. Godfrey, who denies his child, must stay childless for the rest of his life. In the end, the gold Silas seemed to have lost in order to gain the golden child reappears as though to say he couldn't have blessings enough.

Making Up Society

The state of life that is recovered is not at all like Job's—the literal return of what was lost. Instead of the fiancée and friend of the Lantern Yard, Marner, an old man now, has the sexless family in which the single emotional tie is the child. His life is lost and he has only a simulation that, like the metaphor of gold and golden hair, is true only on the plane of the imagination.

5

Romola

Romola and *Felix Holt* are both experiments in social vocabulary. Although both fail, each constructs one part of the epic method that leads to the triumph of *Middlemarch*. In *Romola*, Eliot invents a novelistic vocabulary that has its roots in a world midway between truth and lie, between reality and pretense: the world of hypothesis. What might be true is risked as a speculative certainty to see if, in time, reality will accumulate around what is possible until, set in place, it becomes real. A hypothesis is at once a description and a proposal. It is our primary technique for dealing in a participatory way, rather than a prophetic way, with the future. Just as trial and judgment are the tools for the establishment of truth about the past, so hypothesis and the risk of personal intervention, are the techniques of future truth. The truth of the past becomes known by exposure, discovery, or confession. The truth of the future is constructed or made up. As Eliot turned to the description of society as an open-ended future, she paradoxically chose to write a historical novel; this was the testing ground for the striking originality of her experimental vocabulary of hypothesis, fiction, and social self-invention, and her master equation between the artist's work in making up a world and the character's work of inventing and then solidifying a personal or political reality.

111

Making Up Society

By contrast, *Felix Holt* deepens, by making more extreme, the social vocabulary of discovery and detection, the vocabulary of the past. A retrospective social form surprises the reader with the hidden order of a past that is now certainly lost. While the detective form is our familiar name for the social vocabulary of *Felix Holt*, we have no technical term for the experiment in making up society represented by *Romola*. It is, of course, a historical novel, one in which the author makes up rather than remembers the world of the novel, constructing the social world that is the medium of her characters by a laborious process of study and synthesis. But to reach the formal center of Eliot's work in *Romola*, we should call the book not a historical novel but a hypothetical fiction: one in which both the overall reality for the author and the moral and political possibilities for the central figures are risked in the fictional form, lived "as if" true, ventured, and subjected to confirmation or collapse much as scientific hypotheses are.

Eliot's project in *Romola* involved abandoning the familiar English rural world of her earlier novels and her own childhood. This rustic world was both the location and the source of moral piety in her previous work. With *Romola*, she authors a world as well as a book. She makes up in her mind the solidity of circumstances, customs, and moral possibilities that yield her construction of Florence in 1494. The more ample moral and intellectual possibilities of Florence are purchased at the cost of their lack of connection by memory and piety to Eliot's own life. The sacrifice of memory and the legibility that the continuity of memory makes possible were themselves the central social themes of her early work.

The disconnection of memory as the price of entrance into the world of Florence is a major problem of the novel. In fact, in ways that modern novels have made familiar, Eliot has seized on her own project and used it, in disguised form, throughout her novel as a major instance of the moral difficulty of the world she is describing. She becomes, as an artist, self-consciously at stake in the book, exactly because her own project is the clearest example of the moral and social ambiguity the novel sees in Florentine life. In her earlier work, Eliot's re-creation by means of realistic, loving memory of the world she was familiar with was a major instance of the self-continuity and legibility that defined the central virtue of the characters' inside lives. Likewise, here her own discontinuity and invention of Florence are at one with the acts of discontinuity and invention recorded by the novel.

With *Romola*, construction replaces memory for the author. Invention or fictionalizing of a total world becomes the goal of writing at the same moment that the novel creates a moral indictment of the role of construction and fictionalizing in individual or political life. Tito, who has abandoned his stepfather and the ties of loyalty in another country in order to make his way in Florence, repeats the author's choice to create a new world and leave behind the loyalty and familiarity of the home country of her earlier novels. However, it is not only the villain of *Romola* who constructs and fictionalizes. The hero, Savonarola, is equally a figure of hypothetical, anomalous realities.

Both Eliot and the reader are outsiders in Florence: both, like the central character, Tito, in chapter 1, wake up strangers, lying on the sidewalk of Florence. Reader, author, and character have been shipwrecked into this new world, which they must learn and master with their wits. All three have abandoned or left in captivity their relations of piety and loyalty, represented by those stepfathers who, should we take too many steps into this world, will be forgotten and will return unexpectedly to take revenge. Three repetitions of the same act, a stranger's arrival, occur in *Romola* to underline the force of the beginning. Baldassare arrives as a chained prisoner, then makes his way to Florence. Romola, late in the novel, sets off in a boat and lands in a world of plague and death where she becomes a madonna. Finally, Tito, swimming off into the unknown, reaches shore just where Baldas-

Making Up Society

sare waits with a knife to slay him. All four acts cast ashore the stranger, but the opening of the novel, with the stranger awakening on the sidewalk at the moment when the reader begins to read, intensifies the arrival by means of a triple pun: arriving in a new land, waking up, and beginning to read; entry in space, in time, and in art.

The beginnings of Eliot's novels often allude to the position of the reader, orienting him by means of a system of situational puns. *Adam Bede* begins with the end of a work day, just as the reader might be expected to have opened the book after putting down the last of his tasks for the day. Locking up and leaving the closed room of the workshop is a reverse analogy to the reader's act of opening up the closed room of the novel. Most scenes within *Adam Bede* occur after work, after school, on Sunday, on a holiday, or as brief interruptions of work by visits or crises. The implicit relation of reading to working, in the reader's life, is insisted upon to intensify the central importance of work within the novel. *Middlemarch* begins with Dorothea and Celia opening a box of jewelry and opening their own adult lives of courtship and marriage. The rich objects in the opened box promise the reader, who has just opened the boxlike book, that what follows will be rare and beautiful. Both *Felix Holt* and *Daniel Deronda* begin with an attentive observer waiting for or fascinated by a central figure of the plot that follows. The waiting and fascination are mirrors of the reader's own state. However, it is with *Romola* that the reflection is most emphatic, precisely because the writing of the book by its author and the reading of it by the reader are instances of the discontinuity that, within the novel, defines the social world.

The breaking of ties occurs in both evil and honorable forms within *Romola*. The powerful commercial opposite of ownership, disowning, is one essential term of the novel. Tito disowns his stepfather, but of course so does Fra Luca disown his role as his father's son to enter the monastery. Romola herself ceremonially disowns her marriage twice, and all Florence disowns patriotic loyalties to enter the world of factions and parties. Abandoning the world, as monks do or as those in flight do, or as those who, like Baldassare, have forgotten everything, do, represents the inverse of the shipwrecked arrival, the awakening of a stranger on the sidewalk.

The morally negative terms of disowning, discontinuity, disloyalty, and abandoning the world represent only the surface configuration of *Romola*. Were they its limits, the novel would not have reached a single step beyond *Silas Marner* with its many-sided destruction coupled to an idyllic, hazy recovery. At the center of Eliot's vision is the description of the moral possibilities of breaks, like her own break in entering, as a novelist, the alien world of Florence. Tito and Baldassare represent the willed and unwilled villainy of breaks. Tito has two families, several names, and many lives. He atomizes his life. He lies, sells off the tokens of the past to make breaks within time, disowns his stepfather, and moves, or plans to move, from place to place. Baldassare is broken by acts outside his will, becoming the passive mirror of Tito's chosen discontinuity. Captured by pirates, prisoner of the French, disowned by his son, driven mad, his memory erased, Baldassare, although a victim rather than a master of atomization, nonetheless becomes an instrument of obsessive violence. The two men are linked symbols: the one of outer, the other of inner discontinuity. What happens in the social world for Tito occurs in the mind for Baldassare. Neither exhausts the moral possibilities of the novel. The moment of entering a monastery and changing one's name, the moment of entering or renouncing a marriage, the changes of loyalty and life that are the novel's strongest instances of discontinuity, are mixed or even positive acts. The models of Tito and Baldassare cannot define the situation of the author working between two worlds or that of a monk at work within both the present political world and a transcendent vision.

Eliot creates one self-portrait within the novel in the life of the scholar Bardi, who exists cut off from the world of Florence, which he has abandoned to live in books and collections that let him reconstruct the life of Greece. Eliot, surrounded by books about Florence in her London study, creates the figure of Bardi, who sits within his Florentine study creating the life of Greece.

The most profound breaks represented by the novel are those within the wholeness of experience. Such breaks are marked by the failure of the senses. In many scenes, characters are together in space while sensory breaks confine them to separate worlds. In his study with his beautiful daughter, Bardi is blind and cannot know her beauty. He cannot see the glances between Tito and Romola. Tessa lives with Mona Lisa, who is nearly deaf and cannot hear the ripples of talk that define the pleasure of the simple girl. Tessa herself is so simple-minded that, when Tito is with her, he is in effect with someone whose experience lacks any power to infer or construct the meaning of events. At other moments in the novel, the painter Piero di Cosimo stuffs his ears with wax so as not to hear the world at all. The madman, Baldassare, sits in a trance, lacking memory, a power that the book represents as equal to that of all the senses put together. Deaf, blind, mad, simple, lacking memory or sense: the novel is rich in the varieties of discontinuous experience. In Florence, cultural prestige lies with the alien Greek language, and for much of the period of the novel the city is occupied by political aliens, the French. The metaphor of foreign occupation, whether by the power of the past—the Greek cultural world—or by the power of the future—the French political world—is at the same time a reiteration of the intrusion of author and reader, who also occupy Florence.

At each stage of Romola's life, she is dominated by a social alien whose relation to the Florentine world repeats components of Eliot's own relation. First, as the daughter of and assistant to Bardi, Romola is under the authority of a man blind to his own city, one who has withdrawn to his hoard of foreign texts that he uses to construct the world of the past. The blind, single-minded cruelty of the scholar, his miserlike relation to his collection, his rejection of the son who would not submit to him, and his contempt for the daughter who has done so all portray the morally troubling elements of what might be called stationary emigration: the mental but not physical abandonment of one's own world. The marriage of Tito and Romola collapses with Tito's sale of the now dead scholar's library to the departing French occupation troops. This meeting point of three alien forces is symbolically complex but, in Eliot's treatment, psychologically uninteresting. The second stage of Romola's life is passed under the power of the shipwrecked parvenu. Tito is an accumulation of all the opportunistic vices of the stranger, including his search for short-term advantages and his continual calculation of the right moment for flight. As an immigrant, Tito inverts the estrangement of the scholar Bardi.

In her final stage, Romola submits to the visionary Savonarola, a man withdrawn physically to a monastic distance, yet troubling the social world with his vision of a reformed and ideal society. Savonarola's hypothetical society suggests the most positive and yet the most troubling model for Eliot's own relation to Florence and her use of Florence as a model for her English readers. Savonarola withdraws to the future as Bardi has withdrawn to the past. All three strangers die: the scholar dies of old age, Tito is murdered by his stepfather, Savonarola is executed by his own townsmen.

The antithetical term to the many forms of intrusion and disconnection remains for Eliot the central term on which her earlier social novels had been based—memory. In fact, the abandonment of memory for construction, an abandonment surrounded with such guilt in *Romola*, became the moral basis of the great social fiction of *Middlemarch*. Making up is the opposite of remembering. It is a crisis of memory that overtakes Baldassare when he is disowned by Tito. The broken outward tie severs all inner links of the mind and finally severs the mind's relation to itself. Baldassare is for most of the time Nola or no one; then, restored to himself, he is a man rich in memories, languages, and links between experience and self.

Making Up Society

Memory, seemingly the most inner and self-sufficient component of identity, rests ultimately in the hands of others and the world of objects. Tito's denial erases his stepfather's memory. Objects, at risk in the world, center and guarantee the stability of memory as the mill or the penknife did in *The Mill on the Floss*. After her father's death, Romola accepts Piero's painting of the scholar, inaccurate as it seems to her to be, while she remains in the immediate period of loss. In the long run, the image of memory will depend on the external image or on tokens of life that are capable of regenerating memory. Even in the act of removing her wedding ring because of her husband's treachery, Romola finds that the ring evokes the happy life of the moment of betrothal in a way that, for a moment, eclipses the very betrayal that caused her to remove it. The crisis in Romola's marriage resulting from Tito's sale of her father's collections is the most dramatic version of the reliance of memory on both objects and the acts of others. With Baldassare the force of memory is stated in its most extreme form. The choice is between memory and madness: to be oneself is to remember who one was.

The act of recovering who one was, or being recalled to oneself, recurs throughout in scenes of waking, like the one with which the novel begins. Tito, on the sidewalk, is first met as a "suddenly awakened dreamer" (I, 12). Waking is the key everyday experience in which remembering one's life reinstates it. Continuity reappears, but as a victory. The rhythm of sleeping and waking that is stressed again and again addresses conditions in which, in a larger way, one's self is periodically lost and recovered, broken and reconnected. Tito falls asleep with Tessa under the plane tree. Late in the novel, it is Romola who, having abandoned Florence and chosen the worldless surrender of a drifting boat, lies down to sleep and then awakes. "She lay motionless, hardly watching the scene; rather feeling simply the presence of peace and beauty. While we are still in our youth there can always come, in our early waking moments when mere passive existence is itself a

Lethe, when the exquisiteness of subtle, indefinite sensation creates a bliss which is without memory and without desire" (II, 177). The intensity of sensation and pleasure in the absence of memory and connection defines one of the moral terms of the novel. Tito destroys memory and creates a life of pleasure. He blots out the memory of Baldassare and sells the scholar's library. His most pleasant life is lived with Tessa, a creature so simple that she has no intact world at all.

The self-recovery of waking is only the most common form of reconnection. In her first flight, Romola removes the tokens of her marriage and disguises herself in religious garb to set out on the road from Florence.

> For the first time in her life she felt alone in the presence of the earth and sky with no human presence interposing and making a law for her.
> Suddenly a voice close to her said—"You are Romola di Bardi; the wife of Tito Malema."   (I, 374)

The voice of Savonarola recalls her to herself by naming her first in relation to her father and then as the wife of her husband. His demand that she return begins the third period of her discipleship, a religious submission to Savonarola himself. In his political role, Savonarola recalls Florence itself to its identity. His sermons call for the regeneration of the church, and he dies less than twenty years before Luther's Ninety-five Theses.

By means of the interwoven religious, political, psychological, and sensory languages of break and resumption, departure and return, forgetting and remembering, decay and reformation, Eliot defines the moment before the onset of the Protestant Reformation and gives a striking psychological interpretation of the inner meaning of the reestablished connection to the past that both the Renaissance, in the sphere of culture, and the Reformation, in the sphere of religion, effected. She makes complete use of the 1490s, both as a moment of moral darkness just before the Reformation, and as a moment of cultural vitality in the midst of personal, familial, and political decline.

THEATER OF REALITY

Were Savonarola the only character taken from history in Eliot's novel, the events would, in effect, be an interpretation of the moral analysis given in his sermons. The weariness with treachery, decline, and complexity that is one of the novel's recurring moods becomes a major argument for the Protestant world that the sixteenth century would bring into being. Savonarola plays the part of John the Baptist to this new order. He previews its themes and inner psychology even in the process of being overwhelmed by the formulas of the discredited order that he is unable to reform from within. As a character, Savonarola is a first version of Daniel Deronda, just as *Romola* is a preliminary version of Eliot's final novel with its severe account of the England of her day. In *Deronda*, the first seeds of Zionism, like the preview of the Reformation in Savonarola, occur within a morally bankrupt civilization. The intense need for a regeneration that neither novel can represent as occurring in fact creates, instead of hope, an increased darkness in the given social patterns of decay and evil. For Eliot, the patterns she found both in Florence in the 1490s and in the England of her own day lead her to attempt to write heroic and tentatively hopeful novels. In fact, with *Romola* and *Daniel Deronda* she created only moderately convincing heroes, but absolutely convincing portraits of evil, her two great villains, Tito and Grandcourt. Nonetheless, the aim in both novels was for an urgent representation of the possibility of rebirth and reformation.

Romola opens in 1492. The Renaissance was the analogue the Victorians chose at their moment of greatest clarity. The expansive energy and individualism, the flourishing art and science, the skepticism and political turmoil were the perfect analogues in which to review the psychology of the nineteenth century in England. Where the Victorians used the Renaissance, as Browning and Eliot did, a vigorous statement of the crisis of the age was possible. In contrast, the use of the Middle Ages was elegiac, whether in Carlyle's *Past and Present*, Tennyson's *Idylls of the King*, or Arnold's "Scholar Gypsy" and "Grande Chartreuse." With the Middle Ages, they saw their negative, the paradise they had lost. Even into the twentieth century, Pound and T. S. Eliot continued the idyllic fiction of the age of Dante. But in the Renaissance was the image of the present itself, not the paradise from which the present had been expelled. The great explorations are one with the colonial frenzy of the mid-nineteenth century. Even the materialism, the force of personality, and the strains of will against order unite the two ages. Both produced the greatest characters of English literature (the prerogative of an age of individualism). Both created high, popular art: the drama of the Renaissance, the novel in the Vicorian period.

In her choice of the 1490s, Eliot has taken a paradoxical period. *Romola* takes place in the six years between 1492 and 1498. Her introduction reminds us of Columbus, and the year 1492 is the beginning of the New World, the world open to exploration and development, the round world that we know in the act of conquest. An exuberant date to begin with. But it is not October 11 that is the starting point, but April 9, not the discovery of America, but the death of Lorenzo the Magnificent, Lorenzo de'Medici. Paradoxically, when we consider the date, the novel sets itself in a period of decline, the end of the greatness of Florence. The Victorian preference was for surveys from decline. Tennyson's *Idylls of the King* are set in the years of dissolution of the Round Table; the years of greatness are remembered only in contrast. Like "Dover Beach," that poem with one of the deepest emotional patterns of the age, *Romola* includes the glorious past only to remind us more completely of the "diminished thing" that remains. By 1498, the end of the book, Dolfo Spini, the most worthless of men, has risen to power. In the novel, men die in order of their nobility, and the greatest of all, Lorenzo, has died before it begins.

Making Up Society

Like the other analogue Eliot used (in *Felix Holt* and *Middlemarch*), the period of the first Reform Bill in England, the situation in Florence in the 1490s is developed as a parallel, an indirect historical commentary on the political and moral life of England in the 1850s and 1860s. In what is surely one of the most daring (and to our sense of the period, accurate) reductions imaginable, Eliot does not identify the new world of 1492 with Columbus and Michelangelo, but with three figures who embody less of the historic thrust of the modern world and more of its problematic side: Machiavelli, Savonarola, and the decadent artist, Piero di Cosimo.

The choice of Piero di Cosimo, out of the many far greater painters alive during these years,[1] involves an identification of the spirit of art in the novel with his fantastic and cynical style, the minor strain of sinister, alienated perception that Piero embodies best in the period. Like Philip Wakem, whose deformity is the price and source of his art, Piero is essentially alone, eccentric, and testy whenever a visitor approaches his house. Piero keeps his ears plugged so as not to be intruded on by the world. His studio and home are the only rooms described in the novel.

> The double door underneath the window that admitted the painter's light from above, was thrown open, and showed a garden, or rather thicket, in which fig-trees and vines grew in tangled trailing wildness among nettles and hemlocks, and a tall cypress lifted its dark head from a stifling mass of yellowish mulberry-leaves. It seemed as if that dank luxuriance had begun to penetrate even within the walls of the wide and lofty room; for in one corner, amidst a confused heap of carved marble fragments of rusty armor, tufts of

---

1. In 1492 Michelangelo fled Florence to join Leonardo da Vinci in Milan. Raphael did not arrive in Florence until 1504, but Botticelli remained throughout the period and became a follower of Savonarola in the late 1490s.

long grass and dark feathery fennel had made their way. . . .
All about the walls hung pen and oil sketches of fantastic
sea-monsters; dances of satyrs and maenads; Saint Margaret's
resurrection out of the devouring dragon; Madonnas with
the supernal light upon them; and on irregular rough shelves
a few books were scattered among great drooping bunches
of corn, bullocks' horns, pieces of dried honeycomb . . .
skulls and bones, peacock's feathers, and large bird wings.
(I, 198)

Piero has a fantastic world of mythology and inner vision. Private
to the point of eccentricity, he lives on boiled eggs, which are
delivered to his door every morning. Cut off, by choice, he releases
installments of his peculiar inner world in the art that is his only
contact. His ears are plugged, his door locked. When spoken to he
has a favorite gesture: "He grinned, stretched out the corners of
his mouth, and pressed down his brows, so as to defy any divina-
tion of his feelings" (I, 198). Piero's most famous pupil was
Andrea del Sarto, that other secondary figure, envious of Michelangelo and Raphael, who served Browning as a model for the artist.
    Piero and Machiavelli, two of the three historical figures in
Romola, are both only choral figures. Nowhere do they alter the
plot or have any relationship other than professional with the
characters who act in the book. In balance with Piero, Machiavelli
embodies the new, openly pragmatic system of political realism.
Interested only in technique and means, only in policy, never in
goals, Machiavelli represents the public life drained of both moral
and human reference. Power and interest are the two terms of his
system; only what is effective has value. Tito is the double of
Machiavelli, and he is constantly compared to the more theoretical
mentor, usually by his coconspirators. " 'Niccolo Machiavelli
might have done for us if he had been on our side, but hardly so
well. He is too much bitten with notions, and has not your power
of fascination. All the worse for him. He has lost a great chance in

life and you have got it' " (I, 364). Politics is spoken of in the language of the theater or as a game. "You have only to play your game well, Malema, and the future belongs to you" (I, 365). Tito's allies temporarily speak of a "wise dissimulation" (I, 362) as the key to public life. Conspiracy and betrayal, loyalties that shift day by day, plot and treachery are the terms of social existence. (Although none exists in the novel, poison was one of the staples of public life in the Italy of the period.) No one has any goal but power, and, as in the French Empire contemporary with Eliot, the slogan of life was *Enrichissez-vous.*

Through Machiavelli, the novel represents the entry into relations within society of the disorder that had always governed relations among societies. Diplomacy, with its alliances and secret agreements, its facade of civility covering the unrelenting search for advantage, had been one of the specialties of the Renaissance. Machiavelli internalizes diplomacy and makes the relations between factions within a state mirror the anarchy of relations among states. No community exists, only parties that embody selfish interests. At one point, the Medici party allies itself with the French king, allowing Florence to pass into the hands of the French because it will serve the Medici interest. In such a state, treason literally no longer exists, but the charge of treason and the execution of rivals in its name continue as a shoddy patriotism concealing yet another interest. By recognizing within the state the same tactics that had always existed in relations among states, Machiavelli exposed the state and showed it to be as hollow a pole for loyalty as the word *mankind.*

In *The Mill on the Floss,* Eliot uses lawsuits in public life and quarrels in private as the images of disorder. In *Romola,* the images are the more extreme ones of intrigue in the state and violent splits in the family. Within this world of faction and deception, the essential man is the inscrutable and absolutely ruthless man of daring. In another context he would be called an adventurer, but within the broil of Florentine politics, he combines a hunger for power and wealth with an almost bravura delight in the intricacy of the game he plays. Ben Jonson drew many such characters. His Mosca is the essence of the type. In Shakespeare's Iago, the traits are made mysterious in the absence of the usual motives, but throughout the Renaissance the schemer, the "motivated malignity," to reverse Coleridge's phrase, was the identified danger of the new political life. The inscrutable man who plays the game of life, living two or many roles, his life cut into sectors each of which has its own logic but is isolated from and incompatible with the others—this is the type Eliot drew on for Tito Malema.

The essential self-made man, Tito is first seen sleeping in the streets, an alien from somewhere prepared to live by his wits. He rises to the highest circles of Florentine life in the six years of the novel, advancing by his ruthless skill as a plotter and by making himself useful to others. In the final pages he falls, plotted against and ruined by a change in the currents he rose by. Tito's usefulness is based precisely on his being an outsider. " 'In truth Malema,' Tournabuoni was saying at this stage, . . . 'No man in Florence can serve our party better than you. You see what most of our friends are: men who can no more hide their prejudices than a dog can hide the natural tone of his bark, or else men whose political ties are so notorious, that they must always be objects of suspicion' " (I, 364). When he has been taken into the intrigue, Tito realizes the source of his power. "His position as an alien, his indifference to the ideas or prejudices of the men among whom he moved, were suddenly transformed into advantages; he became newly conscious of his own adroitness in the presence of a game he was called on to play" (I, 366). Spy and informer, plant and triple agent, betraying the plots he himself has created, his entire value rests on his having no identifiable opinions, loyalties, or interests of his own.

An outsider who has erased his ties by abandoning his foster father, Tito lives three roles in Florence. Married to Romola, keeping Tessa with whom he has gone through the fake marriage ceremony at the carnival, and uniting and reversing alliances among the parties of political life, Tito has no final goal but to get out of Florence and move into a more complex life, that of Rome. Without a home, he has no interest in one. As Romola's uncle says of him, "It seems to me he is one of the *demoni*, who are of no particular country. . . . his mind is too nimble to be weighted with all the stuff we men carry about in our hearts" (I, 206).

The one characteristic repeatedly stressed is that he is not moved by associations, he "had the unimpassioned feeling of the alien towards names and details that move the deepest passions of the native" (I, 229). The same lack of passion is identified as the ground of his attitude to life. "As the freshness of young passion faded, life was taking on more and more decidedly for him the aspect of a game in which there was an agreeable mingling of skill and chance. And the game that might be played in Florence promised to be rapid and exciting; it was a game of revolutionary and party struggle, sure to include plenty of that unavowed action in which brilliant ingenuity, able to get rid of all inconvenient belief . . . is apt to see the path of superior wisdom" (I, 330). The metaphor of theater is side by side with that of the game. Living several lives, Tito finds it convenient to have a second name: to Tessa he is Naldo. When assaulted by Baldassare, he creates a fictional identity, Jocopo di Nola, for his foster father, and condemns him as a madman. Disguises, forged letters, rumors and counterrumors are all part of the theater and created identity that Tito's new world fashions.

Far more important than these mechanical props of theater is the aspiration to counterfeit life: to create what is imagined, and force, in Oscar Wilde's phrase, life to imitate art. When Tito feels the grasp of the prisoner he recognizes as his foster father, the man who raised him and was abandoned by him, he turns to his companions and explains the man's apparent recognition: "*Some madman, surely*" (I, 233). To explain the man, he creates a false identity for him, but in the act of denying his own foster father he makes that identity come true: the denial drives Baldassare mad. Similarly, the bogus wedding Tito goes through with Tessa becomes, when he decides against telling her it was only a joke, a marriage far more authentic in fact than his legal marriage to Romola. When he plans to flee Florence secretly, it is Tessa and the children he will take, not Romola.

The counterfeiting of life that is occasional in private life is the essence of public reality. In *Romola* there are no institutions, no patterns of behavior and feeling that externalize life, only theater and the attempt to manipulate appearances to create an imagined reality that might then come into being. Savonarola must stage a miracle when his prestige declines. Dolfo Spini stages a riot that is in fact a carefully directed attack on the houses of his enemies. The mountebank who marries Tito and Tessa is only a harmless version of the manipulation that creates public life throughout Florence. Savonarola can be tried and convicted as a traitor because the letters he entrusted to Tito were opened, re-sealed, then given to a messenger, who will be "surprised" at the border by agents who will seize and reveal the letters without implicating Tito. The sequence becomes an arranged little drama controlled by invisible hands.

What Tito embodies as a counterfeiter of realities can be seen even in the lives of the more sympathetic characters. Baldassare creates the scene in which he will expose Tito, plotting as much as any conspirator for dramatic effect. The most honorable man in Florence, Romola's uncle, joins conspiracies that involve pretended allegiances to one party so as to crush another, leaving his true allies to deal with their pretended allies in the sequel.

Nothing of Florence exists in the novel but its streets and private rooms. Even Savonarola, whom we see preaching in church, is a man in a purely personal relationship to his audience. His power lies in his personality; he is a celebrity. To the church he is a heretic. The final theater is located in the streets of Florence. Crowd and then mob, the people are joined by the currents that sweep them, not by any relationships that mold their lives. Emotional, violently blind, open to manipulation by those who can simulate the realities they desire, the people of Florence are a rabble like those of ancient Rome or Paris during the revolution, two historical situations where public spectacle and drama and staged reality were also central. Instead of society, there is the theater shared by the few and the many: the few magicians—public artists—who create imaginary realities, and the many who respond and therefore confirm the reality or do not respond and dispel it like the fiction it is. The word *charisma* describes the sinister power of the few. Savonarola, with his magic, his charisma in its literal Greek meaning of "divine gift," lives in the imaginative sweep of his power of vision, his sense of the infinite. But this power is never displayed in the intimate, plain, human context, as Dinah's enthusiasm was in *Adam Bede*. Like the host in Catholic rituals, Savonarola appears only in the most theatrical settings. One third of his force is personality, one third is theater, and the final third is miracle.

When his position is sinking and questions arise about the loyalty his followers can give him as an excommunicated priest, a miracle is advertised. The crowd gathers. Monks begin to enter near the pulpit that has been placed above the church door. All know what to expect.

> But while the ordinary Frati in black mantles were entering and arranging themselves, the faces of the multitude were not yet eagerly directed towards the pulpit: it was felt that Savonarola would not appear just yet, and there was some interest in singling out the various monks, some of them belonging to high Florentine families, many of them having fathers, brothers, or cousins among the artisans and shopkeepers who made the majority of the crowd. It was not till the tale of monks was complete, not till they had fluttered their books and had begun to chant, that people said to one another, "Fra Girolma must be coming now."

Romola

. . . The next instant the pulpit was no longer empty. A figure covered from head to foot in black cowl and mantle had entered it, and was kneeling with bent head and with face turned away. It seemed a weary time to the eager people while the black figure knelt and the monks chanted. (II, 131–32)

Prepared entrance, mystery, solemnity, even the tactic of delay, all heighten the tension, and of course the timing is perfect. The monks begin chanting as though this were an annual event for which they were well rehearsed. Only a few in the crowd kneel when Savonarola begins to bless them: the church has declared that any who accept absolution from him will be cast out. Savonarola senses another gesture is needed. "After the utterance of that blessing, Savonarola himself fell on his knees and hid his face in temporary exhaustion. Those great jets of emotion were a necessary part of his life. . . . all faces were intently watching him" (II, 133).

The "miracle" that follows is an ambiguous one, mixed with opportunism and exaggeration. Savonarola stands holding the host in front of him.

Everyone else was motionless and silent too, while the sunlight, which for the last quarter of an hour had here and there been piercing the grayness, made fitful streaks across the convent wall, causing some awe-stricken spectators to start timidly. But soon there was a wider parting, and with a gentle quickness, like a smile, a stream of brightness poured itself on the crystal vase, and then spread itself over Savonarola's face with mild glorification.

An instantaneous shout rang through the plaza, "Behold the answer!"

The warm radiance thrilled Savonarola's frame, and so did the shout. It was his last moment of untroubled triumph. (II, 134)

Making Up Society

The entire significance of the event lies in the expectations created by the staging and Savonarola's emotions. In itself the event is natural and uninteresting, but it is transformed into a miracle. No lame man is cured, no laws of nature are suspended as they were when Christ walked on the water. The event is banal, and only the interpretation of the chance occurrence makes it important.

The downfall of Savonarola is staged by his enemies in the same way his friends have staged his triumph. A rival monk calls on him to submit to an ordeal by which God will make known whether or not he speaks the truth. Each will walk through fire. The enemies care nothing for the life of the monk who offers himself as bait, but Savonarola will be forced to destroy himself either in the fire or in the scorn that will follow if he refuses. Even when he does refuse, the enemies double their triumph by appointing a day for the test to dramatize his absence. They place the wood for the fire in the square. Once the expectations of the crowd are aroused, the theater must occur or Savonarola will lose entirely the faith of the people in the divine protection he claims. Like the test for substance that drowns the witch in *The Mill on the Floss*, the test by fire must destroy Savonarola. A ludicrous scene develops on the day of the test when both sides quibble over details until rain soaks the wood. But Savonarola is ruined and shortly thereafter is burned to death as a heretic in the square filled with the crowd shouting "gross jests, taunts, and curses," the same mob that had been the source of his power as leader of the Popular party.

In the streets of Florence, processions follow carnivals, executions follow miracles, and in each case the bonds that unite those present are fugitive and emotional. In most cases the bonds are artificial, created with an interest that the crowd itself is ignorant of. The crowd in the streets moves without will, and those caught in it are described with language like that used for Romola's floating boat. "Tito . . . again found himself pushed towards the middle of the piazza and back again without the power of determining his own course. In this zigzag way he was carried along to the end of the piazza opposite the church, where . . . a girl was being pushed forward into the inner circle with apparent reluctance" (I, 153). As the historian E. P. Thompson has shown in *The Making of the English Working Class*, the English drew an important distinction between a crowd and a mob. In the mob no man is any longer himself, no man is responsible for the events that only the chemistry of the group can explain. Like drunkenness, the mob is a negative selflessness. Violence and irrationality are the marks of this new community. Both *Romola* and *Felix Holt* have climactic public scenes that are full-scale riots. No more extreme antithesis could exist to the court of law that is the final public center in *Adam Bede*. Riots, like processions, carnivals, miracles, and executions, are not spontaneous, although they are often out of control. Those who give themselves up in the mob do so with a half-knowledge of what they do and a trace of suspicion that they act out events that are staged.

Machiavelli was a playwright as well as a philosopher. When his values rule public life, and they do in the Florentine society pictured in *Romola*, we are no longer faced with an obscure public life. Mr. Tulliver's phrase, "It's a puzzling world," does not apply here. The "world" no longer exists. Artifice and image dominate everywhere; fictions combat fictions just as party does party. The state no longer exists, and with it treason disappears. Likewise, since no true state of affairs exists to be untangled, public life is a set of projections waiting for confirmation. Intangible, as full of bluff as a game of cards, every pretense is equally true and equally false. Which one will *work?* Machiavelli's question not only alters the tactics of social life, it also troubles its being. When either game or theater becomes the rule in public life, no outside world exists to return to.

In *Romola*, the factions of Florentine life are rival troops of actors who attempt to entrap one another and enlist the mob into making fact out of what so far is only scenario. The "charisma," the magic of public life, is literal: the magic is to call events and meanings into being. In the test by fire and the heresy trial that follows, the opponents of Savonarola outwit him and force him into a role in their script. Once he is trapped and executed, a fiction has enlisted reality to follow. Like Tito's word *madman*, a lie makes itself fact through the drama by which it seizes reality. The very terms that characterize the moral evil of public life in *Romola*, terms like fiction, theater, and the testing of reality by means of inventions, became, with a slight shift of emphasis, the elements of a positive and experimental notion of social reality in *Middlemarch*. The distance from the fictive to the hypothetical is defined in *Romola* by the contrast between Tito and Savonarola. Both men have abandoned continuity and invent their roles by inventing a social reality that is unprecedented. Heroic and villainous lives are equally distant from the social norm and are, in fact, variants of one another.

ADEQUATE VILLAIN, ADEQUATE HERO

Like Heathcliff, that other great usurper of the Victorian novel, Tito is found on the street and enters a society he comes to dominate by embodying in an undiluted form the forces of that social life. Where Heathcliff rises to own and rule the world of the heights, Tito aims for that peculiar modern kind of power that is invisible behind a set of symbolic figures: the power of the adviser. His life is a sequence of betrayals with only money or a precarious dominance as his goal. In his private life, the treachery we have traced in the social conspiracies takes on a more complex appearance. Tito is the best, the most ruthless of a set of men in public life who have lost any loyalty beyond private interest and gain. More refined, he differs only in degree from the rest, even from Savonarola, because it is the condition of public life that creates the possibility of his career. Unlike the criminals whose acts register as crimes against a frame of order and legality, the conspirators of Florence are natural. Where there is no state, there is no treason;

in the absence of law, there is no crime.

In the more restricted bonds of society, a difference between Tito and the rest begins to appear. Marriage and the family retain force in the Florentine world. In fact, the three political parties are family parties based on loyalty to the Medicis or to other prominent families who have a chance to rule. The dissolution of society is general but not local. Only Tito makes even the relationships of father and son, husband and wife, subservient to absolute convenience and self-interest. As his marriage to Romola shows, the force of his indifference to loyalties contaminates and weakens those bonds in the lives of others until he reduces life everywhere to the temporary fiction it is for him.

When Tito proposes to Romola that they leave Florence, she is startled, and her emotion brings from him the image of their marriage. " 'I like people who take life less eagerly; and it would be good for my Romola, too, to see a new life. I should like to dip her a little in the soft waters of forgetfulness' " (I, 289). The waters of forgetfulness, Lethe, are to weaken the ties in others that Tito no longer feels in himself. When Baldassare is denied by his son, the form his madness takes is loss of memory, a loss so complete that he becomes "no one," Jacopo di Nola, as Tito names him. Unable to remember even his name, the old man sits on the riverbank with a knife in his hand waiting for he no longer remembers what. What Tito denies consciously he obliterates in others. In Baldassare the world vanishes in the one moment of shock when Tito says, "*Some madman, surely.*" The process is slower and more subtle in Tito's relationship to Romola, but at the point where she lies down in the boat in an imitation of death, her life, her world, has been erased as completely as the old man's. Tito dips Romola as though in a bleach, in the waters of forgetfulness. In Tito's third relationship, that with Tessa, nothing exists to erase because Tessa is simple and ignorant to the extent that she never knows who Tito is or where he lives. He appears and disappears in her life under an assumed name, then vanishes she

Making Up Society

knows not where. Of course, this relationship is ideal for Tito, and he plans to take Tessa along when he leaves Florence; it is with her he has children, not Romola. Tessa's is a mind too innocent to create records that later need be erased.

In Romola's marriage forgetfulness is, from the start, the key, a deliberate erasing of the past that is thematically liked to sensuality. In one of the most obtrusive symbols of the novel, one that points out the destructive influence of Hawthorne and particularly his *Marble Fawn* on *Romola*, Tito has Piero di Cosimo create a shrine to depict his marriage to Romola. It consists of a triptych of the story of Bacchus and Ariadne, paintings in which the two characters have been given the faces of Tito and Romola. Inside the shrine Tito locks the crucifix given to Romola by her brother on his deathbed. " 'It is a little shrine, which is to hide away from you forever that remembrancer of sadness. . . . We will bury it in a tomb of joy' " (I, 212). Romola at this moment in her life agrees. "She had no wish to prevent his purpose; on the contrary she herself wished to subdue certain important memories and questionings which still flitted like unexplained shadows across her happier thoughts" (I, 213). At first she cooperates in locking the past away. She seems even to accept the image of life the painting offers, an image that contrasts startlingly with the boat she finally rides in. " 'And now, while I am away, you will look every day at those pretty symbols of our life together—the ship on the calm sea, and the ivy that never withers, and those Loves that have left off wounding us and shower soft petals that are like our kisses; and the leopards and tigers, they are the troubles of your life that are all quelled now: and the strange sea-monsters with their merry eyes' " (I, 214). Bacchus, god of the three Greek forms of ecstasy ("standing outside the self")—drunkenness, cruelty, and sexual passion—was also the god who destroyed all loyalties. In Euripides' play *The Bacchae*, Pentheus is torn apart by his own mother. In the story the painting depicts, Ariadne had just abandoned her father to choose Bacchus.

Romola

We see little of the sensuality and joy the symbol of Bacchus suggests. The few embraces the book mentions are exchanged at moments of relief and darkness suddenly lifted. The moment of greatest intensity happens when Romola returns from the deathbed of her brother and, crushed with despair over the vision he has told her about, she seeks consolation from Tito. What Tito says of Florence is true of Romola. " 'There is something grim and grave to me always about Florence . . . and even in its merriment there is something shrill and hard—biting rather than gay. . . . I should like to see you under that southern sun, lying among the flowers, subdued into mere enjoyment' " (I, 194–95). Joy is always pictured in this reductive way, and even when it is being urged, it is called "mere enjoyment." Linked to forgetfulness and an oblivion that is deliberate, like that of Tennyson's Lotus Eaters, pleasure is neutral to life, incapable of creating or expressing any more than transient situations. In this it is the equivalent of the mob in public life, a loss of the self that allows the pure present to carry away the surrendered will.

None of the joy of the marriage appears. The novel represents Romola and Tito's life together only at the moments of crisis when it is being destroyed. Each crisis arises from Tito's attempts to dip Romola, against her will, in the "waters of forgetfulness." Without telling her, he sells her father's library, the past itself to the invading French. The old scholar had spent his life collecting and editing it, with Romola's help, intending to leave it permanently in Florence as a memorial to his life. Through the sale, Tito creates a willingness in Romola to destroy ties, and she prepares to leave him, "the act of breaking a tie that no longer represented the inward bond of love. . . . But that force of outward symbols by which our active life is knit together so as to make an inexorable external identity for us, not to be shaken by our wavering consciousness, gave a strange effect to this simple movement towards taking off her ring" (I, 338).

The removal of the ring and the loss of the library point to an important difference between memory and the tokens of memory in *Romola* and *The Mill on the Floss*. The wedding ring is purely symbolic; it is not a lived, used token like Bob Jakin's knife or the mill itself. In our reading experience, the ring never existed until the moment it is removed. Our process of attachment and familiarity does not come into play as it does through the repetitions of experience in *The Mill on the Floss*, repetitions that create in the reader a miniature attachment of the same kind as that felt by the characters. A wedding ring is abstract, and the library, although it has personal meaning for Romola, or so we assume, has none for us.

The entire departure scene is a parade of symbols rather than things. In a trunk Romola finds two dresses: her wedding dress and the coarse gray robe of a nun. Her final act is to unlock the shrine of Bacchus and Ariadne and remove her brother's crucifix to take it with her. Allegory has replaced memory in the novel. The meaning Eliot created in her earlier novels through echo scenes and development arises instantly here through Hawthorne-like "meaningful" objects. The need to externalize psychology is a real one, but the realism created by natural objects has disappeared, leaving us only the pseudo-objects like the shrine in which the crucifix is locked, objects we understand but do not believe in.

Romola's flight is stopped by Savonarola, who calls on her to return. " 'You are flying from your debts: the debt of a Florentine woman; the debt of a wife. You are turning your back on the lot that has been appointed for you—you are going to choose another. But can man or woman choose duties?' " (I, 376). When Romola accepts his argument that outside the imposed duties there is only lawlessness and wandering, she reaches the position of Maggie Tulliver when she returned to St. Ogg's. But Tito betrays her again by giving false evidence against her uncle, Bernardo de Nero, the noble man who had acted like a father to her. Romola flees a second time to drift in the boat that will determine her future.

Romola

Romola's father, husband, and spiritual master are equally tyrannical. None of the relationships has any middle ground between self-annihilating submission and total defiance. In the fourth stage of her life, the one with which the novel ends, Romola has taken the upper hand, living surrounded by the simple-minded Tessa and her two children. At last the patron herself, she seeks no equals, but speaks and moves with the authority others had ruled her with in the earlier three phases.

Romola's life, with its submission and dominance, its too simple reliance on duty and charity, casts no more appeal in the book than do the more flawed or evil lives of the artist Piero di Cosimo, the scholar her father, or the Machiavellian Tito. Like Silas Marner, Romola, her father, and Piero di Cosimo substitute a simplification for the confused world they no longer understand. Piero's ears are plugged, the old scholar is blind, and Romola moves from person to person seeking a mastery or submission that will release her from the need to deal with the larger confusion. Tito is the center of the confusion; self-created, he makes those around him as worldless as himself. Erasing and rewriting as the moment demands, he lives a life where not only are his own moves improvised but the reality in which they take place is imaginary, a fiction hoping to be repeated often enough to sound familiar and finally be accepted as true.

Only one character breaks beyond the fatal opposition visible in the rest: the choice between an evil, self-interested fictionalizing of and a reduced enclave of reason. This is Savonarola, at once the most fascinating and the least realized character in the novel. Eliot's interest in his life was the motive behind her decision to spend the long years researching and writing a novel so completely different from her earlier novels of memory, the novels of English rural life that brought her fame. Like Tito, Savonarola does not retreat but works within the half-realities of public life, creating and bluffing, using plots and alliances to work for his ends. But his ends are a moral order, not self-interest, a renovation of society and church that would cleanse Florence and remake all of Italy.

However, the fascination of his character lies in Eliot's refusal to create a simple dichotomy of selfless moral vision—Savonarola— and selfish material ends—Tito. Possibly, Savonarola's real interest is power and the lofty ends he mentions are in fact incidental in the true balances of his psychology. As often as not, Savonarola acts out of the intermediate goal of power. He must first dominate before he can begin to create his new moral order, and to gain power he uses the same ruthlessness, the same conspiratorial duplicity his enemies use. He, like Tito, must make himself. He is "a man who had sought his own glory indeed, but sought it by laboring for the very highest end—the moral welfare of man—not by vague exhortations, but by striving to turn beliefs into energies that would work in all the details of life" (II, 200). His vision of moral good leads him through actions that are themselves evil, like the execution of Romola's uncle, acts for which he can plead only expediency. " 'The end I seek is one to which minor respects must be sacrificed. The death of five men—were they less guilty than these—is a light matter weighed against the withstanding of the vicious tyrannies which stifle the life of Italy' " (II, 117).

The miracle Savonarola stages exists alongside his fear to accept the test of the fire. Highest and lowest are inextricable in the man. When excommunicated, he does not submit, but begins a plot to overthrow the pope. The cautious rebels of Eliot's earlier novels give way here to absolute defiance, a defiance that cannot cloak itself in the knowledge of its high motives and generous means. For in Savonarola vanity and the need for power, despicable means, and even betrayals or alliances with the least moral parties all obscure with doubts our judgment of the man. Dinah Morris or Maggie Tulliver stand outside society in occasional and completely sympathetic moments. Savonarola is heretical and beyond evaluation, as enigmatic to himself as he is to others. "But at this moment such feelings were nullified by that hard struggle which made half the tragedy of his life—the struggle of a mind possessed by a never-silent hunger after purity and simplicity, yet caught in a tangle of egoistic demands, false ideas, and different outward conditions, that made simplicity impossible" (II, 115). In his final days in prison, Savonarola confuses even further the truth of his life. Under trial by torture he confesses, retracts, and confesses again. No matter, he will be burned as a heretic in either case. But the question remains: did he act believing God spoke through him, or was he a charlatan disguising his search for power under noble pretenses? Even he does not seem to know. In each moment of analysis, Eliot reminds us of the mixture. He was "a consciousness in which irrevocable errors and lapses from veracity were so entwined with noble purposes and sincere beliefs, in which self-justifying expediency was so inwoven with the tissue of a great work that the whole being seemed unable to abandon . . . that it was perhaps impossible, whatever course might be adopted, for the conscience to find repose" (II, 148). When offered the chance to prove his divine sanction in the test by fire, Savonarola backs away; no test is subtle enough, no substance can ever be proved.

The greatness of the character of Savonarola does not lie simply in the complexity of motives, the mixture of high and low, the enigmatic nature of his life within the confused social reality of Florence. He goes beyond every earlier character Eliot created in his courage to act in the absence of the ability to justify himself. He cannot express his path as a series of choices between good and evil alternatives, and no rationalism can describe the degeneration or growth of his character. Only his goal can be evaluated, but is he sincere about it? His goal is his hypothesis about both himself and his social world. Every step he takes toward his goal remains suspended. Each will be judged good should his fiction become truth, his hypothesis become confirmed, but each will be judged evil should he fail. Totally beyond both strict morality and the rationalism that insists on understanding in order to justify, he balances Tito until he is destroyed by him. Finally a martyr, he dies not because of the particular turn of accidents that betrayed him to his enemies, but in testimony to the authetically tragic nature of the life he has the courage to lead. Tito and Savonarola are in conflict to cast the meaning of the life within their grasp. Unable to clear himself of the accusations of a hypocrisy that would make him no better than Tito, Savonarola continues nonetheless, content that the goal itself creates something of a moral protection.

With Savonarola, Eliot passes beyond that primary goal of the social novel written up to her time: the goal of judgment. Her earlier characters, like Maggie Tulliver or Silas Marner, held a private certainty of their own innocence that the reader was expected to share even when the weight of social judgment went against them. The judgment was always a function of understanding, of knowing the complete truth that the method of realism, through its attention to details, could give. The moral rationalism that underlies both sympathy and judgment gives way to a more suspended relationship, that of analysis and fascination, in the case of Savonarola. In a later chapter, that on *Middlemarch*, interpretation will be seen as the mode that replaces judgment. Interpretation, however, is a provisional resting place in the history of the social novel. From judgment through interpretation the novel passed to imagination, as the life it was forced to comprehend became more obscure.

Like the public life of Florence, the inner life of Savonarola is without substance. Substance has been replaced by process, character by career. Savonarola takes on the dizzying ambiguities of both his own motives and the public life to create a heroic career, one filled with arrogance and doubt, certainty that he knows the divine plan and mistrust of even his simplest act. Every test for truth offered him is irrational. He must produce a miracle, he must walk through fire, he must tell the truth under torture. He confesses, he retracts, he confesses.

Romola

Nietzsche, in the notes now known as *The Will to Power*, described the will to truth as one subordinate to the will to power. Savonarola claimed the reverse, that for him power was the means to truth. Nietzsche's summary is important for the description given here of Florentine public life and Savonarola's character.

> Will to truth is a making firm, a making true and durable, an abolition of the false character of things, a reinterpretation of it into beings. "Truth" is therefore not something there, that might be found or discovered—but something that must be created and gives a name to a process, or rather to a will to overcome that has in itself no end—introducing truth, as a *processus in infinitum*, an active determining—not a becoming conscious of something that is in itself firm and determined. It is a word for the will to power.
>
> Man projects his drive to truth, his "goal" in a certain sense, outside himself as a world that has being.[2]

Savonarola's heroism consists in his need to act without being able to predict the meaning the act will finally have; he creates results, meanings, and moral values simultaneously.

One demand every hero must fulfill is that he be adequate to the world he is represented within. The complexity of the life he dares to live must reach into every corner of the reality against which we see him. He must exhaust the truth of that world by standing at a pressure point where the energies and contradictions of the world become most viable. The hero cannot accept what Milton scorned as a "fugitive and cloistered virtue." Savonarola is Eliot's first adequate hero. Everywhere in her novels, the temptation to renounce the painful mixture her analysis discloses leads her to stress characters who either withdraw, like Romola, or never even

---

2. Friedrich Nietzsche, *The Will to Power*, ed. Walter Kaufmann (1911; reprint ed., New York: Vintage Books, 1968), p. 298.

perceive that complexity, like Dolly Winthrop, Silas Marner, or Bob Jakin. Romola can only act where she is certain that a strict local moral bookkeeping will approve each component of her action.

Among Shakespeare's tragic heroes, only Othello is inadequate, and he is, like so many heroes of the last hundred years, a victim of the complexity he is too innocent to suspect. Hamlet, perhaps alone among Shakespeare's heroes, is too complex for the reality surrounding him, and, like Quixote, projects imaginatively his reading of the life around him until he creates the disorder and nuance that are rich enough for his moral being. The adequate hero lies between the innocent who cannot register the complexity of the reality and the too imaginative man, such as Quixote, Hamlet, or the hero of James's *Sacred Fount*, who proposes a version of the reality around him so subtle and seductive that he is able to disturb that reality at last into a momentary alignment with his sensibility.

Often in the Victorian novel it is the villain who most completely matches the intricacy of the social reality. Knowledge and intricacy are part of the equipment of evil. Goodness is associated with innocence, a sweet ignorance, with children or childlike women who are unworldly, intuitive. In *Romola*, both villain and hero match the strength of the world they struggle for. When goodness is associated with simplicity, with exemption from the need to come to terms with the full measure of experience, and when only villains seem adequate to that measure of life, then the novel has built in an evasive otherworldliness. Romola is left with the life of a nurse or patron. Her life is close to the miniature, rational world of Silas Marner or her father's life in his library. The world is abandoned. Similarly, Bob Jakin and Dolly Winthrop, like the color-blind who perceive a simplified version of the visual world, exist within a flat moral universe of trust, loyalty, and intuition. Where these characters are emphasized, another type of inadequate hero is offered.

Romola

Conrad's Kurtz, Lord Jim, and Nostromo and Stendhal's Julien Sorel are all, like Savonarola, adequate heroes. Romola and many of Savonarola's followers attend his execution certain that, at the last moment, he will make a definite sign that under the solemnity of death will be the truth. His face is blank, and he makes no gesture.

6

Felix Holt, the Radical

In *Felix Holt*, Eliot abandons almost everywhere the ambition to create mixed characters, situations, and responses. A story of hero and villain, distinct choices between right and wrong futures, and a truth about events that is clear and can only temporarily be prevented from coming to light, *Felix Holt* is her most optimistic novel. It ends with its hero and heroine newly married and its villain exposed and disgraced.

Not since *Adam Bede* have the external signs of happiness, order, and justice been so prominently displayed. Even Bede suffered through the broken relationship with Hetty, but Holt is balked only by a temporary cloud of misunderstanding about his part in the election riots, a part we know from the beginning was entirely noble and aimed at restoring order and preventing damage. His temporary disgrace is thematically parallel to Esther's temporary elevation to heiress, which occurs at the same time. He is in jail, she at the manor house, and each is externally given a false identity that will be dispelled: hers by the choice that renounces all claims to the Transome estates, his by the unification of the "best families" behind his plea for pardon. The story of Cinderella is twice mentioned in connection with Esther, a story of magical changes of social position, changes that conceal or temporarily deny a true social nature within. Esther's aristocratic refinement, taste, and even reading habits reveal even before the plot does that she is out

Felix Holt, the Radical

of place in her life with the dissenting minister she thinks is her father. Inheritance is stronger than experience: illegitimate children reproduce the natures as well as the features of their hidden fathers. The novel is one of substance and illusory conditions that hide, but never prevent anyone from finally discovering, who or what he really is. A world of secrets and detectives—the foremost of whom is the reader himself, trying to guess who is related to whom before the author has dropped too many obvious clues in his path—the world of *Felix Holt* is one of discovery, not change.

The novel of secrets and discoveries, the detective novel, creates a time scheme of revelation. The complexities are all over before the novel begins. What the reader is invited to follow is the discovery, thread by thread, of the past. The elements of mystification are the common ones: old love affairs with the resulting illegitimate children, hushed-up scandals, ancient legal tricks that deprived the true heirs of property they now no longer know they once had a right to, murders never solved, false imprisonments, and exchanged identities. The enigma of the present would disappear if we could learn the buried past from which it springs, or so the detective form in *Felix Holt* promises. Many critics have stressed the bourgeois optimism, the confidence in rationality and perseverance that the detective form rests on. Every detective novel, beginning in mystery and ending in total clarity, reassures and dispels for a moment the fear of half-truths and false surmises, the obscurity and final enigma of social life.

Felix Holt takes place over a six-month period, from the return of Felix and his foil, Harold Transome, to Treby until Esther's final choice between them—a correct, moral, unambiguous choice of poverty, true love, hard work, and happiness over riches and a loveless, boring, idle life as an heiress and wife to Transome. The detectives have done their work in the six months. The lawyers Jermyn and Johnson, the servant Christian, and the reader, all have learned the secrets of the past and understand the configurations of the present that were obscured by those secrets.

An image that expresses the underlying assumptions of the detective form is used twice in *Felix Holt*. "He felt very much like an uninitiated chess-player who sees that the pieces are in a peculiar position on the board, and might open the way for him to give checkmate if he only knew how" (p. 255). The story begins in the middle of the end game; we see a certain arrangement that implies a mysterious set of past moves. The novel moves in two directions: forward, making us aware of each new move as it is made, and backward, revealing (after coyly holding back for a while) selected key moves from the past. The game is even more complex than the first use of the chess image suggests.

> Fancy what a game of chess would be if all the chessmen had passions and intellects, more or less small and cunning: —if you were not only uncertain about your adversary's men, but a little uncertain also about your own; if your knight could shuffle himself on to a new square by the sly; if your bishop, in disgust at your castling, could wheedle your pawns out of their places; and if your pawns, hating you because they are pawns, could make away from their appointed posts that you might get checkmate on a sudden. (P. 289)

This chess in the style of Kafka is further complicated by assumed identities. Some of what we think are knights turn out to be rooks, some allied enemies. Harold Transome is really the son of the lawyer Jermyn. Esther Lyon is not the daughter of Rufus Lyon. In fact, going back two steps, she is really the heiress to the Transome estates. Maurice Christian, who has dropped the last name Byecliffe, is neither Christian nor Byecliffe, but Henry Scaddon. The other name or pair of names he got by trading identities with a fellow prisoner once long ago.

Of course, traced far enough back, every name is an assumed name, just as every piece of property is, in Proudhon's ringing phrase, a theft. When Jermyn thinks about the legal tricks behind

Felix Holt, the Radical

the inheritance, he makes the general point that "as for right or wrong, if the truth were known, the very possession of the estate by the Durfey-Transomes was owing to the law tricks that took place nearly a century ago" (p. 228). Even Esther's rights to the estate are only the results of slightly more remote crimes.

Of the important characters in the novel, all are outsiders. Harold has returned after making his fortune in the colonies, in Smyrna. Felix comes to Treby from Glasgow, where he leaves behind a mysterious period of dissipation. Seven years earlier, Rufus Lyon had arrived in Treby leaving behind somewhere else his complex earlier life of ministerial promise, scandal, resignation, the death of his wife, and, at last, his return to the ministry. His past is told to the reader in a separate chapter, at the end of which, in that final community of reader and writer, Eliot states, "This was Rufus Lyon's history, at that time unknown in its fulness to any human being besides himself" (p. 95). Harold's father, the lawyer Jermyn, is credited only with a rumored past. He was "a young lawyer who came from a distance, knew the dictionary by heart, and was probably the illegitimate son of somebody or another" (p. 48). The servants Christian and Dominic are foreigners and even more remote and mysterious than the rest. Of Dominic, Harold says the last word in rootlessness.

"Oh, one of those wonderful southern fellows that make one's life easy. He's of no country in particular. I don't know whether he's most of a Jew, a Greek, an Italian, or a Spaniard. He speaks five or six languages, one as well as another. He's cook, valet, major-domo, and secretary all in one; and what's more he's an affectionate fellow. . . . That's a sort of human specimen that doesn't grow here in England, I fancy." (P. 39)

At the end of the book, the departures from Treby are listed. "For Felix and Esther did not take up their abode in Treby Magna; and after a while Mr. Lyon left the town too, and joined them where they dwelt." We do not learn where Mr. Jermyn has vanished, gone "to reside at a great distance" (p. 491). Christian goes off somewhere with the money from the secrets he sold. The Transomes leave and return later, only to die. Treby Magna is not, then, a place like Hayslope or St. Ogg's; rather, it is a stage on which enough of the ingredients have assembled by accident for the flash point to be reached. In the drama of revelation, the past is opened, each learns who he is, and all depart. Treby Magna is not a community but a temporary configuration, like the pieces of a map long ago scattered, of which enough pieces suddenly come together for the whole to be assembled on a table. Formed of mystery and mystery dispelled, secrets and revelations, the tactics of *Felix Holt*, like the optimism of the detective form that begins at this period in England, stem from the escapist need to imagine a reprieve from the obscurity and half-knowledge of discontinuous social life— one where every arrangement of chess pieces we see is that of the middle of a game that began somewhere else under conditions we cannot imagine.

Whether stage or chessboard, Treby Magna is not the permanent, static community of Hayslope in which substance exists and is embodied in visible, continuous styles of life. Equally, Treby Magna is not the stage of Florentine public life where no substance exists, only images and fictions competing for confirmation. Truth, substance, and absolute moral choices still exist in Treby Magna. Life is a matter of station, not career; the social identity is that of Hayslope prolonging its existence after Hayslope itself has disappeared. But Felix and Esther choose their places, or rather they choose not to change their places. Felix's choice underlines the central fact. " 'If there's anything our people want convincing of, it is, that there's some dignity and happiness for a man other than changing his station. That's one of the beliefs I choose to consecrate my life to' " (pp. 447–48).

Truth of blood determines heritage and heritage determines station. " 'My father was a weaver first of all. It would have been

Felix Holt, the Radical

better for him if he had remained a weaver. I came home through Lancashire and saw an uncle of mine who is a weaver still. I mean to stick to the class I belong to—people who don't follow the fashions' " (p. 67). He explains his contempt for the middle class with an absurd exaggeration. " 'Why should I want to get into the middle class because I have some learning? The most of the middle class are as ignorant as the working people about everything that doesn't belong to their own Brummagem life. That's how the working class men are left to foolish devises: the best heads among them forsake their born comrades, and go in for a house with a high door-step and a brass knocker' " (p. 67).

What Felix has chosen is, however, an odd occupation—that of watchmaker. Apprenticed to an apothecary, he later refused to become a professional, a pharmacist, and joined the working class. He has, unlike Adam Bede, joined that part of the working class that produces goods only the middle and upper classes can afford. Watches are quite different from Bede's doors, benches, and coffins. Silas Marner produced special, luxury cloth for which he was paid in gold. Does Holt do more for the world by producing jewelry— and a watch is jewelry—than by providing medicine? His idealism is more than a little hollow. The choice he so rhetorically describes is not the one he actually made, and at any rate he chose his place, he did not inherit it. Adam Bede's father was a carpenter, and Silas Marner comes from a community of weavers. Holt makes a symbolic choice of the working class, but we are told of his work, we never see it. He exists for us in conversation and descriptions like the clergymen in the novels of Austen, ministers we never see in church or near a Bible. What being a workingman means is that, in conversation and courting, the two realms of activity in this novel of manners, he is gruff and boorish, occasionally insulting, and has the lack of taste to wear a cap and heavy boots.

If Felix chooses the working class, Esther fulfills her nature by discarding the snobbery and estheticism that too much reading of Byron and French novels, and too long a residence in continental boarding schools, had cast over her as an unreal identity. "She was alive to the finest shades of manner, to the nicest distinctions of tone and accent; she had a little code of her own about scents and colours, textures and behaviour, by which she secretly condemned or sanctioned all things and persons. And she was well satisfied with herself for her fastidious taste, never doubting that hers was the highest standard." She could not "use without disgust any but the finest cambric handkerchiefs and freshest gloves. Her money all went in the gratification of these nice tastes, and she saved nothing from her earnings" (p. 81). But her choice, like Felix's, is a peculiar one. The novel ties her choice about the inheritance to a decision for or against marrying Harold Transome, an absolute Turk in his relations with women, a man whose illegitimate son was born to a woman who "had been a slave—was bought in fact" (p. 431). Life would be a "well cushioned despair" with him (p. 480). In fact, the choices are distinct: she could accept the inheritance without marrying Transome. But by joining the two, Eliot creates a pseudo-choice that evades the problem.

No one has an identity or place, not even a natural set of values. Harold Transome arrives home and announces himself as a Radical candidate for Parliament. When the election campaign around which the book is organized is over, Eliot neglects to say who has won. Through Holt and Esther, Eliot propagandizes for a simplistic notion of moral choice; for social stability through literally reactionary choices whereby those who have deserted the working class return, as Holt does; and finally, for melioristic improvement of faults that are, in the phrase Holt likes to use, "under our noses." One of his projects is a school, like Bartle Massey's in *Adam Bede*, to be set up by the miners themselves. "If we could move these men to save something from their drink and pay a schoolmaster for their boys, a greater service would be done for them than if Mr. Garstin and his company were persuaded to establish a school" (p. 138). Self-help, sobriety, and education. Holt has a feel for obvious wrongs and corrects them; he prefers spending his energies cor-

Felix Holt, the Radical

recting trifles that are morally clear and demonstrably wrong to wrestling with the anomalous and morally ambiguous major problems. We see him stop his mother ("reform begins at home") from selling quack remedies; later he pesters the Radical candidate about his low tactics; then he shames Esther Lyon into giving up her snobbery and aristocratic pretensions. In each case, including his final act (the attempt to lead the rioters away from the town), wherever he acts there is clarity, right and wrong alternatives, and only a symbolic relationship to the deep problems of the society.

Holt's four public acts are carefully chosen. They repeat the imagery with which the Victorians seized political life in their imaginations, an imagery they owed in many cases to Carlyle. The quack medicine Holt forces his mother to stop selling is the metaphor Tories used for the ballot. Changes like the extension of suffrage were "nostrums," quack medicine, panaceas that were irrelevant and dangerous. When H. G. Wells hunted for a metaphor to sum up the entire new fabric of English life, he found it in a patent medicine, Tono Bungay.

The mob, both literally and symbolically, is the directionless energy of the working class and all those demanding change. When Harold Transome returns home a Radical, he explains his conversion from Toryism by using the metaphor of the mob. " 'If the mob can't be turned back, a man of family must try and head the mob, and save a few homes and hearths, and keep the country up on its last legs as long as he can' " (p. 36). Later in the book, this is what Holt must try to do.

Holt's third and fourth public acts are more profound metaphors than those of the mob or quack medicine. In converting Esther Lyon from her social pretensions, he achieves what Carlyle would call the destruction of "sham." In Carlyle's peculiar version of German idealism, humanity moves toward a harmony between the appearances of public life—hierarchies, manners, institutions—and the realities of human relations those appearances are designed

Making Up Society

to express. Revolution happens when sham and lies create a split between forms and the energetic reality no longer expressed (in fact denied) by the forms of public life. Carlyle had an almost Hegelian trust in history, in the pressure of impersonal forces that will tear off the masks and allow true life to become visible. In *Felix Holt*, the plot utilizes this metaphor of shams and realities, appearances and substances. The plot accepts also the faith that shams will not endure. Substances are hidden by names, manners, even apparent relationships. Neither Esther Lyon, Harold Transome, nor Christian carries a true name. Most live in relationships that appear to be families but are not. The Transomes are really the Durfeys, and they live on estates really belonging to Esther Lyon, who, if the truth were known, is really Esther Byecliffe. The providential history that, for Carlyle, shatters all that is false and brings the truth to prominence without human intervention, parallels the texture of accidents, discoveries, and detections that reveals the true lords and commoners of Treby Magna. When Holt ridicules Esther's aristocratic pretensions, he is saying, "be what you are." Ironically enough, she is an aristocrat, but by choice she repudiates both the fortune and the dainty life she led before meeting Holt.

In his fourth act, Holt insists on the purest tactics for the Radical cause. He will speak truth to the workers, urge them to sobriety, self-help, and education for their children. The bribery, flattery, and wet elections with their appeals to envy and class division— the tactics of the Radical party as well as all the others—bring out his anger far more than does exploitation of the workers in the mines. The desire to be above suspicion, this moral rationalism and strict bookkeeping, make him irrelevant to the deep problems posed. In his public acts as well as in the choice of a working-class life, Holt is a straw hero.

Through Holt, Eliot states and then skims a set of problems. Just as in *Silas Marner*, the pressure of the perception holds only with the individual images, not with the fate of those images in combi-

Felix Holt, the Radical

nation. The hopelessness of life in Treby Magna is amply demonstrated by the flight at the end, of every major character. And yet, in the regressive choices of Holt and Esther, in their marriage as well, there is the false implication of stability and renewal.

The best example of skimming a complex problem is the trial of Holt. At a critical moment in his attempt to control the riot, Holt was forced to knock down a constable. He did it only to prevent worse happening, but the man died. Holt is on trial for murder, and however much his motives can explain the other crimes he is charged with, there is no doubt he is guilty of at least manslaughter. Like Savonarola, Holt was forced to do evil in reaching for good. But the novel gives no moral analysis of the act or of Holt's feelings afterward. The constable was "nobody we know," and no sympathy is created for him. At the trial Holt produces his account of the riot and is believed immediately, even though, a few hours earlier, he appeared to be the most dangerous agitator in the county. Still it is not enough. He cannot deny he killed a man—a fact that doesn't seem to trouble him at all. He says nothing of the act. To save him, a surprise witness is needed, an appeal to feeling. With great drama, Esther Lyon steps forward at the last moment and touches the hearts of all. When Holt is sentenced to four years, a mild sentence, all the best Tory families appeal to London for a pardon for the most dangerous Radical in the district. As Sir Maximus Debarry puts it, " 'I tell you what, Gus! we must exert ourselves to get a pardon for this young fellow. Confound it! what's the use of mewing him up for four years? Example? Nonsense. Will there be a man knocked down the less for it? That girl made me cry' " (p. 466).

No more absurd moment exists in all of Eliot's novels. The complex questions of Holt's or any man's responsibilities in events he only partly controls are papered over by the sentimental melodrama of the surprise witness and the primitive psychology that allows sentimental Tories to think "no good will be done." The plot deflects our attention to the superficial question of how Holt will be freed, and away from the moral one of whether he is guilty. Although the trial is the best example of the skimming of problems, it is by no means the only one. But in the line of trials that have been described in the preceding chapters as an index of social legibility, Holt's trial is a more absurdly confident one than even that of Hetty. From Hetty's to that of the witch in *The Mill on the Floss*, to Marner's trial by the casting of lots, to Savonarola's trial by torture, there is a clear progression into enigma. With Holt, wishful sentimentality breaks the logic, and creates, out of the need Eliot felt to propagandize for an almost journalistic set of opinions about the condition of England on the eve of the Reform Bill, an exercise in legal and political fairy tales that well deserves Cinderella as its presiding figure.

IMAGES OF SOCIAL MYSTERY

Among the quotations that Eliot attached to her chapters in *Felix Holt*, the most curious is that at the head of chapter 39.

> No man believes that many textured knowledge and skill—as a just idea of the solar system, or the power of painting flesh, or of reading written harmonies—can come late and of a sudden; yet many will not stick at believing that happiness can come at any day and hour solely by a new disposition of events; though there is nought least capable of a magical production than a mortal's happiness, which is mainly a complex of habitual relations and dispositions not to be wrought by news from foreign parts, or any whirling of fortune's wheel for one on whose brow time has written legibly. (P. 381)

Ponderous as it is, this observation harmonizes with the best of Eliot's work and restates the value of conditions and continuity and the irrelevance of the magic of events. Why then has she written a novel with a plot based exactly on the assumption that the magic of events determines all? Identity, inheritance, and love: these three

Felix Holt, the Radical

components define a very special Victorian novel, the novel of magic and place. The two most important examples are *Jane Eyre* and *Great Expectations*. In the first, Jane discovers who she is, finds her family, receives an inheritance that makes her moderately rich, and marries Rochester. Pip, in *Great Expectations*, chooses in love between Estella and Biddy, receives an inheritance that gives him a place, and moves between three families, Gargery, Havisham, and Magwitch.

An absolute, binary quality, completely at odds with the "mixed conditions" Eliot believes in morally, underlies this type of novel. The inheritance is never just a little money: it is plenty, a kind of social magic that makes the difference between toiling in a forge and living like a gentleman, between a menial job as a governess and complete security and independence. With the inheritance Esther will rule the Transome estates; without it she will live in cramped rooms with the dissenting minister. Fortune is binary: one is rich or poor. So with identity. Pip's benefactor is either Miss Havisham or a transported criminal. In the world, he knows he is either at the top or the bottom. In *Jane Eyre* and *Felix Holt*, identity is equally absolute. While Jane is an orphan, she is abused, tormented, and deceived by every person who has power over her. Once she has found who she is, she becomes the generous patron and, thanks to the fire that cripples Rochester, the master of her much reduced and repentant husband. The identity one finds is either pride or disgrace. Pip made a gentleman, a Havisham, swells with arrogance. Discovering his benefactor is Magwitch, he is crushed with disgrace. Harold Transome leaves Treby Magna totally vanquished by the information that he is the illegitimate son of Jermyn. Jane Eyre rises when she learns of her wealth and relations. In esteem or shame, wealth or poverty, these transformations are as extreme as those of fairy tales. Cinderella is either the exploited, contemptible drudge or she is the princess.

The third element alongside identity and inheritance, love, is similarly absolute, a source of unconditioned happiness. The epilogue to *Jane Eyre* assures us she and Rochester have had ten years of complete happiness. When Felix Holt marries Esther, no more need be said except to assure us there is a young Felix. All three novels, as the two endings of *Great Expectations* show, create countercurrents that undermine the satisfaction of the absolute terms they are based on, but, even against the grain, the three elements of love, inheritance, and identity impose the alternates of dichotomy. The three are the signs of a novel of place, a fixed universe of high and low. Tom Jones is either a bastard without money, wife, or future, or he is Squire Allworthy's heir and nephew, married to Sophia, and the happiest of men. A great loss of confidence has occurred between *Tom Jones* and the three Victorian novels that all seem troubled by the motifs they yet feel compelled to use. Novels in the tradition of *Tom Jones* are set to the energies of life between sixteen and twenty-five. One of the greatest accomplishments of realism was the introduction of the thirty-nine-year-old hero. Where realism moved past identity and inheritance and marriage, it argued for the openness of life, its continuing complexity, the lack of a freeze somewhere about the age of twenty-five that resolved every problem of interest.

In *Felix Holt* a second set of characters exist, the thirty-nine-year-old heroes. Because of the six-month span of the novel, the complex of relationships that have been created in time can only be given through summary and reprise. What would be needed to dramatize, to embody, this side of the novel would be at least the eight- to ten-year span of *Romola* or *The Mill on the Floss*. In psychological complexity, the characters of interest in *Felix Holt* are Mrs. Transome, Rufus Lyon, and the lawyer Jermyn in his relationship to his former mistress, Mrs. Transome. But here the action is of a kind the time scheme cannot contain. The detective form, with its obsession with scenes of revelation and discovery, its preoccupation with secrets and mysteries, always takes place after the action is completed. The murder mystery begins with a corpse. The complications of experience and passion that lead to that ultimate act are over, and we follow the process of inference and reconstruction, of intellectual discovery. We do not participate in the dramas, in the emotional life that led up to the event. The detective form lives on a sterile, purely mental curiosity about events. Only when we begin to doubt the ability of the detective to maintain the objective competence his job demands, as we do with James's Strether or Kafka's K, do we reenter the form to experience events completely. Conrad goes to absurd lengths in *Lord Jim* and *Chance* to maintain direct experience in spite of the detective form and its technique of indirect, reconstructed accounts of experience.

The three characters whose inner experience is examined in the novel are known only to the reader. Alone, silent, hiding the past, neither Rufus Lyon, Mrs. Transome, nor Jermyn has any longer even a chance at initiative. Each lives in a world of concealment and absolute solitude, locked into relations they know to be false. In the past are the sexual transgressions that have created the mysteries of parentage and identity in the present. The affair between Jermyn and Mrs. Transome and the peculiar relationship between Lyon and Annette Ledou produce by symmetry the two confusions—Harold's ignorance about his relationship to Jermyn and Esther's false assumptions about Lyon. The chapters that describe Mrs. Transome are among the best in the book, but they become tedious because she only dreads and waits. She cannot act, she has no life; she exists in the novel to receive shock after shock. Given no one but a servant to talk to, she suffers most from the time scheme because the rich progression of her past is the meaning of her life, not the empty present.

With Rufus Lyon and Jermyn, the situation is different only because in each case the complex, psychologized past is superimposed on a stock comic or melodramatic character. In fact, each man is two characters. Lyon is the foolish but touching minister in the tradition of Fielding's Parson Adams or the Vicar of Wakefield, a comic type pacing his book-lined study and challenging rivals to absurd debates about the true church. Jermyn is a composite lifted out of Dickens, a blend of Jaggers and Tulkinghorn, and when he appears in the novel he is a stock villainous plotter. Each man, in addition to the superficial role the form favors, is given a past that fascinates.

The relationship between Jermyn and Mrs. Transome has degenerated from passion to business to a complicity that the lawyer can exploit in his management of the estates. When the two are together the past remains tacitly disturbing.

> Today she was more conscious than usual of that bitterness which was always in her mind in Jermyn's presence, but which was carefully suppressed:—suppressed because she could not endure that the degradation she inwardly felt should ever become visible or audible in acts or words of her own—should ever be reflected in any word or look of his. For years there had been a deep silence about the past between them: on her side, because she remembered; on his, because he more and more forgot.   (P. 120)

When challenged about his mismanagement, Jermyn turns to bluster, and the real feelings become more and more invisible.

> "*My* management of the affairs!" Mrs. Transome said, with concentrated rage, flashing a fierce look at Jermyn. She checked herself: she felt as if she were lighting a torch to flare on her own past folly and misery. It was a resolve which had become a habit, that she would never quarrel with this man—never tell him what she saw him to be. . . .
> Jermyn felt annoyed and nothing more. . . . He was anything but stupid; yet he always blundered when he wanted to be delicate or magnanimous; he constantly sought to soothe others by praising himself. . . .
> "My dear Mrs. Transome," he said, in a tone of bland kind-

ness, "you are agitated—you appear angry with me. Yet I think, if you consider, you will see that you have nothing to complain of in me, unless you will complain of the inevitable course of a man's life. I have always met your wishes. . . ."
Every sentence was as pleasant to her as if it had been cut in her bared arm. Some men's kindness and love-making are more exasperating, more humiliating, than others' derision. (P. 121)

To render the moment, the author has to enmesh the few commonplace words and the almost invisible gestures within a commentary that presents each character through what is habitual to him. Eliot must add these qualities of the self because the compressed time scheme makes it impossible to dramatize through repetition, echo scenes, and development, as she did in *The Mill on the Floss*. A disproportion that can reach almost Jamesian proportions begins to appear between action and commentary. The first chapter has no action but the wait Mrs. Transome endures when her son is expected home. The drama that this scene would have naturally in a novel of development must be created artificially by dropping hints about the past and giving summaries that place the event as the climax of years of separation. Eliot creates narrative suspense by withholding facts in a coy way to create anticipation, then supplying several paragraphs later the fact she has withheld. The opening sentence reads, "On the 1st of September, in the memorable year of 1832, someone was expected at Transome Court" (p. 12). The deliberately vague "someone" creates a false suspense that is based only on the reader's question: "Who?" In the chapter, every character first appears as someone, somewhere, doing something.
Both authorial intrusions—the cheap suspense we call mystification rather than mystery, and the commentary that reveals habitual psychic life to allow the reader to comprehend the few cryptic words exchanged by the characters—are elements of the detective

form. They are the result of the author's choice of that form, which consists of secrets and revelations, as a solution to the novel of society in the discontinuous and therefore obscure social life of Treby Magna. Mrs. Transome has not seen her son in fifteen years, Mrs. Holt's son has been in Glasgow for years, and Rufus Lyon's daughter has spent only the past two years with him. When Mrs. Transome's son returns, "he volunteered no information about himself and his past life at Smyrna, but answered pleasantly enough, though briefly, whenever his mother asked for any detail" (p. 33). Felix Holt only hints at his dissipation in Glasgow. Instead of following each through time and creating a legibility of art where one no longer exists in society—the technique of *Middlemarch* and *Romola*—a magical six months of discoveries and revelations is projected to unravel and reconstruct the facts if not the experience of the lives.

A description of the evolution of landscape painting in Friedlander's study, *Landscape, Portrait, Still-Life*, creates the three possibilities of representation that I believe also belong to the novel of society.

So long as belief in the Bible ruled unshaken, the "Maker" . . . was regarded as having fashioned the cosmos, meaningfully and planfully, with organisms that are God-willed and immutable in form and substance. But when the world was regarded as having evolved, when the cause of evolution was lodged in nature, the eye fastened itself on coming-to-be and growth and passing-away, change, one the relations of things to one another, for instance the relation between soil and growing vegetation, terrain and the course of rivers, the might of elements and their effects. In all Being the "having become" was detected. At last, the existent having become questionable, and even the object without a subject dispossessed of existence, the vision that depended on the subjectivity of the observer gained in significance.

Felix Holt, the Radical

Thus Being was superseded by Becoming and Becoming by Seeming.[1]

Adam Bede is the novel of being, and, once that being is lost, a vacillation between becoming and seeming follows, a vacillation between the novel of development and that of detection. Both are forms aimed at discontinuity, and each is a solution outside reality. The novel of development creates a coherence and legibility on the plane of art, while that of detection pretends that a reprieve by magic occurs here and there within the overall obscurity.

The introduction to *Felix Holt* ends with an image that is a parable of the obscurity of the lives that follow in the book. "The poets have told us of a dolorous enchanted forest in the underworld. The thorn-bushes there, and the thick-barked stems, have human histories in them; the power of unuttered cries dwells in the passionless-seeming branches, and the red warm blood is darkly feeding the quivering nerves of a sleepless memory that watches through all dreams" (p. 11). The hidden realities, the unuttered cries, the absolute break between insensate, timeless appearance and inner facts: all three argue for the strong word *enchanted*. The break between behavior and experience in daylight hours has become, in the parable, as absolute as that between the silent, motionless body and the deepest energies that remain in motion in the dreams within.

Enchantment in fairy tales is often accompanied by sleep that lasts many years. In sleep each is absolute, alone, no longer even himself. No society exists, no behavior. Yet experience continues, experience more central to the self than the mere analogues of daylight existence. The island of Philoctetes and the ultimate island of the drifting boat Romola chose are both images beyond the social, exemptions that temporarily deny. But in sleep each is the final

---

1. Max J. Friedlander, *Landscape, Portrait, Still-Life* (New York: Schocken, 1963), pp. 151–52.

Making Up Society

otherness that cannot even be remembered or communicated except in the suspect memories of the morning. Where the blank unintelligibility of the sleeper gives the metaphor for social life, the notions of magic and enchantment are near at hand. A break of substance exists between the forest and the unsuspected human reality it contains. No clues exist, no inference is possible. The truth is not obscure; it is unavailable except to a magic that reverses the enchantment. The lives of Rufus Lyon, Mrs. Transome, and Jermyn are locked in enchantment that only a magical combination of witnesses can release for a moment.

The final important character among the elders is the feeble-minded Mr. Transome. In the entire novel he says only one sentence. Otherwise he arranges and rearranges his collection of beetles and allows himself to be ridden like a horse by Harold's son. Opaque, unfathomable as another species, he seems present in every scene at the Transome estates, and he contains the full force of the enchanted forest, an enchantment and a sleep of the self that even the magic of the detective novel cannot touch.

7

Middlemarch

One of the passing exchanges in *Hamlet* that should trouble our sense of the play occurs between Polonius's message, "My lord, the Queen would speak to you, and presently," and Hamlet's delayed reply, "Then I will come to my mother by and by." The message and acknowledgment are part of the business of life, the social surface. Such mechanical parts of role and civility never satisfy Hamlet, and so he probes beneath it to make a reality that he believes exists behind the everyday expose itself. Between Polonius's message and Hamlet's casual reply there is the following gratuitous probe.

> *Hamlet.* Do you see yonder cloud that's almost in shape of a camel?
> *Polonius.* By th' mass and 'tis, like a camel indeed.
> *Hamlet.* Methinks it is like a weasel.
> *Polonius.* It is backed like a weasel.
> *Hamlet.* Or like a whale.
> *Polonius.* Very like a whale.
>
> (III, ii, 384–90)

The accommodations the lord chamberlain makes from camel to weasel to whale point out that his sense of reality, like the food on his table, is dependent on those he serves. "It is what you say it is," he is answering. His loyalty is stronger than his sense of reality, or at least he publicly pretends it is. But what of Hamlet's part? Why does he create tests so peculiar: the exchange here, the play at court, the terrible harrowing of Ophelia? In police work, there is a clear distinction between capture and entrapment. In the second, the detective creates the crime he solves. Does Hamlet capture or entrap Polonius, Ophelia, his mother, and Claudius? Hamlet proposes constructions of what is random, imagining he can read all things, he insists on reading the clouds. He interprets then imposes, creates hypotheses and then sets up experiments, like this exchange or the play, to perturb reality into confirming or denying his reading. Because he must perturb, no one can any longer tell whether he has found the truth or created it. With Ophelia he creates it: the inner life she exposes, once mad, does not confirm the accusations that drove her mad. By acting as though there are plots he finally brings them into being when Claudius and Laertes league against him.

Hamlet's complement in interpretation is Othello, the innocent who cannot read until he misreads. Each man interprets, judges, and executes, and each creates a carnage of social life. Both live like all modern heroes amid obscurity and perhaps even random events that can be read only to a point, but they must be read, and there is no certainty where the point is. Othello, inadequate hero, cannot decipher the codes, cannot tell true from false, cannot trust and suspect wisely. He is at home elsewhere, in the military life. In social life his eyes record and miss at random. But Hamlet, the more than adequate hero, makes meanings even in clouds and sees corruption even in innocence. In everyday life a paranoid sees conspiracies, makes accusations that disturb those he lives with until, in fact, they become secretive and consult doctors in what becomes a plot to commit him. He accuses others of power over him until they seize power.

The clouds Hamlet reads and insists Polonius read so as to mock him are one image of that disturbing resistance to meaning we find everywhere once passivity and accommodation are given up and human will enters to determine, project, and annex reality. Don Quixote, like Hamlet, is a "reader," and like Hamlet he is perhaps mad. Where will governs, we see constellations instead of stars, growth instead of succession, conspiracy where there is only association. In *Middlemarch*, one image repeats the thrust of Hamlet's cloud. "Probabilities are as various as the faces to be seen at will in fretwork or paperhangings: every form is there from Jupiter to Judy, if you only look with a creative inclination" (I, 316). In fretwork, however, most would agree the faces are imagined, imposed by the "creative inclination," the will, and in any case it does not matter, for nothing urgent depends on whether it is Jupiter or Judy or nothing at all.

In other cases, in medicine for example, the need to imagine is urgent—the need to infer from a few marks we call symptoms, to dissociate the accidental from the essential, to find and identify coherence where only clues exist. Imagination is necessary in order to go from symptoms to syndrome to diagnosis to treatment— here reading is urgent, meaning, we hope, exists, and disturbing action is essential. A doctor like Lydgate must read the probabilities, work on his sense of things, and continue even in the face of mistakes. A doctor reads diseases. Symptoms are a language he learns, a code where there is a continued disagreement among readers and yet the absolute necessity for action. There is no certainty. When Lydgate treats Fred Vincy or Raffles, his diagnoses differ from those of the other Middlemarch doctors. The diagnosis is based always on provisional knowledge where yesterday's certainty is tomorrow's error; the doctor, even when his scrutiny is exact and complete, interprets within a historical net that has no higher standard than the best treatment according to current, provisional knowledge. The best diagnostician (reader) among doctors is still only at the front of an army that might be moving in the wrong direction.

Like a doctor with the language of disease, a valuer like Caleb

Garth reads and infers, adjusts and reconstructs according to his own learned skill and to the general historical needs and values. "Caleb Garth, having little expectation and less cupidity, was interested in the verification of his own guesses, and the calmness with which he half-smilingly rubbed his chin and shot intelligent glances much as if he were valuing a tree, made a fine contrast with the alarm or scorn visible in other faces" (I, 344). The value of a tree is partly absolute according to size, straightness, and health, but it is also partly relative to current taste, which might shift from oak to maple for its furniture.

In art, too, there is a language, one that some read and others do not, a language that changes its vocabulary from period to period and style to style. In Rome, Dorothea hears Ladislaw describe a painting he plans.

"I take Tamburlaine in his chariot for the tremendous course of the world's physical history lashing on the harnessed dynasties. In my opinion that is a good mythical interpretation." Will here looked at Mr. Casaubon, who received this offhand treatment of symbolism very uneasily and bowed with a neutral air.

"The sketch must be very grand if it conveys so much," said Dorothea. "I should need some explanation even of the meaning you give. Do you intend Tamburlaine to represent earthquakes and volcanoes?"

"Oh yes," said Will, laughing, "and migrations of races and clearings of forests—and America and the steam-engine. Everything you can imagine!"

"What a difficult kind of shorthand!" said Dorothea, smiling toward her husband. "It would require all your knowledge to be able to read it." (I, 223–24)

Earlier, at their first meeting, Dorothea looked at a sketch of Will's and, even where there was no symbolism to read, spoke of the language of art.

Middlemarch

"I am no judge of these things. . . . You know, uncle, I never see the beauty of those pictures which you say are so much praised. They are a language I do not understand. I suppose there is some relation between pictures and nature which I am too ignorant to feel—just as you see what a Greek sentence stands for which means nothing to me." Dorothea looked up at Mr. Casaubon. (I, 81)

Her inability to read paintings is temporary. Training and experience, just as in the case of a doctor, begin to make art legible to her.

Dorothea felt she was getting quite new notions as to the significance of Madonnas seated under inexplicable canopied thrones with the simple country as background, and of saints with architectural models in their hands, or knives accidentally wedged in their skulls. Some things which had seemed monstrous to her were gathering intelligibility and even natural meaning. . . .
"I think I would rather feel that painting is beautiful than have to read it as an enigma." (I, 224)

The obscurity is not simply the Christian scheme of symbolic notation, the problem of allegory: the sketch Will showed her at their first meeting had been a simple landscape.

In her first marriage, Dorothea is ignorant of many languages. She proposes to read Greek to her husband, but her uncle suggests she learn only the sounds, not the language, so that it will be less of a strain. Ladislaw points out to Dorothea two fatal gaps in Casaubon's work. The first is his inability to read German, the language in which most current work in his field of mythological studies exists. The second gap is Casaubon's reactionary scholarship: he is as out of date as a doctor who would propose letting blood in the twentieth century, or a painter doing historical allegories in the time of the Impressionists. " 'The subject Mr. Casaubon has chosen is as changing as chemistry; new discoveries are constantly making new points of view. Who wants a system on the basis of the four elements, or a book to refute Paracelsus? Do you not see that it is no use now to be crawling a little way after men of the last century —men like Bryant—and correcting their mistakes?'" (I, 232). Like medicine, scholarship bases itself on rooted, historical, provisional techniques of interpretation as changing as style in art. Where Lydgate is an up-to-date doctor, Casaubon is ahistorical and therefore reactionary and irrelevant. Also, he is provincial, unaware of German contributions, whereas Lydgate knows the latest French medical advances. Casaubon is unable to do the one thing possible: to be as accurate and pertinent as his moment of history allows.

Casaubon reads the past, the human imagination; he seeks or creates coherence; he seeks the Key to All Mythologies. Like Goethe, who, in biology, searched for the *Urpflanze* that all other plants are derived from by transformation but related to by morphology, Casaubon and so many other scholars of the nineteenth century sought the final synthetic unity of mental life. Under the shadow of Hegel, men like George Eliot's friend Herbert Spencer wrote encyclopedic summaries of knowledge, grand, almost baroque systems that released the final secrets of human history. Hegel, Spencer, Marx, and, in mythology, Frazer: the taste for many-volumed works of synthesis is as striking as the preference for monumental, slow-moving, orchestral and operatic music like that of Wagner or Mahler, or for ambitious, ultimate social novels like *Middlemarch, War and Peace, The Brothers Karamazov,* and *Remembrance of Things Past.*

Like Casaubon, who seeks the key to all mental life, Lydgate's researches are aimed at the single final key to organic life. He plans to follow Bichat, who demonstrated the essential nature of tissues. "The great Frenchman first carried out the conception that living bodies, fundamentally considered, are not associations of organs which can be understood by studying them first apart, and then as it were federally; but must be regarded as consisting of certain primary webs or tissues, out of which the various organs—brain, heart, lungs, and so on—are compacted, as the various accommodations of a house are built up in various proportions of wood, iron, stone, brick, zinc and the rest" (I, 153). The breakthrough of Bichat is the same as that of *Middlemarch* in the social novel: for the organs (selves) first studied and defined separately, then seen federally in the body (society) Eliot substitutes a primary web, which will be called here the web of interpretation, that is prior to both organ and body. The primacy of the web over the threads and the junctions of threads is one point of the use of this repeated image throughout the book.

Lydgate plans to attempt the final step beyond Bichat. "This great seer [Bichat] did not go beyond the consideration of the tissues as ultimate facts in the living organism, marking the limit of anatomical analysis; but it was open to another mind to say, have not these structures some common basis from which they have all started. . . . What was the primitive tissue?" (I, 154). In chemistry that step had recently been taken: after all substances were seen as combinations of the (then) eighty-nine elements, the atoms of those elements themselves were all seen as variations on the one primitive atom, the hydrogen atom. Lydgate seeks to do the same for organic matter: he would find what we now call the cell.

Casaubon's scholarship, which Dorothea calls "this questionable riddle-guessing" (I, 351), is the pursuit of the same coherence and simplicity as that sought by Lydgate's research and science in general.

Superficially, the image of the languages of art, disease, valuing, scholarship, and scientific research might seem variations on the idea of the detective form. Nothing could be further from the truth. In detection there is a criminal, a crime, and a solution. The interest lies in the deductive skill and the confusing impediments that *temporarily* block the detective's access to the truth. In medicine, art, scholarship, valuing, and science, there is no final truth, only well-informed, trained opinion, historical correctness, skill in the light of currently held ideas and the state of the art. All absolutes are gone, and the detective form is riddled with absolutes.

In a passing exchange that is essential to the meaning of *Middlemarch*, Eliot shows how deliberate she was in the choice of images of language and interpretation.

> "What must Rosy know, mother?" said Mr. Fred. . . .
> "Whether it's right to say 'superior young men'," said Mrs. Vincy. . . .
> "Oh, there are so many superior teas and sugars now. Superior is getting to be shopkeepers' slang."
> "Are you beginning to dislike slang then?" said Rosamond. . . .
> "Only the wrong sort. All choice of words is slang. It marks a class."
> 'There is correct English: that is not slang."
> "I beg your pardon: correct English is the slang of prigs who write history and essays. And the strongest slang of all is the slang of poets." (I, 102–03)

Rosamond claims there is an objective language, a claim identical to the absolute claim of an accessible truth. Parallel would be a true history of the French Revolution, a "correct" diagnosis of symptoms. Fred's claim is that of *Middlemarch:* there is no language, only slangs, no correct word, only relatively correct ones that vary from place to place, circumstance to circumstance. There is the best history of the French Revolution for now, there is the currently accepted diagnosis of these symptoms. Not the absolute, true interpretation, but the best possible for now, under these circumstances, from this point of view. For the absolute world of detection, *Middlemarch* offers a world of interpretation, and one guarantee of the best possible interpretation is the widest possible experience.

Middlemarch

THE LANGUAGE OF BEHAVIOR

The central language of which those of art, medicine, science, valuing, and scholarship are anticipations is the everyday language of behavior. With behavior as with every language in the novel, the attention is on interpretation, not detection. The contrast between these two activities is of such importance that beneath the difference can be seen the entire nature of legibility and therefore of society. Detection is absolute, as it is, for example, in James's *Portrait of a Lady*. Isabel is ignorant of a set of secrets: the source of her inheritance, the past relationship between Mme. Merle and Osmond, and Pansy's parentage. Between ignorance and knowledge stand the shock moments of revelation. The truth exists, it is hidden by others, then it is revealed. Knowledge, total control over the important facts, replaces ignorance.

But with interpretation, as with diagnosis in medicine, there is only provisional, historical likelihood. The language of behavior is a system of signs. When Lydgate arrives in Middlemarch he is "a cluster of signs for his neighbours' false suppositions" (I, 105). To Dorothea, Casaubon in the days after their first meetings is a similar cluster of signs. "Signs are small measureable things, but interpretations are illimitable, and in girls of sweet, ardent nature, every sign is apt to conjure up wonder, hope, belief, vast as a sky, and coloured by a diffuse thimbleful of matter in the shape of knowledge" (I, 24).

Fragmentariness, far more than conscious deception (the essential problem of the detective form), is what turns behavior into a set of hieroglyphs. After her marriage, Dorothea's first pain stems from the coherence she had assumed, the way her mind in courtship had filled in the blanks.

The fact is unalterable, that a fellow-mortal with whose nature you are acquainted solely through the brief entrances and exits of a few imaginative weeks called courtship, may, when seen in the continuity of married companionship, be disclosed as something better or worse than that you have preconceived, but will certainly not appear altogether the same. . . . I suppose it was that in courtship everything is regarded as provisional and preliminary, and the smallest sample of virtue or accomplishment is taken to guarantee broad stores. . . . In their conversation before marriage Mr. Casaubon had often dwelt on some explanation or questionable detail of which Dorothea did not see the bearing; but such imperfect coherence seemed due to the brokenness of their intercourse. (I, 204–05)

Rome itself becomes for her a nightmare of fragmentation that projects the terror of the mysterious gaps of inner life. In the effect of Rome, Dorothea's self-coherence begins to vanish within the incoherence of the setting and marriage.

She was beholding Rome, the city of visible history, where the past of a whole hemisphere seems moving in funeral procession with strange ancestral images and trophies gathered from afar.

But this stupendous fragmentariness heightened the dreamlike strangeness of her bridal life. . . . She had been led through the best galleries, had been taken to the chief points of view, had been shown the grandest ruins and the most glorious churches, and she had ended by oftenest choosing to drive out to the Campagna where she could feel alone with the earth and sky, away from the oppressive masquerade of the ages, in which *her own life too* seemed to become a masque with enigmatical costumes. (I, 201–02, emphasis added)

The elements of meaning pass a point of fragmentation where

there is no longer any meaning at all. When enough letters are missing, there are no words at all but blanks in a string. At last Dorothea can find no coherence at all.

The long vistas of white forms whose marble eyes seemed to hold the montonous light of an alien world: all this vast wreck of ambitious ideals, sensuous and spiritual, mixed confusedly with the signs of breathing forgetfulness and degradation, at first jarred her with that ache belonging to a glut of confused ideas which check the flow of emotion.   (I, 202)

Only at one extreme is the illegibility of others pictured as a function of deliberately hidden secrets. The entangled relationships and identities of Bulstrode, Raffles, Ladislaw, and Featherstone amount to an obscurity of repressed facts, mysteries dependent on Bulstrode's attempt to erase his past. Here *Middlemarch* touches the elaborate parentage and inheritance plots of *Bleak House* or *Portrait of a Lady*. But in *Middlemarch*, this type of obscurity is one end of a spectrum that includes the most complete analysis of the psychology of partial truth and interpretation in the history of the novel. The center of unintelligibility is the new society itself, society built on change, selves in process of growth and transformation.

Unstable, discontinuous, the life of *Middlemarch* is the life of becoming and process, not of being and place. Of the central characters, all but the Vincys and Garths are outsiders, and most are orphans. Dorothea and Celia are orphans newly arrived to live with their uncle; Lydgate, another orphan, is a newcomer. Mrs. Cadwallader describes Ladislaw's blood as a "frightful mixture . . . the Casaubon cuttle-fish fluid to begin with, and then a rebellious Polish fiddler or dancing master, was it? and then an old clo—' " (II, 409); he has lived everywhere and nowhere. Bulstrode, too, an orphan and an outsider, is the self-made man in the tradition of Dickens's Bounderby, the man with a rewritten past and a hypocritical, canting version of himself. No institutions exist: no churches, only clergy; no banks, only bankers. Life is intangible, not visible. Psychology and not sociology is needed to render it. Where events are reflected in psychology they have a value and meaning that are mediated. Truth becomes version, and each event or character exists in the mind through which we see it. Ladislaw's visits to Mrs. Lydgate are for her a continuation of the romance of her life. Love for her is a game of power and one that is extended wider and wider. Her husband, then his cousin, then Ladislaw— each is a conquest or possible admirer. For Dorothea, who twice enters Rosamond's drawing room to find Ladislaw there, his presence throws into question the feeling she imagines he has reserved for herself. In a very subtle way, Dorothea also half begins to believe that her husband was right to suspect Ladislaw as a trifler. But most important, she fears Ladislaw prefers Rosamond to herself. The event disappears into the assumptions each character holds about its meaning in his own experience. A trivial example, but one that shows the strength of passing detail in the novel, occurs when Mr. Vincy thinks of Featherstone's death.

> Mr. Vincy, who, just returned from Stone Court, was feeling sure that it would not be long before he heard of Mr. Featherstone's demise. The felicitous word "demise," which had seasonably occurred to him, had raised his spirits even above their usual evening pitch. The right word is always a power, and communicates its definiteness to our action. Considered as a demise, old Featherstone's death assumed a merely legal aspect so that Mr. Vincy could tap his snuff-box over it and be jovial, without even an intermittent affectation of solemnity; and Mr. Vincy hated both solemnity and affectation. (I, 315)

The three factors—interpretation, psychological presentation, and fragmentation—are three levels of the same situation. The fragmentation or discontinuity, the "few entrances and exits" that are all the characters know of one another, creates the need for inference and imagination, which can penetrate the unknown part of experience to create a coherence, a predictability, a self behind the cluster of signs. In behavior, each person is a doctor progressing from the few, confused, visible symptoms to an inferred cause that gives coherence and can be reacted to. Each is also a scholar like Casaubon, synthesizing fragments through inference. When Celia watches her new baby she sees "remarkable acts . . . so dubious to her inexperienced mind that all conversation was interrupted by appeals for their interpretation made to the oracular nurse" (II, 63). The child's acts are like Hamlet's cloud: nothing is intended at all, but the antithesis of experience and inexperience underlines the essential center of interpretation. The baby's acts are the other side of that invisible limit where we no longer read meaning but invent it.

The acts of the miser Featherstone tempt the Vincys to the interpretation that Fred will be his heir; Featherstone exploits the half-meanings of his position for power over others, the power of Volpone. Dorothea's partisanship for Ladislaw innocently misleads Casaubon, whose inflamed jealousy determines the restriction in his will that implies that Dorothea and Ladislaw meant to marry.

One effect of the suspicion is to create the thing it most feared.

> It was a sudden strange yearning of heart towards Will Ladislaw. It had never before entered her mind that he could, under any circumstances, be her lover: conceive the effect of the sudden revelation that another had thought of him in that light—that he himself had been conscious of such a possibility,—and this with the hurrying, crowding vision of unfitting conditions. (II, 67)

The suspicious interpretation creates the prohibition, which suggests for the first time what is prohibited and proposes it to

Dorothea as something she should be tempted by. Surmise, gossip, conjecture, prejudice, implication, presentiment: most interpretation is misinterpretation. Dorothea is naively unaware of her husband's jealous conjectures about Ladislaw. After Casaubon's death, she makes the opposite mistake when she assumes that Ladislaw knows about the prohibition in the will. Knowing too little, assuming too much, in either case there is misinterpretation. When Ladislaw plans to leave Middlemarch, he speaks ambiguously about "certain things a man can go through only once in his life" (II, 216). He means to allude to his love for Dorothea, but she misinterprets the ambiguity and assumes that he is speaking about Mrs. Lydgate. At most moments, no observer is subtle enough and the narrator intervenes.

> Mr. Farebrother noticed that Lydgate seemed bored, and that Mr. Vincy spoke as little as possible to his son-in-law. Rosamond was perfectly graceful and calm, and only a subtle observation such as the Vicar had not been roused to bestow on her would have perceived the total absence of that interest in her husband's presence which a loving wife is sure to betray, even if etiquette keeps her totally aloof from him. When Lydgate was taking part in the conversation, she never looked towards him. (II, 224)

Nuances that are visible to one person are invisible to another who lacks experience of the situation. Rosamond "was keenly offended, but the signs she made of this were such as only Lydgate was used to interpret. She became suddenly quiet and seated herself, untying her hanging bonnet and laying it down with her shawl" (II, 366).

One part of the reality is not just subtle, it is deliberately repressed. Bulstrode's secret past is the most melodramatic example, but a more positive one is Mr. Farebrother's repression of his own love for Mary Garth when he goes to plead for Fred. Ladislaw too has "a delicate generosity that warned him into reticence" when he speaks with Lydgate about the money Bulstrode had loaned to

Lydgate. Ladislaw "shrank from saying that he had rejected Bulstrode's money, in the moment when he was learning that it was Lydgate's misfortune to have accepted it" (II, 372).

Elusive and complex as the signs of behavior are, the waywardness of interpretation might be moderate if it were not forced to deal with change. The turbulence of life and character demands not only interpretation but continuous reinterpretation that adjusts and sometimes reverses versions of experience. After Dorothea learns of her husband's will, she revises completely her interpretation of their life together.

> Her life was taking on a new form; . . . she was undergoing a metamorphosis in which memory would not adjust itself to the stirring of new organs. Everything was changing its aspect: her husband's conduct, her own duteous feeling towards him, every struggle between them—and yet more, her whole relation to Will Ladislaw. Her world was in a state of convulsive change; the only thing she could say distinctly to herself was, that she must wait and think anew. One change terrified her as if it had been a sin; it was a violent shock of repulsion from her departed husband, who had had hidden thoughts, perhaps perverting everything she said and did. (II, 67)

After Bulstrode is exposed, the town inverts its reading of his life. These dramatic revolutions of interpretation are extreme cases of what occurs everywhere, in the smallest events. Until Featherstone dies, "tacit expectations of what would be done for him by Uncle Featherstone determined the angle at which most people viewed Fred Vincy in Middlemarch" (I, 243). Once the will is read, a severe judgment replaces the leniency Fred met before. After his marriage and the death of their child, Lydgate reinterprets Rosamond's character, and sees the charming submission he had known during their courtship as a decoy that covers an obstinacy against which he is helpless.

Making Up Society

To summarize, the elements identified so far as contributing to the elusiveness of behavior and the difficulty of interpretation are: first, the ambiguity of acts and the way experience and motive only partly express themselves in behavior; second, point of view, which means each interpretation is someone's partial reading of the behavior; third, reinterpretation that stems from the lack of fixity. Setting and growth and development recombine and redistribute the meanings of characters and events.

A brief history of Lydgate's medical reputation in Middlemarch will underline the complex connections of all three factors. Since Lydgate is a stranger, his first patients must take his competence on trust. Some favor him because of his family connections, some because he is new, and others oppose him for the same reasons. His refusal to base his fee on the number of prescriptions he writes seems to imply a criticism of the other doctors, and they become hostile. He feels he must make a direct charge for visits, and this alienates some who think his "reform" is a hypocritical way of charging double. His reform of medical fees creates confusion and suspicion where it was meant to clarify. All opinion of him, up to this point, his entire reputation, is based on irrelevancies or misinterpretations. In his first days, Lydgate is, luckily, credited with miraculous cures.

The trash talked on such occasions was the more vexatious to Lydgate because it gave precisely the sort of prestige which an incompetent and unscrupulous man would desire, and was sure to be imputed to him by the simmering dislike of the other medical men as an encouragement of his own part of ignorant puffing. But even his proud outspokenness was checked by the discernment that it was as useless to fight against the interpretations of ignorance as to whip the fog; and "good fortune" insisted on using those interpretations. (II, 22)

After his correction of Dr. Wrench's mistaken diagnosis of Fred Vincy's illness, Lydgate gains more patients, but Wrench and the other doctors increase their hostility. Forced to choose between parties in the medically irrelevant question of the hospital chaplaincy, Lydgate allies with Bulstrode, thus gaining and losing patients among allies and enemies for another irrelevant reason. Finally, the scandal after the death of Raffles ruins Lydgate in Middlemarch. Gossip and inference take over to simplify a set of ethical and medical questions so intricate as to be almost beyond judgment.

At no moment in the course of his professional life does any other character have the experience or the objectivity to give a "true" appraisal of Lydgate's skill or incompetence. The other doctors lack modern and continental medical knowledge, and they are biased by the tacit condemnation of their own methods implied by Lydgate's new practices. One interesting minor point is the scandal that arises when Lydgate proposes autopsies: that is, he proposes to check whether diagnoses and treatments were correct. But to do so he must desecrate the dead; no one will allow this.

In the key words *reputation, respectability*, and *name*, we see that the substance of each character is a floating, communal fiction, a blend of interpretations each of which is partial, temporary, and based on a "cluster of signs." The more critical term *world*, as used in the earlier quotation about Dorothea ("Her world was in a state of convulsive change") is likewise a construction of interpretations. When Casaubon adds the codicil to his will, he casts a shadow over Dorothea's "name" and he transforms her "world." When she marries Ladislaw anyway, she confirms the imputation. The novel speaks often about Bulstrode's "respectability," and his most desperate acts are done to preserve his projected fiction, his "name." "Who can know how much of his most inward life is made up of the thoughts he believes other men have about him, until that fabric of opinion is threatened with ruin?" (II, 274). In one of the most crucial phrases of the novel Eliot quotes from a source she does not identify. "Even much stronger mortals than Fred Vincy hold half their rectitude in the mind of the being they love best. "*The theatre of all my actions* is fallen," said an antique personage when his chief friend was dead" (I, 251, emphasis added).

Interpretation works, then, in both directions: from the self outward, when we assure and adjust actions according to what we think they will mean in the theater others make for us; and, equally, from the outside in, when reputation and name limit the freedom of action. Bulstrode, Lydgate, Dorothea, and Ladislaw all leave Middlemarch at the end imprisoned by interpretation they can no longer break.

Projected Meaning

The elusive complexity of behavior, with its range of possibilities from Hamlet's cloud, into which we inject meaning, to Bulstrode's past, where meaning has been erased, and including the intermediate but far more important blends of everyday life— this complexity is only one side of the difficulty of interpretation. The other half is the range of sources for the meanings we see. Why does Hamlet see camel, weasel, and whale, not peddler mountain range, and hunchback? Meanings are gratuitous where no certainty exists. Where signs are ambiguous and spare, we see and project at the same time, we find ourselves everywhere, as Dorothea does when she assumes Casaubon's lofty goals and intellectual life are an enlarged version of her own ardor. When her marriage turns to despair, she has learned the otherness of what appeared an affinity. Or with Fred and Uncle Featherstone: "Fred fancied that he saw to the bottom of his uncle Featherstone's soul, though in reality half what he saw there was no more than the reflex of his own inclinations. The difficult task of knowing another soul is not for young gentlemen whose consciousness is chiefly made up of their own wishes" (I, 124). When Mr. Brooke wants to keep Ladislaw in Middlemarch to run his campaign in spite of the gossip about Casaubon's will, he sees a convenient truth. " 'As to gossip, you know, sending him away won't hinder gossip. People say what they like to say, not what they have chapter and verse for,' said Mr. Brooke, becoming acute about the truths that lay on the side of his own wishes" (II, 60–61).

The base of interpretation is, then, self-interest, an acuteness that depends on the convenience of the truth to our own aims or on an assumption of the same state in others we know in ourselves. Fred is afraid Mr. Farebrother will court Mary Garth and use the advantage of his wealth as vicar, not because he knows Farebrother to be treacherous but because he knows how tempted he himself would be in the circumstances. Rosamond Vincy's word for her husband, "moody," shows the way description itself is interpretation, particularly when everything is understood only through its effects on oneself. "Lydgate, relieved from anxiety about her, relapsed into what she inwardly called his moodiness—a name which to her covered his thoughtful preoccupation with other subjects than herself, as well as that uneasy look of the brow and distaste for all ordinary things as if they were mixed with bitter herbs" (II, 165–66). The most famous metaphor of the novel captures brilliantly this first level of interpretation.

> Your pier-glass or extensive surface of polished steel made to be rubbed by a housemaid, will be minutely and multitudinously scratched in all directions; but place now against it a lighted candle as a centre of illumination, and lo! the scratches will seem to arrange themselves in a fine series of concentric circles around that little sun. It is demonstrable that the scratches are going everywhere impartially, and it is only your candle which produces the flattering illusion of a concentric arrangement, its light falling with an exclusive optical selection. These things are a parable. The scratches are events, and the candle is the egoism of any person. (I, 274–75)

Egoism is a fixed point, a point of view in narrative vocabulary, and implied in the novel is the idea that, at the lowest level, there is no meaning without point of view, but only delusive meaning if there is only a single point of view. The candlelight that makes a pattern and coherence in the signs, the scratches, is not, in the novel, simply a question of direct egoism or selfishness. The disguised, secondary egoism of Casaubon's work or Bulstrode's religion (both men favor elaborate impersonal forms of speech that disguise their relentless reduction of the world to selfish terms) are also examples of single candles, "keys to all experience." Bulstrode's central word is *Providence;* he assumes he can read not only human experience but the invisible, divine goals of action. *Providence* is, of course, only his canting way of referring to what he wants. When Farebrother is chosen over his own protégé Tyke, he translates the event into his private language, a language as specialized as a style in art, or a slang, a language that imposes openly on reality. "Mr. Bulstrode, when he was hoping to acquire a new interest in Lowick, had naturally had an especial wish that the new clergyman should be one whom he thoroughly approved; and he believed it to be a chastisement and admonition directed to his own shortcomings and those of the nation at large" (II, 97).

The novel is particularly hard on any subjectivity that passes itself off as an objective, impersonal reading of events. Casaubon's language is almost pathologically devious. When in Rome, he suggests visiting

"*celebrated frescoes*, designed or painted by Raphael, which *most persons think* it worth while to visit."

"But do you care about them?" was always Dorothea's question.

"They are, I believe, *highly esteemed*. Some of them represent the fable of Cupid and Psyche. . . . He is a painter who *has been held* to combine the most complete grace of form with sublimity of expression. Such at least I have gathered to be *the opinion of cognoscenti.*" (I, 206, emphasis added)

He refuses to choose, to reflect honestly a bias or an egoism that is candid, willful, and subjective.

The fixed candles of interpretation, Rosamond's egoism, Bulstrode's disguised egoism, and every character's moments of selfishness and self-interest, are joined by one important, final, fixed point of reference: hidden obsession.

The pathos of Casaubon's life rests on our seeing that his every move is defensive. He lives in fear that others will recognize his failure, and he himself knows but cannot accept that, in the theater of others, his work has come to nothing. He marries Dorothea in a surprised moment; he has found an admirer, a believer, a theater in which he can see the illusions, which he knows are false, still living. Soon he begins to suspect she knows his secret doubts, and her every word becomes filled with innunendo.

> In Mr. Casaubon's ear Dorothea's voice gave loud emphatic iteration to those muffled suggestions of consciousness which it was possible to explain as mere fancy, the illusion of exaggerated sensitiveness: always when such suggestions are repeated from without, they are rejected as cruel and unjust. . . . And this cruel outward accuser was there in the shape of a wife—nay, of a young bride, who, instead of observing his abundant pen-scratches and amplitude of paper with the uncritical awe of an elegant-minded canary bird, seemed to present herself as a spy watching everything with a malign power of inference. (I, 210)

His secret world is as vulnerable as Bulstrode's, his "reputation" and life in the eyes of others is as fragile as Lydgate's medical name. Where anyone's feelings are hidden, all events seem related to

Making Up Society

them; everyone might know or be hinting that he knows the secret. Before Lydgate declares himself to Rosamond, his love for her is a concealed, fixed point. An innocent joke of Farebrother's takes on a full meaning. "A few days before Lydgate would have taken no notice of these words as anything more than the Vicar's usual way of putting things. They seemed now to convey an innuendo that confirmed the impression that he had been making a fool of himself and behaving so as to be misunderstood: not, he believed, by Rosamond herself; she, he felt sure, took everything as lightly as he intended it" (I, 312). Later, when his debts overwhelm him, money replaces love as the candle that arranges the scratches around him.

In Rome, Ladislaw's friend Naumann reads all reality in the light of what he could make of it in one of his allegorical paintings. When he sees Dorothea, he says to Ladislaw, " 'If you were less artist, you would think of Mistress Second-Cousin as antique form animated by Christian sentiment—a sort of Christian Antigone—sensuous force controlled by spiritual passion' " (I, 198). But Ladislaw jokes at the false centricity of Naumann's way of thinking. " 'Yes, and that your painting her was the chief outcome of her existence—the divinity passing into higher completeness and all but exhausted in the act of covering your bit of canvas. I am amateurish if you like: I do *not* think that all the universe is straining towards the obscure significance of your pictures' " (I, 199).

Point of view creates meaning out of clusters of signs, and it creates drama, the movement of action toward and away from purposes that are projected as goals. Point of view creates perspective: details become foreground and background, characters turn into principals and subordinates. Old Featherstone no longer exists except as a utility in the expectations of those who hope to be included in his will. Naumann deceived Casaubon and Dorothea to get a sketch of Dorothea. It is one of the great epic insights of the novel that point of view and drama are tied to reductive views of others that are views based on interest.

The first stage of interpretation, then, is the self-centered, dramatic version of events where egoism, secondary egoism, or some fixed obsessional point collects events concentrically around itself. "We are all of us born in moral stupidity, taking the world as an udder to feed our supreme selves" (I, 221). This moral stupidity of innocence (which is literally "ignorance") comes as a startling contrast to the usual Victorian identification of superior moral sense with childlike innocence and inexperience, an identification that continues by equating wide experience, worldliness, with corruption. In that identification is assumed a stage of the self prior to egoism and self-interest that mature life obliterates, a stage that is visible in certain women and small children. Bob Jakin and Dolly Winthrop are examples from Eliot's own work. The starting point of *Middlemarch* is the acceptance of the irrelevance of those fictions of selfless innocence. "Moral stupidity," like ignorance of language, is where each must begin. Equally absent from *Middlemarch* are those characters of absolute moral goodness like Romola, Silas Marner, and Felix Holt, characters that seem to have entered a stage of existence absolutely distinct from normal selfish or mixed existence, a state beyond point of view.

The dialogue in *Middlemarch* is not between selfishness and selflessness, but between innocence and experience. That is to say, *Middlemarch* is not concerned with moral substance but with growth and expansion. The word *experience* is the great goal of the novel, and the alternative to the egoism of a fixed point of view is not some other charitable, selfless, fixed point of view, but an epic comprehensiveness that weakens the drama of the self by developing the drama of a "world," a comprehensiveness that replaces the single candle with a prismatic, complex way of reading experience that reaches behavior. This epic exhaustiveness is the method of the novel itself.

Casaubon's great fear is of the possibility that Dorothea sees him comprehensively. "There had entered into the husband's mind the certainty that she judged him, and that her wifely devotedness was like a penitential expiation of unbelieving thoughts—was accompanied with a power of comparison by which himself and his doings were seen too luminously as a part of things in general" (I, 436). Where there is a key to all experience, one key, whether it is the self or one idea or one project that gives meaning to life (and even Lydgate's research is after the one source of life), there is a lie about experience, a narrowness that construes falsely because it can see only one thread to which all others are in the dramatic relationship of being incidental. The method, not the goal, of Lydgate's research is one paradigm for flexible, adjusted accommodation to multiple truth. " 'There must be a systole and diastole in all inquiry. A man's mind must be continually expanding and shrinking between the whole human horizon and the horizon of an object-glass' " (II, 222).

A far more important statement, because it indirectly describes the novel itself, comes in Ladislaw's contrast of painting and literature.

> "Language gives a fuller image, which is all the better for being vague. After all, the true seeing is within; and painting stares at you with an insistent imperfection. I feel that especially about representations of women. As if a woman were a mere coloured superficies! You must wait for movement and tone. There is a difference in their very breathing! they change from moment to moment—This woman you have just seen, for example; how would you paint her voice, pray? But her voice is much diviner than anything you have seen of her." (I, 199–200)

Language does not render substance; it gives aspects, growth, and change of perspective—the variety of life, not a summarizing gesture. The different lenses that Eliot mentions several times are the different points of view, each fixed, each ignorant of and often in conflict with the rest. Out of the mixture of imprecision and bias, out of the range of points of view, a fiction is created, a construction, a world: Lydgate's reputation as a doctor, Dorothea's name. The novel seldom summarizes or blends opinion into reputation. Each fixed point is named, and the fiction develops slowly. In the first book, the shifting readings of Casaubon are unfolded. To Dorothea he is a great soul, but to her sister Celia he is an ugly old man. Mr. Brooke, Sir James Chettam, Mrs. Cadwallader, Mr. Cadwallader, and Lydgate: each judges absolutely. And Dorothea, of course, acts on her judgment. But, for the reader, Casaubon turns through the spectrum; only the reader has the *unreal* objectivity to summarize, because only he has no point of view, no interest. Judgment is not idle or esthetic. The question of the first book is whether Dorothea should marry, and, for the others, whether they should act to prevent the marriage. Each estimate prescribes a course of action; every diagnosis, a treatment.

In combination, points of view make up one prism: time gives another. By *time*, is meant not objective change but differences noticed from points of view with interests. The opinions of Casaubon in the first book are static; each attempts to summarize the man's character. Dynamic character, however, is one of the great accomplishments of the novel, and the growth of the reader's knowledge and opinion of Dr. Farebrother is a more complex guide to the essence of interpretation than the chorus of opinions about Casaubon. Our knowledge of Farebrother is a sequence of impressions seen in turn by three characters under the demands of different situations over the course of the novel. First seen through Lydgate's eyes, then Fred Vincy's, then Dorothea's, the character of the man changes and deepens with every move. Each judgment is *active*, based on an interest and the need for a course of action. Lydgate must come to an opinion in order to vote in the hospital chaplaincy election. He first sees Farebrother gambling, and notices that his face is a mixture of the "shrewd and the mild" (I, 169). His second impression comes when he visits Farebrother at home and sees him amid his family of widowed mother and eccentric old-maid sisters. The new setting brings out his generosity and quiet indulgence of the whims of his family. Lydgate and Farebrother move to the study, a third setting, where, in the presence of Farebrother's collection of natural history specimens, an entirely new side of the man appears. He is misplaced as a clergyman and has sacrificed his interests to his need to support his family and maintain the comforts of life.

Further sympathetic elements of the minister's character come out when we see him from Fred Vincy's point of view in the problems of Fred's relation to Mary Garth. The minister suppresses his own love to aid Fred's. But, in the final chapters, the less sympathetic side of Farebrother dominates. When seen from Dorothea's point of view in her attempt to rescue Lydgate's reputation after the scandal of Raffles's death, Farebrother is too cautious. The diffidence so winning when we saw him willing to step aside for Fred is now seen in new circumstances as a flawed lack of assertion, a passivity that is negative.

Farebrother is revealed aspect by aspect, and along with interpretations from new points of view there is reinterpretation as time changes the meanings of events already complete. Every judgment is from a point of view and under the compulsion of action. No one in Middlemarch knows Farebrother; only the reader of the book, perhaps, has access to enough points of view to make a synthesis, but new events would make even that synthesis incomplete.

Were the multiple points of view of epic, of art, the only alternative to the single candle of egoism or obsession, the novel would offer a hopeless dichotomy. The truth of art depends on its objectivity, its detachment, but, as the novel expresses it, the only truth is lived truth, urgent, relative and partial, and the only important judgment is that made necessary by the need to act, not that reached in the leisure of esthetic contemplation.

The enlarged truth that lies between that of egoism and that of art is the still incomplete truth of experience. Most characters in

Middlemarch

Middlemarch are "twice-born," to use William James's word. Dorothea's second marriage is her less deluded choice; Caleb Garth fails in business the first time but will prosper after his bankruptcy. Fred Vincy's true life begins when he no longer presents himself as the future heir, when his great expectations fail. Lydgate leaves Middlemarch to begin a second life, as Bulstrode years earlier had come to Middlemarch to begin a second, better, life. The first world is destroyed, the world of false confidence and romantic images of the self. In this sense, Dorothea's idealism, Fred's expectations, Rosamond's romance of her life, and Lydgate's ambitions in research: all are equally false worlds, the first world that is only a projected self writ large. The moments of growth are often so minor as to escape notice. When Fred must tell the Garths he cannot pay back the debt for which they signed the note, his perception in the crisis is jolted into a larger vision. "His pain in the affair beforehand had consisted almost entirely in the sense that he must seem dishonourable, and sink in the opinion of the Garths: had he not occupied himself with the inconvenience and possible injury his breach might occasion for them. . . . But at this moment he suddenly saw himself as a pitiful rascal who was robbing two women of their savings" (I, 258–59).

Rosamond's fantasy world, a construction as false as Bulstrode's respectability or Casaubon's intellectual eminence, is shattered when Ladislaw shows her the contempt he feels for her alongside Dorothea, and in the next few days Rosamond acts generously for the first time. In Dorothea, the process of enlarged perception is traced most lucidly. Her own hidden pain in the eighteen months of her first marriage allows her to infer the breakdown between Rosamond and Lydgate. "All the active thought with which she had before been representing to herself the trials of Lydgate's lot, and this young marriage union which, like her own, seemed to have its hidden as well as evident troubles—all this vivid sympathetic experience returned to her now as power: it asserted itself as acquired knowledge asserts itself and will not let us see as we saw in the day of our ignorance" (II, 377). Beyond the moral stupidity into which each is born is a secondary power: the light of experience. This power is the knowledge not of right and wrong, but of the psychological possibilities of life, and its varieties.

Once again there is an important, a crucial analogue with scientific method. Eliot describes the scientific method of Lydgate's researches. "But these kinds of inspiration Lydgate regarded as rather vulgar and vinous compared with the imagination that reveals subtle actions inaccessible by any sort of lens but tracked in that outer darkness through long pathways of necessary sequence by the inward light. . . . He was enamoured of that arduous invention which is the very eye of research, provisionally framing its object and correcting it to more and more exactness of relation" (I, 171). Beginning with a provisional framing, it adjusts slowly to perfect focus, or as near as it can come. Hypothesis and experiment. Yet the idea will always be provisional and approximate. His truth will always be tentative. The greatest accomplishment of the book is the subtlety with which it practices this method, the force of its reinterpretations. In behavior, that final sphere of inquiry, it is Dorothea who is credited with the impulse of precision and expansion. "But in Dorothea's mind there was a current into which all thought and feeling were apt sooner or later to flow —*the reaching forward of the whole consciousness towards the fullest truth*, the least partial good" (I, 212–13, emphasis added). The fullest truth is not the absolute truth, it is an activity that reaches and enlarges its domain, like that of science. Like science it is transitional, tentative, and always provisional; but its goal is the least provisional, least relative, least subjective vision.

The three terms that describe the ideal of interpretation would not be those used to describe ideal judgment in *The Mill on the Floss*: *patience, discrimination, impartiality*. The three words used throughout *Middlemarch* are *ardent, tentative*, and *generous*. The terms of *The Mill on the Floss* are those of detachment and objectivity; they would describe an ideal court of law. Those of *Middle-march* are a language for those within a battle, those engaged in the moment of life itself.

When Dorothea wants to clear Lydgate's reputation, she makes a criticism of Farebrother: "For the first time she felt rather discontented with Mr. Farebrother. She disliked this cautious weighing of consequences, instead of an ardent faith in efforts of justice and mercy, which would conquer by their emotional force" (II, 320–21). The word *ardent* is used dozens of times, usually to describe Dorothea, Ladislaw, or Lydgate. In the final chapter, we are told "Will became an ardent public man" (II, 424). Ardor and enthusiasm are the forces behind the restlessness with partial truth, the forces that press for a wider truth. The cautious, passive men like Farebrother, Mr. Brooke, and Sir James Chettam, although inoffensive, are diffuse and finally at fault because they will not extend themselves to enter the struggle to imagine, project, and realize the best selves of those around them. Although not similar to the egoists like Rosamond or Bulstrode or the characters ruled by a single obsession like Casaubon and Featherstone, they end up blamed, as all sideline figures must be in a world of growth and imagination.

The second the three terms, *tentative*, is crucial because of the limits of point of view and the continuous change that demands reinterpretation. The years in which *Middlemarch* takes place, 1829–1832, are not used, as the same years are in *Felix Holt*, to draw a specific analogue to the year the book appeared. Beneath the choice of that turbulent moment is the great insight of the century that every age is an age of transition. Medicine, scholarship, reputations: all are in flux.

Character, too, is not a substance but a process.

"But, my dear Mrs. Casaubon," said Mr. Farebrother, smiling at her ardour, "character is not cut in marble—it is not something solid and unalterable. It is something living and changing, and may become diseased as bodies do."

"Then it may be rescued and healed," said Dorothea. (II, 322)

The point Will Ladislaw made to Naumann vindicates language over painting because language is tentative and can show change. Interpretation is tentative because, in the great phrase of the novel, "we are on a perilous margin" (II, 372). The self is the margin where it is in motion and transformation, just as the age is its transitions, and science is the frontiers of science. Activity is on the margin. Since the self is in flux, interpretation plays a more active part than simply following behind, as judgment does, to record what has occurred. A scene of quiet brilliance occurs in the novel when Lydgate gambles in the billiard parlor. A good player, he is betting on his shots and winning consistently. "Lydgate, by betting on his own strokes, had won sixteen pounds; but young Hawley's arrival had changed the poise of things. He made first-rate shots himself, and began to bet against Lydgate's strokes, the strain of whose nerves was thus changed from simple confidence in his own movements to defying another person's doubts in them. The defiance was more exciting than the confidence, but it was less sure. He continued to bet on his own play, but began to fail" (II, 257). Hawley's bets against him are an interpretation that destroys his poise and creates the very failure the bettor is wagering on. Each has the theater of his actions in the doubts or confidence of others, and the balance of their interpretation acts as a lift or weight on every action.

In the days after the scandal of Raffles's death, Lydgate finally recovers himself only in the presence of Dorothea, who believes that self exists. "The presence of a noble nature, generous in its wishes, ardent in its charity, changes the lights for us: we begin to see things again in the larger, quieter masses, and to believe that we too can be seen and judged in the wholeness of our character. That influence was beginning to act on Lydgate. . . . He sat down again, and felt that he was recovering his old self in the consciousness that he was the one who believed in it" (II, 350–51). Similarly, Fred Vincy is saved because, even when he appears at his lowest point, Caleb Garth interprets his future generously. Farebrother's best self becomes his visible self when Lydgate convinces Dorothea to give him the living. More than faith or trust is involved. An interpretation that anticipates the best goes several steps toward producing it. The gambler who bets Lydgate will fail causes the failure, then collects on it.

The most sustained example of the effect of generous interpretation in the novel is the insistent claim Mary Garth makes on Fred Vincy. She will not marry him if he becomes a minister, for he would not be "himself." By identifying his true self and then insisting that he reach it, she brings him to a confirmed image of what he is. Being, as he is, on the margin of himself, Fred has the choice not between higher and lower selves but between true and false ones. Should he become a minister, he would be what he can only simulate. Mr. Brooke, when he runs for office, chooses a false self, and his bungling attempts to act the politician are corrected and finally eliminated by the mockery of others. At his speech, his opponents hold up a puppet of Brooke—a false self—and echo his words with comic emphasis. Fred as a minister would be simulating, as Mr. Brooke is. The false self acts, memorizes, performs. Mr. Brooke's speech is written for him by Ladislaw, who has him memorize it, but the puppet wipes his memory clean.

To be permanently a false self is the fate of Casaubon, Bulstrode, and Rosamond Vincy. From the first, Rosamond is represented as acting out an imaginary being. "Every nerve and muscle in Rosamond was adjusted to the consciousness that she was being looked at. She was by nature an actress of parts that entered into her *physique*: she even acted her own character, and so well, that she did not know it precisely to be her own" (I, 122). The metaphor is sharpened later. "For Rosamond, though she would never do anything that was more disagreeable to her, was industrious; and now more than ever she was active in sketching her landscapes and market-carts and portraits of her friends, in practising her music, and in being from morning to night her own standard for a perfect lady, having always had an audience in her own consciousness" (I, 174). Her own role is only one element in an imagined romance of life for which she recruits others. Lydgate courts her, but in fact she conscripts him. She wins, of course, and Lydgate ends up a society doctor. Not satisfied with only one actor in her play, she attempts to recruit Ladislaw as a secondary admirer. Like Hetty Sorrel, Rosamond commits the final sin against life when she takes a life, when she causes the miscarriage by going out riding with Lydgate's foppish cousin. The little rituals of her social fantasy mean more to her, her conquests and airs are chosen over the baby's life.

Rosamond's imagined world, the thater of the world she lives in, is like Bulstrode's. It is an unreality that spreads out from the self to contaminate, conscript others, and destroy everything that cannot be included. It is the final egoism: that of an imagined self. As theater it is the reverse of the "theatre of my actions," that respectful attention to the meaning of acts in the interpretations others will make of them. Fred Vincy, who could have gone the same route into unreality as his sister Rosamond, begins with great expectations. But, when Featherstone's will gives him nothing, he begins to live in the light of, and to adjust to, the generous interpretations of his possibilities held out by Mary Garth, Farebrother, and Caleb. The final meaning of generosity, then, is not a choice between higher and lower selves, not a moral choice at all, but a call to affirm a true self over the range of false roles. Interpretation, the "theatre of my actions," when it is community reaching in and not the self reaching out to recruit others (as Casaubon recruits Dorothea), is exactly the call to form a self, not a role.

The three qualities of interpretation, once it has reached out in experience beyond the candle of self, are all elements of fact. *Tentative, ardent,* and *generous:* all three are based in the rootedness of truth and the power to create meaning. Like the diagnoses of medicine, the best interpretation is the best according to the materials at hand. Tentativeness acknowledges that relativity, ardor forces the increased knowledge that experience brings, and generosity guarantees that the best side of the margin on which each exists will stay in sight.

The first reality of community in *Middlemarch* is the community of interpretation, the power of others to blight or foster the marginal part of the self. Described as a "huge whispering gallery" (I, 429), the world is always contested, theories and hypotheses are engaged in capturing reality. This interpretation, however, is not the gossip and commentary of idle observers. "Commonness," a word which Eliot uses to predict Lydgate's failure, she defines as "that personal pride and unreflecting egoism." Growth is not from the commonness of the self to the commonness of society, that lowest denominator of idle speculation. If the egoistic readings the self makes are common, so is the reductive, negative reading of gossip. In an important dialogue between Dorothea and Mrs. Cadwallader, the relation of language to interpretation is stressed.

"You will certainly go mad in that house alone, my dear. You will see visions. We have all got to exert ourselves a little to keep sane, and call things by the same names other people call them by."

"I never called everything by the same name that all the people about me did," said Dorothea stoutly.

"But I suppose you have found out your mistake, my dear," and that is a proof of sanity."

Dorothea was aware of the sting, but it did not hurt her. "No," she said, "I still think that the greater part of the world is mistaken about many things." (II, 113–14)

At a minimal level all language is slang, all description interpretation, but language which contains a certain generalized human

Making Up Society

reading of experience is one pole beyond the self, one community of thought and appraisal. Whether the word *murder* applies to the death of Raffles, whether *Providence* describes Mr. Bulstrode's purchase of Stone Court, only a second level of interpretation will determine.

THE HOME EPIC

The title of the novel is the name of the community, *Middlemarch*, not of any hero or heroine. The first level of this community is that of the "huge whispering gallery," the "theatre of my actions," the others in whom each sees a version of himself that calls to him to become that self. A second level is far more concrete. *Middlemarch* is a novel of complete actions. At the same time, it is one of the great novels of character. In the image of the web that Eliot uses for her novel, each character is a thread and can be traced here in primary, there in subordinate, here in visible, there in invisible positions in the web. In the same way, we can begin with an action, a knot, a tie in the web, and trace the different strands that meet there. The greatest affirmation of community in Eliot's work comes from her success in *Middlemarch* in creating actions in which characters are truly interdependent, in which a complete action always refers to a motion in which many selves aid or hinder one another.

No finer demonstration of the limit of de Tocqueville's predictions for the age of individualism exists. Whereas he had identified the new self-reliant man as one who has only himself to thank for the conditions of his life, one who imagines a self, wills to create it, and energetically succeeds only to find himself alone within a world that is uniquely his but sealed off from all others, in *Middlemarch* every ambition that is self-reliant or dependent purely on will fails. Casaubon's scholarship, Lydgate's research, Bulstrode's self-made world, even Dorothea's projects: all collapse or abort. As Dorothea says, " 'I never could do anything that I liked. I have never carried out any plan yet' " (II, 410).

Middlemarch

The contrast to self-reliant, willed plans is the complete act. When Mr. Brooke runs for Parliament as a reformer, his opponents ridicule him as a self-styled reformer whose own tenants live in squalor. His son-in-law, Sir James Chettam, tries to convince him to hire Caleb Garth to manage his lands but fails. Sir James then talks to his sister-in-law, Dorothea, who urges her uncle to hire Garth. Brooke weakens but puts her off. Finally, a tenant insults him and breaks through Brooke's hazy self-image of a good landlord. He hires Garth, who, because of the extra work, needs an assistant. He takes on Fred Vincy, who is now able to give up any thought of the ministry. The extra money Caleb earns also means his daughter Mary won't have to go into service and his son Andrew can be apprenticed.

Even this far the act is incomplete, but the key to the action is apparent. A dozen people, accidents, relationships, moments of experience, all contribute to the results, and there is no one result. Many lives feel echoes of Brooke's decision to run for Parliament. Many lives go into any one result. The web, not the thread; community, not any one life that fulfills its ambitions—its will and imagination and projected self; Middlemarch, not Dorothea or Lydgate or Fred Vincy. When the texture of life is as dense as it is in *Middlemarch*, an epic contentment begins to appear. Compensation appears to work in the long run and without any particular effort of will. Garth reaches prosperity in spite of his bankruptcy. Accidents eventually expose the villain Bulstrode. Lydgate first votes against Farebrother for the hospital chaplaincy, but several years later he can urge Dorothea to make him vicar, a ten times more valuable situation. It is through a chain of other accidents that Farebrother gets the living. The most startling compensation of the novel comes when Fred Vincy goes to live in Stone Court after all. The estate he once hoped to inherit from Featherstone is now his. What he loses in the will he eventually earns and is given by the interventions of others and the accidents of life. To trace the chain of those who work to get Stone Court for

Fred would involve a list of half of the characters in the novel. The complete act is not willed or earned. Compensations are not willed or earned, but they are deserved. The interpretations others have of Farebrother or Fred are the impulses that, when combined with their ardor, create the gifts that come to them. We never see Caleb Garth seek work, but every major job comes to him along a chain of those who respect his work. He does not compete, or bid, or advertise himself.

Eliot's earlier novels often preached or allegorized the limited power of the self and will in the final life each has; she contrasted the willful, egoistic self to unreal and pious alternatives of duty, selflessness, resignation, and sympathy. In *Middlemarch* the community of becoming and interpretation is realized: interpenetration of lives exists in the smallest details. This society of becoming and interpretation, this new community, is not one of permanence, visibility, place, and rootedness. It is not the community of *Adam Bede* or the community lost in *The Mill on the Floss*. The continuity imposed by memory in *The Mill on the Floss* does not exist in *Middlemarch;* a community of others replaces that of memory. Most important, in *Middlemarch* both the self and the community it exists in are chosen.

Fred Vincy must choose between his parents' projection of his life, the socially approved life of a minister, and that projected by Mary Garth, Farebrother, and Caleb. Casaubon, after recruiting Dorothea in his fantasy world, leaves instructions that are a projection of her future after he is no longer alive. His will insists that she not marry Ladislaw. To continue the fiction of his scholarship, which neither he nor Dorothea any longer believed in, and which is a false world with roles exactly like Rosamond's, he leaves behind a "synoptic tabulation" for the use of Mrs. Casaubon. He attempts to be the audience for her life even beyond the grave. Since he insists, she addresses him as though he were alive, and, in a scene as chilling as that in *Vanity Fair* when old Osborne takes down the family Bible to cross out his son's name, Dorothea writes an answer on Casaubon's instructions: "I could not use it. Do you not see now that I could not submit my soul to yours, by working hopelessly at what I have no belief in?" (II, 113). She chooses to live beyond the reach of his eyes.

Dorothea, Ladislaw, Rosamond, Lydgate, and Bulstrode all choose new communities in leaving Middlemarch. Bulstrode goes to end his life amid the "indifference of new faces" (II, 413). That indifference too is provisional. Exile can be purely negative, not being where one was, or it can in time be another home, as London is for Dorothea and Ladislaw. It is one of the great achievements of Eliot's career that she came to affirm choice, freedom, and experience.

The key to this reversal lies in her breakthrough into epic form, which places characters within a felt context wider than themselves, and which therefore destroys the connection between, on the one hand, choice and freedom and, on the other, will and the tyranny of the unique world each self-made man brings into being. The force of epic is to embody the truth that it is possible to create a common world as well as a private one that is only ego or fantasy writ large. The common world of *Adam Bede* or *The Mill on the Floss* is given, each must accept it, as Adam and Dinah do, or become a worldless wanderer like Hetty. The world of *Middlemarch* is the second world, a world that is, in both senses of the word, a construct. Fiction and artifact, made and imagined, the new world is shaped and chosen, fought for and brought into being. And, because it is provisional, it is made and transformed at every moment. From this common world the defective types are exactly those we see in *Middlemarch*. First are the misers who hoard what they can accumulate and reserve for themselves, separate from the common world. Second are those who insist on unreality and conscript others, as Casaubon does Dorothea or as Rosamond does Lydgate, into a false world that depletes and finally destroys the common one. And third are those who lack ardor, those who have no energy or enthusiasm for the construction. Each of the three holds back from the aspiration toward, in the words that are used of Dorothea, "the fullest truth, the least partial good."

Making Up Society

In the final chapter, Eliot speaks of the "home epic," which she defines as the "gradual conquest or irremediable loss of . . . complete union" (II, 420). The home epic is the epic of intimacy and estrangement when we stress the word *home*. Eliot's other epic, her other great novel, is *The Mill on the Floss*; like *Middlemarch*, it is named not for a hero but for a unity larger than the self. *The Mill on the Floss* is also a home epic, an epic of the loss of home; it has the epic rhythm of the first world, the world of childhood that is the world always lost, scattered, and finally obliterated. The first world is the world of familiarity, a world "there before we choose it." It is the epic of the first home, the home always lost. The second world is constructed and is not familiar but intimate. *Middlemarch* has the epic rhythm of this second world. The two books together are the complete span, the home epic. James Fenimore Cooper titled two of his novels with phrases that enhance the meaning of Eliot's: *Home as Found* and *Homeward Bound*.

The second word of her phrase, the word *epic* points to the comprehensiveness and, even more important, to an advance beyond what I have called local, moral bookkeeping—the rationalism that insists each act be lucid, every crime punished, every motive pure or punished. The epic strain favors a relaxed sense that things are right on the whole. Of the two marginal selves in the novel, Fred Vincy is won and Lydgate is lost to the "spots of commonness." Of Dorothea's marriages, one is a nightmare, the other good. Farebrother does not get the hospital job but eventually he is vicar. As Eliot uses it, epic is the refutation of drama that sees events in single directions, in terms of single interests. "Scenes which make vital changes in our neighbours' lot are but the background of our own" (I, 337).

Nothing could be further from the power of epic than that journalistic trick that shows in so many news photographs an old woman calmly knitting, unaware that behind her someone has just jumped from a bridge. These synchronized ironies testify to the indifference of things, to their confusion, and to an isolation so deep that they continue in circles of their own, unaware. The epic comprehension is that of one texture, one web of events. Because of the scandal that destroys Bulstrode and Lydgate, Fred Vincy is able to move into the now vacant Stone Court. Eliot's final summary of the character of Casaubon is filled with understanding of what all those who live in reduced worlds have lost. "For my part I am very sorry for him. It is an uneasy lot at best, to be what we call highly taught and yet not to enjoy: to be present at this great spectacle of life and never to be liberated from a small hungry shivering self—never to be fully possessed by the glory we behold" (I, 291–92). Metaphors of sight are everywhere in Eliot's novels: blindness, shortsightedness, dim-sightedness. Adam Bede on his hilltop surveys, the novel *Middlemarch* surveys, and both do so because underlying any epic is the feeling of abundance, the richness of life when we are there to see it. The life of Middlemarch is teeming, various; the novel is as generous with life as the best of its characters are with each other.

In the work of a writer as different from Eliot as can be imagined, in Wallace Stevens's poem *Esthétique du Mal*, there is a great summary of the epic feeling that underlies the meaning of interpretation in *Middlemarch*. Stevens first protests against those who live in one idea, in drama, in reduced worlds like those of Casaubon, Rosamond, Bulstrode, and Featherstone.

> He would not be aware of the lake.
> He would be the lunatic of one idea
> In a world of ideas, who would have all the people
> Live, work, suffer and die in that idea
> In a world of ideas. He would not be aware of the clouds, . . .
> His extreme of logic would be illogical.

Those who make all reality into one idea are everywhere in *Middlemarch*. Even the painter Naumann is challenged by Ladislaw, "I do not think that all the universe is straining towards the obscure significance of your pictures" (I, 199). Stevens's last stanza evokes the abundance I have called "experience" in *Middlemarch*, and the richness of interpretation that reaches, at some point, imagination.

> One might have thought of sight, but who could think
> Of what it sees, for all the ill it sees?
> Speech found the ear, for all the evil sound,
> But the dark italics it could not propound.
> And out of what one sees and hears and out
> Of what one feels, who could have thought to make
> So many selves, so many sensuous worlds,
> As if the air, the mid-day air, was swarming
> With metaphysical changes that occur,
> Merely in living as and where we live.[1]

The final step of *Middlemarch* is beyond esthetics, beyond the mental play with the many worlds. Finally we want to live in one. Beyond the experience and the interpretation, beyond the imagination, is the second world, the constructed world, Middlemarch itself.

---

1. Wallace Stevens, *The Collected Poems of Wallace Stevens* (New York: Knopf, 1954), pp. 325–26.

8

Daniel Deronda

In her final novel, Eliot returned to the heroic, returned, that is, to the stream of her work that began with *Adam Bede* and continued through *Silas Marner* and *Felix Holt*. The challenge of the heroic for her was to create around a disqualified hero the clear moral action that could compel the respect and sympathy that her audience would be likely to withhold in real life. The clearest moral action is, of course, suffering, and it is because of his suffering that Silas Marner cannot be dismissed. Bede, Marner, and Holt are workingmen; gruff or taciturn, impatient with or ignorant of the demands of refinement. They are without skill in conversation or lovemaking. They are cloth-cap heroes. Exasperated with the lowness of Eliot's heroes, her publisher, Blackwood, paid her the equivocal compliment of saying in a discussion of *Silas Marner*, "You paint so naturally that in your hands the veriest earthworms become most interesting, perfect studies in fact."[1] From earthworms she progressed to radicals, the heroic agitator Felix Holt. Each hero is disqualified in being inappropriate, except in comic or villainous roles, for the ordinary polite novel. None would be acceptable in polite society, nor in that image of polite society, the novel of manners. Eliot's last hero has the ultimate disqualification.

---

1. George Eliot, *The George Eliot Letters*, ed. Gordon S. Haight, 7 vols. (New Haven: Yale University Press, 1954–1955), III, 379.

Rustic workingmen, strange weavers, boorish radicals: none is as completely unthinkable. Even Blackwood would not have imagined she would create a heroic Jew.

Between *Adam Bede* and the three later heroic novels there is an important difference. *Adam Bede* represents a society that is vulnerable and beginning to change, but one in which loyalty and accommodation still remain an alternative. Further, the hero of this acceptable society stands above it as a sample of its best virtues, a condensed expression of the forces and tensions of the society itself. The optimism of the novel's form, Bede's success in love and commerce, gains force from the worth we feel in the general life of Hayslope. On the contrary, community having disappeared in *Silas Marner*, *Felix Holt*, and *Daniel Deronda*, the uprightness and moral clarity of the heroes, as well as the happiness, finally, of their lives, puzzle anyone considering the background of disintegrating values in the novels. The hero is not a product that epitomizes the best of the society, but a solitary who avoids the contamination that seems the only effect the society can have on the self. In each of the three novels, it is the villain, not the hero, who condenses the meanings of actual public life.

Each book ends with peculiar optimism by picturing an ideal marriage: Eppie's to Aaron Winthrop, Felix Holt's to Esther Lyon, and Deronda's to Mirah. But in every case, the marriage follows a symbolic renunciation of society: Eppie refuses to return to her real father and to become heiress to the Cass estates, Esther Lyon refuses the Transome estates, and Deronda chooses to be a Jew instead of an English gentleman. The marriage suggests a peace outside society, not the renewal of society itself.

The heroic novels, *Silas Marner*, *Felix Holt*, and *Daniel Deronda*, are also the three badly flawed by a clear division into two parts. What is, on the surface, a problem of form is in fact deliberate at another level. The need for sharp moral contrast, for dichotomy and antithesis, creates the break in form. To the Marner half is opposed the Cass half, the Transomes balance the Holts, the

Daniel Deronda

Gwendolen Harleth half is distinct from the Deronda half. The simplification in the heroic novels is not an alternative, more comforting version of the events registered in greater complexity in *Middlemarch*, *The Mill on the Floss*, and to some extent in *Romola* and *Adam Bede*. Instead, there is an abbreviated version of a process that changes in later stages into anomaly, inscrutability, and moral ambiguity. About the first stages of this process Eliot had no doubt, and where she deals only with these stages she creates a false impression of completeness and certainty. The process is that of moral growth, and her view never changed of the "moral stupidity" with which we begin. This stupidity is the stage of the egocentric self—absorbed, dramatic, pleasure-seeking. In every novel there is an absolute moral repudiation of this instinctive egoism. By contrast an absolute moral goodness is felt in individual, local acts of duty, generosity, renunciation, and sympathy: in the constriction of both the will and the search for pleasure by means of choices made in terms of perspectives outside the self. In the contrast of these two stages, the simplified novels find their material. Where the novels are divided into halves, these stages are represented in contrasting characters, not as earlier and later phases of the same life.

In her best work, Eliot moves to the next plateau, where what appeared selfless and external becomes the cover for a disguised egoism of which the agent himself can be ignorant. Tom Tulliver's goals are external but riddled with disguised egoism. In a character like Bulstrode, the selfless cause can be the thinnest pretense. Even beyond disguised or unconscious egoism there are the entangled blends of self and selflessness, high and low, seen in characters like Savonarola and Dorothea. At this level the moral judgment is suspended, the moralist gives way to the psychologist.

A clear example of the way the heroic novels simplify by breaking off only the first steps of a process that, elsewhere in Eliot's work, is expanded into realms of moral complexity is the use of Deronda's Jewish cause. Deronda sets off to restore " 'political existence to my people, making them a nation again, giving them a national centre, such as the English have, though they too are scattered over the face of the globe' " (II, 422). He has merged his own future with that of his people. He has found the wider life, the necessity he lacked earlier. He says of the work he will do, " 'that is a task which presents itself to me as a duty . . . I am resolved to devote my life to it' " (II, 422). Compared to the choices of convenience, pleasure, and selfish ease made by Gwendolen, Deronda's goals are pure and elevated. No hesitation exists in the final chapters, no irony suggests he might be selfish, or delighting in the chances of power, or taking a perverse pleasure in the very Jewish identity that had so horrified others that they hid it from him. On the other hand, no clue is given as to how he will carry out his high purposes. The intentions are elevated and he is given credit, as though that were enough.

The deliberate naiveté of the ending appears in striking focus when contrasted to the case of Savonarola, the character who attempts to carry out a vision that in conception was surely as noble as Deronda's. The Florentine monk entered public life to clear Italy of corruption and return both church and state to their former purity. But in *Romola* his career is engaged at a later point. Here we are beyond noble purposes and into actual tactics and possibilities, into the ambiguous relationship of generous idealistic goals to corrupt or simply dubious means, into the opportunism of day-to-day political life, into the unworthy alliances, into the question, finally, of how different really Savonarola is from a man like Tito, whose only goal is power or pleasure. Not only moral clarity, but finally even the distinction between selfish and selfless is lost. Does Savonarola seek power because he will then be able to accomplish his vision, or does he have a vision as one more tactic in a quest for power? Even he, after years of ever deeper ambiguity, no longer knows.

In permitting the rhetorical finish in which Deronda's intentions are taken at full force, Eliot allows what she never permits in her best work: ideas and impulses are judged without pushing the question of what they create or destroy in the widest sense within life. When, in *Middlemarch*, Mr. Brooke announces his political candidacy and his desire for "some reforms," the announcement is only the first pulse of energy. Direct and indirect results, ironies, and predictable effects follow until the event has exhausted itself in the lives of others. In Savonarola, high purpose (also chosen by Deronda) is seen to lead to a transformation, a more complex restatement of the problem of self, not a solution to it. In permitting Deronda's dedication to his new identity to conclude the novel, Eliot creates the dramatic implication that the cause Deronda takes up is a solution and not a renewal of the problem.

The rhetorical use of conclusions that imply solutions, the use, in other words, of dramatic rather than epic conclusions, is another factor in the clarity of the three heroic novels Eliot wrote after *Adam Bede*. *Silas Marner, Felix Holt,* and *Daniel Deronda* all end with ideal marriages, repudiation of the society, and a suggestion of a new life free of the complications as well as of the moral difficulty of the life represented in the novel. And yet this simplicity has no basis. In Eliot's best work, the endings are mixed or tragic. At best they promise a continued set of chances and errors.

Alongside the moral simplifications, and based equally on a relaxation of pressure, is the unfinished quality that can be felt immediately in the final novel. In *Daniel Deronda* the results of this incompleteness can be seen in the narration rather than dramatization of material. The novel contains many chapters of advice, confession, or encapsulated history. Further, the lack of finish is visible in the numerous false starts and undeveloped material, and most obviously in the clumsy and glaring symbolism.

Typical of the false starts and undeveloped material are the cases of Klesmer, Rex, and Hans Meyrick. Initially, the marriage between Klesmer and Catherine Arrowpoint is developed to contrast with Gwendolen's marriage to Grandcourt. An entire chapter narrates the history of the relationship up to the announcement to the parents. We learn nothing more of the marriage. After an initial development of Klesmer that suggests important parallels to Mordecai, he disappears except for an incidental moment in the second half of the novel. Similarly, Rex Gascoigne, contrasted with Grandcourt as a suitor of Gwendolen's, seems a character whose growth, like that of Fred Vincy in *Middlemarch*, will run as a thread through the novel, but after his failure with Gwendolen and his recovery, he is dropped. With Hans Meyrick, again, there is a suggestion of a study of a shallow cynicism, an artificiality of sentiment, and a willingness to use others that is combined with a painter's dedication to beauty and effect. But only a tedious letter to Deronda and the absurd scene where he stumbles in after a period of dissipation with opium, develop the character after it is introduced.

Of the circle so carefully created around Gwendolen in the first twenty-five chapters, no character has any use in the rest of the novel. Mrs. Danilow, Rex Gascoigne, Klesmer, Catherine Arrowpoint—all vanish or make only token appearances in the remaining fifty chapters. In the first third of the novel, the strategy of *Middlemarch* can be felt. Multiple lives and stories are set out in a pattern of flexible contrasts that can be progressively deepened by sheer addition. That nothing is done to keep alive the periphery of *Daniel Deronda* as the attention centers on the closet dramas of Gwendolen and Deronda deprives Eliot of her most powerful psychological tool. It is only in reading *Daniel Deronda* that one can see how much of the depth of *Middlemarch* is depth not at the center but at the periphery. It is the series of delicately handled emotional surprises involving our feelings about such figures as Farebrother and Brooke, Casaubon and Sir James Chettam, that give the novel its massive psychological accuracy. Equally, it is the author's ability to revitalize and extend in unexpected directions her basic symbolic patterns, rather than the central accuracy of those patterns in their primitive allegorical form, that testifies to her ingenious control over the texture of her novel.

209
Daniel Deronda

In *Daniel Deronda*, Eliot substitutes for the careful shading of
alternatives a kind of profundity gained by the disturbing practice
of using identical symbolic patterns for morally opposite situations.
After developing a series of events in which power and submission
are morally evil, as they are in the power Grandcourt holds over
Gwendolen or Mirah's father over her, the novel moves toward a
submission of Deronda to the fanatical power of Mordecai. Frequently, identical symbols have opposite moral meanings: both
Grandcourt and Deronda are linked to boats. In Grandcourt's case
the boat is an island of absolute power and emptiness. In Deronda's
it is a solitude that opens him to profound identifications of an
unexpected kind. He is first seen by Mordecai as the "intended"
one when, as he stands on a bridge, he sees Deronda rowing toward
him. The box of poisoned diamonds given to Gwendolen is later
mirrored by the trunk of papers, also a family inheritance held
temporarily by the wrong person, given to Deronda in Mainz.
Even the central notion of acting seen again and again as a deception or deliberate emptying of the self, is given a sudden inversion
in the rhapsodic role of Mordecai and his assumption that Deronda
can carry out exactly this "other self."

Clearly one of Eliot's goals is to create a series of disturbing
analogues in the novel by means of formal links between opposed
acts and characters. The novel ends with the deaths of Grandcourt
and Mordecai: the extreme of negation and boredom vanishes
along with the extreme of enthusiasm and creation. But in effect
what is cancelled is the idea of extremity itself, along with the kind
of power over another and absorbtion of the life of another that
characterizes both Grandcourt's relation to Gwendolen and Mordecai's intended relation to Deronda.

This technique of Eliot's might well be called symbolic dis-
sonance, and it is the major one in the novel once the *Middlemarch*
technique of delicately shaded differences and expansive reinterpretation is abandoned after the novel's first twenty-five chapters.
The sign of this change of focus is the diminution of Hans Mey-

rick, Rex Gascoigne, Mrs. Danilow, Catherine Arrowpoint, and Klesmer.

Were it only such lesser and, with the exception of Klesmer, predictable characters that remained unused, the problem would be a minor one. But, in the cases of Deronda's mother and Mirah's father, Eliot created unique and essential parts of the texture of her novel, only to fail to find any use for them. Like many of the most important parts (including the climactic scene on the yacht), Deronda's mother's story is presented in retrospective narration, in one of the many static scenes where one character sits down to tell another of his past history. The story is summarized on the evening of her first meeting with her son in twenty years. The circumstances frame and distort the complexities of the story by revealing them within the sentiment and melodrama, the regret and final defiance that this extraordinary meeting guarantees. The story itself is a painful narrative of choice, of the choice to be oneself, of the cost, and of the endless doubt that follows rebellion. Of equal importance for the thematic concerns of the novel, it is a story of a life lived within art, and for that reason, particularly in the absence of any development of Klesmer's life, it is a crucial pattern of dedication and enthusiasm, an alternative to the life of social and political goals embodied by Mordecai. The old woman's relationship to her father, her own abandonment of her son, her attempt to choose her own life and her son's heritage: all are essential and intricate, touching on the central concerns of the novel. The material, like the character, appears in a single chapter; Deronda never mentions his mother again, nor does he seem to think of her. What both he and the novel find most important is the location of the trunk the old woman tells Deronda he will find in Mainz. The trunk is the one detail of the material that is elaborated and persists through the later chapters.

Mirah's early life with her father, that Dostoevskian man, exists also as a retrospective, framed narrative, a history she tells Mrs. Meyrick after Deronda has rescued her. The dangers and terrors of Mirah's life with the man who used her as a resource he could exploit in any direction he could imagine are neutralized when the story is told in the secure comfort of the Meyrick home. Again it is a story of tyranny and rebellion, of life within art; a family story that defines an extreme of exploitation and submission. When the father later appears in the action of the novel itself, he is only the palest remnant of the figure we see in Mirah's narrative.

In both cases, essential material is blunted in presentation, offered at several removes, evoked and then discarded. The climax of Gwendolen's marriage, the scene on the boat, is recounted in a conversation with Deronda. And yet it is narrated on the evening of the event itself, so that her manner is hysterical and frantic. As a result, the event has neither immediacy nor distance, neither the complex feeling of the moment itself nor the opportunity for reflection and analysis that an account given a week later would have. The six scenes between Deronda and Gwendolen in the second half of the novel all have the same mechanical structure: wise counsel, immediate understanding, and moral perfection on the one side; a helplessness, confusion, and sin on the other.

A final important side of the artistic incompleteness of the novel is apparent in the symbolism. The use of archery throughout the love section of the book underlines the simple lack of action in many parts of the novel. Even more important, it exemplifies Eliot's inability to evoke the texture of the lives of the characters she creates. As a shortcut to the arduous realistic detail that "places" a character, she poses them in highly symbolic, obvious situations. We see Gwendolen at an archery contest or gambling. In the novel no character is in fact a gambler, not even Mirah's father, and yet, because of the use made of the metaphor of gambling, the need is felt to pose a character in a casino surrounded by an assortment of types easily evoked and quickly forgotten. To compare the equally brief but perfectly felt scene of Lydgate's gambling in *Middlemarch,* or the use of gambling as a characterizing detail for Farebrother, is to see how blatant the set-piece opening of *Daniel Deronda* is. Similarly the career of acting, while rich with meanings, is empty of instances in the novel. By way of contrast, Lydgate's medical career, while equally rich in meaning, leads to the concrete medical scenes of Fred's illness, the treatment of Casaubon, the debates about the hospital, the advice to Rosamond about riding, and the climactic mishandling of Raffles. It is one thing to apply, like a costume, meaningful occupations like actor, doctor, and gambler to characters in a novel. It is an entirely different level of accomplishment to impel the momentum of action and make concrete the pattern of daily life by means of those very elements that have symbolic weight.

The many objects of the novel have the same allegorical half-existence the activities have. The diamonds Mrs. Glasher sends Gwendolen on her wedding day, the trunk Deronda goes to Mainz to recover, the boats and horses: each object symbolizes meaning that only action can give any importance to. Where action exists, as it does in the case of Grandcourt's pleasure in mastery, the physical symbol—the whip—is superfluous and crude. Most frequently, the symbolic object substitutes for action. By the end of the novel, we have learned nothing of what is in Deronda's trunk. We are told there are papers in a number of languages, and that the box itself is richly carved with Arabic inscriptions. It is, or rather it symbolizes, Deronda's heritage, his Jewish past, his continuity with his people through the materials assembled by his grandfather. In abstract language the trunk contains society, Deronda's society and the promise of the nation he must work to bring into existence. The trunk is his identity, or it stands for his identity, because in the language of the novel identity is partly reached through identification, the ability to merge onself with an outside force. "It was as if he had found an added soul in finding his ancestry" (II, 360). The trunk is the symbol of this second soul, no matter what it has inside.

A measure of the progressive weakening of the reality of society in Eliot's work can be seen in the contrast of Deronda's trunk with the box in which Hetty stored her jewels and keepsakes in *Adam Bede.* Hetty's box was one of the few spaces immune from the eyes of society, a place to conceal the materials of her fantasy existence. Society in *Adam Bede* rules everywhere but the secluded woods and the deliberately concealed theatrical performances Hetty created for herself in her room. Even in those places, only a short time remains before society discovers, judges, and readjusts itself. The materials for a fantasy self are hidden in a box because the strength of society is such that it will destroy any unreality it discovers. By way of contrast, Deronda's trunk is the fantasy, the "vision" as the novel calls it, of society. Society, once all-powerful except for one trunk, has now shrunk so that it is only present in the locked, ornamental trunk. Mere personal life, the ethical style of self-referent choice, the individualism based on the right to self-realization that has the life of the artist as its supreme and supremely anomalous expression: this is the only life in *Daniel Deronda.* Hetty's acting in front of her mirror is now the acting that everywhere defines public life in *Daniel Deronda.* Acting has replaced working, replaced, that is, the round of tasks that in Eliot's first novel noted and stabilized one's place and therefore one's identity. In *Daniel Deronda* no one has a place, each has only a role. The vocabulary of acting applies to all social life. And just as "place" meant both social occupation and fixed home in Eliot's early novel, so, too, role is both social position and an index of the temporary and homeless quality of public life in her final one.

No society exists, and only the Jews, with their family structure and religion, their care to preserve their heritage, their "added soul" that comes from identification—only they have even the impulses out of which a society might be built. The trunk Deronda finds in Mainz is part of this heritage, but what, for him, does this heritage involve? He makes it plain he will not believe in the religion, and the trunk amounts to only an abstract heritage since he learns of no actual, living relatives.

Like the gambling, the archery, and the diamonds Mrs. Glasher sends before disappearing like so many other characters from the novel, the trunk symbolizes part of the intended meaning without partaking of the texture of life in the novel. When needed it is invented; once expounded it is forgotten. Of Eliot's novels only *Romola* is as cluttered with allegorical set pieces and heavy-handed symbolism. What does, however, exist in finished form is the material for a disturbing treatment of the alternatives of individual style after the loss of society. Most striking is the central contrast of the life of art and the life of visionary social reconstruction. Both art and visionary politics are lives of intensity and enthusiasm. Therefore either life defeats the sterile boredom and negativity centered on Grandcourt, gambling, and the empty mobility of social life. In the character of Mordecai, who is at once a rhapsodic poet and a visionary political thinker, Eliot has blended the two realms. By means of Mordecai she suggests that the highest art is only a temporarily unrealizable politics, a vision that is articulated because it would be premature to enact it. When Deronda takes up the task upon Mordecai's death, action replaces song.

However blended in Mordecai, political vision and art, the bonds of society and the claims of art, are opposed in the novel as a whole. Art is defined by performance and is contrasted with the social. The undeveloped characters of Hans Meyrick and Rex Gascoigne were perhaps intended to map out the youthful version of these two worlds. Rex, who considers the pioneer life of the colonies and ends up in the law, represents the two social roles: founding societies and maintaining already established ones by means of the law. Hans, on the other side, represents the callow young artist whose sense of beauty and bohemian experiments trace the first stages of artistic egoism.

In its mature form, the world of art is defined as singing and acting, whether in the commercial and sordid form of Mirah's life with her father or in the exalted theatrical life of Deronda's mother, or even in the local aristocratic world of musical evenings and charades. All share the vocabulary of acting and roles, a vocabulary

Daniel Deronda

that is morally tainted in the novel. It is Gwendolen who must always act her part and perform as Grandcourt's wife, making entrances and appearances in a simulation of marriage. On the opposite side, Mirah is dismissed by someone in the theater with the statement, " 'She will never be an artist: she has no notion of being anybody but herself' " (I, 218).

The three symbolic components of Gwendolen's life are performing, mastering, and gambling. Each is anchored in a tableau-like scene, and each reaches down into the central moral evils of the novel: pleasure in deception, pleasure in the conquest of another, and pleasure in the losses of another. The world of lies and secrets is linked to performance through Mirah's father, but it is more disturbingly tied to the great singer, who withholds from him the truth about his origin, his religion, and even his name. Deception, whether for sordid gain or in the name of the most daring idea of individual freedom, is allied to art.

It is important to note that the many secrets, deceptions, and lies of *Daniel Deronda* are closest to the detective elements of *Felix Holt* and *Silas Marner*. The far richer notions of fiction and hypothesis that dominate *Romola* and *Middlemarch* are missing in Eliot's final novel. There is no equivalent for the complex sense of truth introduced by means of medicine and the analysis of language in *Middlemarch*. The theater and the acting profession are allied to all that is mose treacherous in social life. Grandcourt is the most accomplished full-time actor of the novel, and his life is a paradigm of cruelty, negation, and secrecy. His real family, like that of Tito in *Romola*, is a secret, hidden family. His formal marriage is a performance for the world.

In the world of the theater, deception is the basis of art itself, and the destruction or exploitation of family is closely tied to the possibility of survival in a career. Thus, in one of her greatest roles, Deronda's mother asks Sir Hugo to *act* as Deronda's father and to bring him up in the *role* of an English gentleman. Similarly, in one of his only great performances, Mirah's father takes her to Prague, pretending there was an engagement there in order to sell her to the count who wants her as a mistress. Beyond the theater, Eliot embodies art only in the shallow and exaggerated young painter, Hans Meyrick, and in the only partially developed figure of the composer Klesmer.

Opposed to the artists is the equally surprising development of society by means of the Jews. In the choice of the Jews—those traditional others, along with gypsies and criminals, throughout the history of the novel—as the only group for whom even the possibility of society exists, the novel has set out the idea not of constructing society in the manner of *Middlemarch*, but of recovering the exact society that has been scattered into fragments, as the Jewish people were scattered by the fall of Jerusalem. The mystery of the Jews that is essential to the novel is that they have remained a people even though they are no longer a concrete society, no longer a nation. The "added soul" registers the fact that, when conquered and dispersed, the Jews did not become individuals, purely personal beings, but internalized—even, we might say, memorized—the values of national life to the extent that that life became portable and finally indestructible. Not individuals, they are fragments of a social order ready to reassemble at a moment's notice: the society they carry in their heads and trunks can write itself out in forms, architecture, institutions, customs, and traditions. The stubborn continuity of reverence and ceremony, family loyalty, and prophesy, all neatly traced in the family of the pawnbroker, Cohen, demonstrates that what seems from one point of view to have disappeared has only become latent and discreet.

It is because a form of society has in fact remained intact among the Jews that Deronda's project to restore a national life makes sense. The geography of society, the politics and economics—what in the Burkean sense are the superficial elements—are all that are lacking. The Jews, however, are a unique case. Their society destroyed by external enemies, their national life one with religion and elaborate tradition, they are tribe and church and nation. The rhapsodic poems Mordecai writes come out of a generalized emotion reached only when identification is complete. His experience of exile and anticipation recapitulate the experience of his people. The emotion has the public quality, the abstraction of prophesy and lament, in which the singer transfers or represents emotions he did not originate but that he has felt as though they were personal experience. That this generalized fate insists on patterning everyone's life, and in so doing blights as often as it creates, can be seen in the example of Deronda's mother. Crushed by the narrow role the heritage insisted she accept as a Jewish woman, she denied that heritage in herself and attempted to hide it from her son. In the second goal she fails, and Deronda becomes the Jew his grandfather had wanted. But the personal claim she represents challenges the otherwise completely unquestioned drive toward identification and submission. In a more complex novel, Deronda's mother would have been as prominent as Mordecai, and the choice Deronda makes would have been troubled by the complex appeal of both lives.

The Evil of Negation

Just as *Romola*, in spite of its many simplifications, retains a complexity centered on the character of Savonarola, so too *Daniel Deronda* is raised above the level of the other two heroic novels, *Silas Marner* and *Flexib Holt*, by an intricate pattern of alternatives that begin to appear once Grandcourt, the central character, is considered. With him, Eliot's sense of moral evil moves onto an entirely new plane. In her early novels, the essential contrast is between those who can forget the self and those whose need for pleasure or fantasy rules their lives. Hetty, Arthur, and Godfrey and Dunstan Cass are the types of moral evil in the first novels. When one element of what was always present in the early sense of evil moves to the center, we have the more interesting notion of evil as any withholding, any hoarding, or any valuing of a project or fantasy over the common life. Pleasure, too, is a private world, but no one would think of Casaubon or Bulstrode as given over to that. In each case there is a choice, whether for pleasure over duty or for some part of life at the expense of life in general. The misers, after all, love their gold, associating it with religious or sexual values expending on it a wealth of internal resources. The fantasy world that begins in unreality and ends in combat with the real world is equally an object of effort and care. Rosamond Vincy has an enthusiasm for the pretenses of her life, an avidity about extending her sovereignty that is, in a distorted way, a compliment to life. Even Tito relishes power and the pleasures of Florentine life. No character in Eliot's earlier work prepares for Grandcourt, the man in league with nothingness, boredom, contempt, and negativity. Whereas in Arthur, Hetty, Tito, Casaubon, Peter Featherstone, Bulstrode, or Rosamond Vincy the force of life is redirected, in Grandcourt that force itself is the enemy.

Throughout *Daniel Deronda*, stress is placed on the type of sudden look that estimates value. Deronda's glance in the gambling casino is felt by Gwendolen as a claim on her, an insistence that she be a better self. Thereafter she feels she is living under the scrutiny of that glance, thinking of every act in the light of whether he would show contempt or admiration for it. "She had learned to see all her acts through the impression they would make on Deronda" (II, 286). His scrutiny and the demand it suggests will, the novel seems to promise, finally create in her the self he assumes she might become.

But where the glance and the assumption it communicates can create, it can equally destroy, wither, and guarantee the minimum it will then use to justify its contempt. This notion of destruction as moral evil goes far beyond what in *Middlemarch* we have as the withholding from common life or the diffidence that is too cautious to risk creation. As active as creation itself, Grandcourt's life has its own intensity. Even lethargy can be strenuous. "He lingered on the terrace, in the gambling rooms, in the reading-room occupying himself in being indifferent to everybody and everything around him" (I, 287). With Grandcourt, to name is to degrade: places are

Daniel Deronda

"kennels"; most other people fall into one of two classes, "brutes" or "bores"; and most feelings and ideas are called "some nonsense." A man of "refined negations" (II, 383), he amounts to a translation of life itself into a kind of spiritual antimatter. To describe him Gwendolen is forced to use negations. "He is not ridiculous" (I, 111), she decides after their first meeting where he amused her by listing the number of pleasures he had given up or could do without. Eliot's own introduction of him lists the string of qualities he is free of.

> There was not the faintest smile on his face as he looked at her, not a trace of self-consciousness or anxiety in his bearing; when he raised his hat he showed an extensive baldness surrounded with a mere fringe of reddish-blond hair, but he also showed a perfect hand. . . . It was not possible for a human aspect to be freer from grimace or solicitous wigglings; also it was perhaps not possible for a breathing man wide awake to look less animated.

His eyes expressed "nothing but indifference" (I, 111).

Grandcourt is by no means presented as a unique moral accident. "Still, the English fondness for reserve will account for much negation; and Grandcourt's manners with an extra veil of reserve over them might be expected to present the extreme type of the national taste" (II, 16). Just as the enthusiasm and intensity of Mordecai, his ardor and idealism, are meant to focus on the extremes of the Jewish national character, so too Grandcourt's studied superiority to surprise and even interest is an extension of the English *nil admirari* and suspicion of "enthusiasts."

Where Grandcourt walks there is always nothing, and he always insists on walking.

> Here Grandcourt, who stood with Gwendolen outside the group, turned deliberately, and fixing his eyes on a knoll

planted with American shrubs, and having a winding path
up to it, said languidly—
"This is a bore. Shall we go up there?"
"Oh, certainly—since we are exploring," said Gwendolen.
She was rather pleased, and yet afraid.
The path was too narrow for him to offer his arm, and they
walked up in silence. When they were on the bit of platform
at the summit, Grandcourt said—
"There is nothing to be seen here: the thing was not worth
climbing." (I, 136)

In his presence the world itself becomes invisible, and, while
Gwendolen lives her moral life under Deronda's gaze, it is Grandcourt's "refined negations" that she chooses and endures.

The beings closest to us, whether in love or hate, are often
virtually our interpreters of the world, and some feather-
headed gentleman or lady whom in passing we regret to take
as legal tender for a human being may be acting as a melan-
choly theory of life in the minds of those who live with
them—like a piece of yellow and wavy glass that distorts
form and makes colour an affliction. Their trivial sentences,
their petty standards, their low suspicions, their loveless
ennui, may be making somebody else's life no better than a
promenade through a pantheon of ugly idols. Gwendolen
had that kind of window before her. (II, 285)

Grandcourt is happiest on the yacht, his prisoner at hand to gloat
over, the yacht surrounded by nothing, empty sea and sky.
Were Grandcourt bored and lethargic, slowly sinking into a
deathlike isolated existence, he would be of no interest. But his
indifference conceals the keenest attention: no man could be more
alert to Gwendolen's every move than Grandcourt. No man is
more drawn to vitality as a challenge than Grandcourt. He marries

Daniel Deronda

Gwendolen because she seems willful, able to resist or at least struggle in an amusing way. She is the center of the little world, its more glamorous treasure. His negativity senses this vitality as an opposition, a spirit to be broken and exhausted. She appeals to his sense of power, as the imagery suggests, in the way wild animals reduced to comical performances in a circus appeal to the Grandcourt in every man.

> She had been brought to accept him in spite of everything— brought to kneel down like a horse under training for the arena, though she might have an objection to it all the while. On the whole Grandcourt got more pleasure out of this notion than he would have done out of winning a girl of whom he was sure that she had a strong inclination for him personally. And yet this pleasure in mastering reluctance flourished along with the habitual persuasion that no woman whom he favoured could be quite indifferent to his personal influence. (I, 328)

In the recurrent imagery of trained animals in the novel, there is a reminder of the casual way in which the pleasures of the negative are accepted in society, the universal pleasure of seeing life and force cramped for satisfactions that are gratuitous except for the delight they give to the sense of mastery.

For Grandcourt the yacht is the absolute domain, a "plank-island" (II, 282) where his victory is complete. He has withdrawn Gwendolen from those she gives pleasure to and from the sources of her own pleasure. On the yacht he indulges in the psychological pleasures of mastery and opposition, the pure enjoyment of his ability to sense what Gwendolen wants and frustrate it. In its own way, Grandcourt's life is strenuous because his desire for mastery is aroused only by worthy opponents. He needs to sense life in order to experience the pleasures of his contempt for it. His death is equally negative: he is not rescued.

Making Up Society

Like so many of Eliot's earlier novels, *Daniel Deronda* has as its climax a highly ambiguous moral act, one for which judgment is nearly impossible. The progressive sequence from Hetty's abandonment of her child in *Adam Bede*, to Maggie's loss of reputation in *The Mill on the Floss*, to Holt's murder in *Felix Holt*, to Lydgate and Bulstrode's part in Raffles's death in *Middlemarch*, to Gwendolen's responsibility in not trying to rescue Grandcourt, shows a refined interiorization of the elements of legal, moral, and psychological responsibility and retribution.

The spirit represented by Grandcourt exaggerates what is essential elsewhere in the social life of the novel. Symbolically, Grandcourt stands to inherit everything, all Sir Hugo's estates. Should enough convenient deaths occur, he would be a baron. His detached superiority and love for idle power are equally important in the character of Gwendolen, or in the lives of the gamblers who go to the tables not out of passion but in search of it. What Gwendolen delights in about Grandcourt at first is the opportunity she will have to reject him: "And it began to appear probable that she would have it in her power to reject him, whence there was a pleasure in reckoning up the advantages which would make her rejection splendid, and in giving Mr. Grandcourt his utmost value" (I, 122). Mirah's father, the one Jew to have renounced whatever of his heritage couldn't be sold, had the habit of amusing friends by mimicking the movements and tones of Jewish prayer.

With its analysis of gambling and the pleasures of mastery, the novel identifies this negative life with a set of profound urges. As usual in the novel, Deronda himself finally explains what the image of gambling is meant to symbolize.

> "And besides there is something revolting to me in raking a heap of money together and internally chuckling over it, when others are feeling the loss of it. I should even call it base, if it were more than an exceptional lapse. There are enough inevitable turns of fortune which force use to see that our

gain is another's loss—that is one of the ugly aspects of life. One would like to reduce it as much as one could *not get amusement out of exaggerating it.*" (I, 346, emphasis added)

Gambling and riding are two of the remaining ceremonies of life. Both show a fascination with what is inevitable and irreducible of the ugliness of life, mastery, and fortune. In both exercises a conscious pleasure is taken in elaborating and civilizing this inevitable evil. At last both are games. Gambling speeds up and manipulates the force of chance in life, and it does so to create a depraved amusement. The pleasure in horses is shown as a similar depraved amusement, savoring what should be regretted, exaggerating what should be minimized. When Gwendolen accepts Grandcourt's proposal he takes her to the window. "They could see the two horses being taken slowly round the sweep, and the beautiful creatures, in their fine grooming, sent a thrill of exultation through Gwendolen. They were the symbols of command and luxury" (I, 314). The appeal lies in the image of the horses led slowly around the sweep, of animal power subdued and waiting for the human command.

After her marriage, Gwendolen's choices reduce themselves to those suggested by the imagery of this life. "By-and-by she promised herself that she should get used to her heart-sores, and find excitements that would carry her through life, as a hard gallop carried her through some of the morning hours. There was gambling: she had heard stories at Leubronn of fashionable women who gambled in all sorts of ways. It seemed very flat to her at this distance, but perhaps if she began to gamble again, the passion might awake. Then there was the pleasure of producing an effect by her appearance in society" (II, 32). Against this life, the life of Grandcourt's world, the novel proposes the alternative to Deronda. Grandcourt's refined negations are contrasted with Deronda's fervor; to Grandcourt's contempt that finds everything tedious, the novel makes at least a claim for Deronda's generous, poetic sense of life. "To say that Deronda was romantic would be to misrepresent him; but under his calm and somewhat self-repressed exterior there was a fervour which made him easily find poetry and romance among the events of everyday life" (I, 209). For what we see in the novel, however, this is no more than a claim. Never is the romantic sense of life realized and articulated in action in the way Grandcourt's negativity is. Instead, Deronda is shown carrying out a series of rescues. To sense the importance of the idea of rescue in the novel it is sufficient to see that, on the boat, at the climax of the novel, what Gwendolen does is to refuse to rescue Grandcourt. She does not cause his death, and perhaps she might not have been able to prevent it, but, at the crucial moment, she refuses to throw the rope, refuses to live out the illusions of a human bond with the man.

Deronda, on the other hand, is almost a professional rescuer. When Hans Meyrick's eyesight puts him in danger of failing to get a fellowship he badly needs, Deronda gives up his own chances to help Meyrick through. In the course of the novel, he rescues Mirah from suicide, Mordecai from poverty, and Gwendolen from the negative life. Eliot summarizes him with special attention to what is almost a need to rescue. "Persons attracted him, as Hans Meyrick had done, in proportion to the possibility of his defending them, rescuing them, telling upon their lives with some sort of redeeming influence; and he had to resist an inclination, easily accounted for, to withdraw coldly from the fortunate" (I, 333). Rescue is a sudden, heroic gesture, not the continuous, creative pressure that Eliot's description of the romantic personality would suggest. Looking back at *Middlemarch*, where the romantic pressure is fully visible, we can see both what Eliot meant by the romantic and why she became impatient with it. The results of generous, local, undramatic, creative pressure are mixed, and they are local. The prominence of moral evil, the blight on life in *Daniel Deronda*, suggests that the only alternative is some new beginning, a new society that is indifferent to the fact that it is the illegitimate son of Grandcourt who inherits the old. The extreme pessimism leads to an exaggerated optimism about the chances of a new start. It leads as well to an indifference to the small pressures of the good man. Instead there is an attempt to outflank the problem by offering the chance to create a nation elsewhere. To this extent, it is not the romantic that opposes the negativity of Grandcourt but the enthusiast: not Deronda but Mordecai.

For Gwendolen, and, to an unpleasant extent, for every character in the novel, moral growth reduces itself to submission. Her choice is between submitting to Deronda and submitting to Grandcourt; no independent course ever exists. When poverty strikes her family, she refuses to submit. "She did not mean to submit and let misfortune do what it would with her" (I, 235). Instead she marries Grandcourt, whom she imagines she can master. But Grandcourt, of course, masters her. "In any case she would have to submit; and he enjoyed thinking of her as his future wife, whose pride and spirit were suited to command every one but himself" (I, 328). By his death Gwendolen is freed; now she can submit to Deronda. Humble, silent, waiting on his judgment, she is, if anything, less morally pleasing than when she was defiant, lively, and egocentric. Of each character we learn first of all whether or not he or she has submitted. Deronda's mother would not submit to her role as a Jewish woman. Mrs. Meyrick describes Mirah after hearing her story: " 'It is not in her nature to run into planning and devising: only to submit. See how she submitted to that father!' " (I, 229). For Deronda the choice is whether or not to submit to Mordecai, to the vision of his future the other man holds out. Similarly, it is important that most of the artists in the novel are interpretive artists, actors, singers, and musicians. The performer submerges his identity into that of the work; he submits in order to incarnate the work of another. This is what Deronda agrees to do with Mordecai's vision.

In the discussion of *Romola*, I have noted the rather unpleasant stress on relations of mastery and submission in Eliot's work. In her final novel, such relations have eclipsed those of love and equality completely. The essential, good relationships are those of Gwendolen and Deronda, and of Deronda and Mordecai. But nowhere are there scenes of positive love between Deronda and Mirah (or between any man and woman in the novel) equal to those between Deronda and Mordecai. The relationship between the two men is described as a marriage. When Deronda returns after learning that he is a Jew, he seems at first to be proposing marriage to Mordecai.

> "I have a joy which will remain to us even in the worst trouble. I did not tell you the reason of my journey abroad, because—never mind—I went to learn my parentage. And you were right. I am a Jew."
>
> The two men clasped hands with a movement that seemed part of the flash from Mordecai's eyes, and passed through Mirah like an electric shock. But Deronda went on without pause, speaking from Mordecai's mind as much as from his own—
>
> "We have the same people. Our souls have the same vocation. We shall not be separated by life or by death." (II, 363)

Later Mordecai speaks, using the word "marriage" directly.

> "It has already begun—the marriage of our souls. It waits but the passing away of this body, and then they who are betrothed shall unite in a stricter bond, and what is mine shall be thine." (II, 367)

The sacred relationship is that of discipleship, complete spiritual submission of the energy of one life to the purposes of another, "so Deronda might receive from Mordecai's mind the complete ideal shape of that personal duty and citizenship which lay in his own thought like sculptured fragments" (I, 119). The image of the

Daniel Deronda

moral life as a chain of masters and followers who are, in their turn, masters to other followers is a disturbing one because of the assumption of absolute goodness that makes submission reasonable. The scenes between Deronda and Gwendolen, with their invariable helpless questions and clear-sighted, selfless replies, show the mechanics of this relationship.

The inconspicuousness of Deronda's wife Mirah and the absolute harrowing Gwendolen endures in her marriage underline the tendency for sexual relationships to be either inessential or filled with horror. With this the novel draws close to *Silas Marner* and *Romola*, both of which ended with what might be called "holy families." The death of Mordecai does leave Deronda to live out his life with Mirah, but she, we learn in the final chapter, appeals most to his force of "blessed protectedness" (II, 427).

The muted quality of the ending is appropriate both to the tame brother-and-sister affection that Eliot portrays between Deronda and Mirah and to the very limited scale of hope that can be claimed for Deronda's project. He will do "something" for his people. He will return to England, he tells Gwendolen, "if I live—*some time*" (II, 422). The actual mood of the ending is determined by the sublime death on the final page, the transfiguration of Mordecai. In this strange novel of property of all kinds, only vision has its rightful heir and only missions are left to be taken up once both roles and places have vanished. Eliot's novels begin with the losing of society. Her central and epic novels provide what is still the best account of the making up of society. Her final novel removes the reality of society to the future where it can only be hoped for or anticipated. Society, which at the start of her work is a rich arena of memory and in the middle a strenuous project of active life, is, in this final work, the most remote of dreams.

9

Social Knowledge

For the social moralist, changes in society appear first as new conditions of awareness, as a new balance between obscurity and legibility in behavior. As society is transformed, the possibilities of knowledge contract and expand, writing the fate of comprehension and equally of those feelings based on understanding. To write of George Eliot as a social moralist is to reach for the point where three lines of primary concern join in her work. These are moral choice, knowledge, and society. Because the pattern of a life is generated by crises demanding moral choice and response, any question of choice is at the same time a question of knowledge —a question, that is, of the conditions under which complete, genuine knowledge of alternatives and implications might exist. For Eliot, reliable knowledge is not derived from introspection and does not depend on skill at self-analysis, on candor and sincerity about and within oneself. Such knowledge is not private, and certainly is not a discipline of a heroic or privileged kind. Any matter of knowledge is a question of society, of knowledge of others, and of the reliability of their knowledge and judgment of oneself. Moral choice, knowledge, and society, as this book has tried to demonstrate, are elements of a single process. The three together are the grounds of character, the medium of selfhood.

The word *social* and the term *social moralist* points to the public character of judgment and knowledge. Our moral tradition insists that sophistication, nuance of motive and result, and awareness of levels within motive and act multiply as we consider events from within. The vocabularies of our moral life are interior, as are our procedures. Examination of conscience, introspection, self-analysis: the private and basically religious character of such activities separates them from the coarse, undeveloped public reconstruction of behavior. In a Confucian or Aristotelian society, the reverse would be true: public strategies, of which the Chinese self-analysis and criticism is the best example, would dominate and force the meanings of acts. Introspective moralists live or die on the question of honesty, but for the social moralist all honesty, even the most heroic, comes to expression already sabotaged by self-interest, by egoism, by pride and false consciousness.

Throughout this study, I have tried to show the elements of public knowledge hidden within the most interior of events. Equally, I have tried to show the failures of that knowledge, particularly those guaranteed by the conditions of society itself.

If one part of the term *social moralist* underlines the public nature of moral ilfe, the other part—the word *moralist*—points to the equally essential fact that what is critical for the novelist in society and history is the way each creates or distorts moral life. George Eliot is equally a social *moralist*. It is the range of experience possible in a society at one moment of history that permits or frustrates that condensation of moral being we call, from the point of view of the self, character, and from that of society, reputation. What makes both character and reputation anomalous is primarily the failure of life to supply crisis, the failure of potential moral being to encounter events pure and decisive enough to allow that condensation to take place.

The opening of *Middlemarch* contrasts Dorothea and St. Theresa. In what at first seems only a contrast of magnitude, Eliot speaks of those who "have found no Epic life" (p. 3). But far more than scale is lost; the difficulty is not simply of realizing impulses in miniature in a domestic rather than public medium. In fact, the failure is to encounter the critical events on any level. Life fails to register the potential moral being of Dorothea or registers it at an angle so oblique that it becomes unrecognizable. Maggie Tulliver, Savonarola, and Felix Holt carry equally distorted characters and reputations in the absence of the complex provocations of experience. Those called out by events (their characters literally *evoked* by crisis), Adam Bede, Tom Tulliver, Bulstrode, and Deronda, are those clarified by experience, by a medium of adequate experience. They reach the meeting point of being and knowledge, character and reputation, through the progressive refinement of circumstance, a refinement joined at every point to a process of revelation that makes public the stages of creation.

The events of Silas Marner's life present the simplest example. The loss of the familiar world of the Lantern Yard destroys his legibility to others until, in his new home, he becomes an isolated, mysterious stranger, his life confused and jumbled in even his own mind. The events that follow release and distinguish his potential being. Experience articulates his character. His work, then his hoarding, the theft of his hoard, the discovery of the child, the near loss of the child, and the final recovery of the money: each catastrophe is a refining fire, an appropriate fate that creates visible character in the act of testing and expressing it. The progressive substitutions of work, gold, and child preserve and develop being while progressively distinguishing the essential from the accidental. What endures is fierce devotion and the need for an object outside the self. The gold allows Marner to exercise his affection and need to love. His attachment grows even in the experience of false objects. Chance substitutes a more worthy object and the already developed devotion can be clarified as a human love only temporarily disguised as avarice. Marner's fate is appropriate because it supplies the means to make essential distinctions of character.

In *The Mill on the Floss*, the identical events clarify and design the elements of one character while confounding those of a second. Every crisis of the novel—the family bankruptcy that forces the

Social Knowledge

children home, the hatred for the Wakems, the threat to the home, the relationships of Maggie to Philip and Stephen—offers Tom the chance to clarify and make solid his character. He is more himself and more visibly himself through the definition each event permits him, definitions of reaction or moral response. Yet the identical events obscure and confuse Maggie's being. Life dresses her in someone else's clothes. Fate will not supply her with defining events. Under oblique and inappropriate tests (the same tests that matched the resources of Tom's being), she becomes more puzzling to others, more invisible, progressively denatured.

In *Middlemarch*, the catastrophes evoke definition, that special gift of focus and register, in Fred Vincy and Bulstrode, while undermining and obscuring Dorothea and Lydgate. The accidents that compose the gain or loss of the chance to have a fate (an action with events suited to define any particular character) are, as Eliot's discussion of Dorothea and St. Theresa points out, historical. For Dorothea, Maggie Tulliver, or Savonarola, the times do not remain silent, denying them any possible fate. Instead each is tempted with a simulation, an approximation of what each needs to reach definition. It is the act of succumbing to the simulation that obscures them completely. Casaubon is that simulation for Dorothea, the life of the gypsies and the romance with Stephen are the equivalent for Maggie, and for Savonarola it is political life. It is as if only the gold had been offered Marner, so that his affection had never distinguished itself from avarice because the false object prevented the clarity.

More interesting than those impulses a society starves are those it distorts beyond recognition. Baudelaire spoke of the dandy as an unemployed Hercules, a potential hero whose world imposed no labors, invented no appropriate ordeals. For Nietzsche the criminal is often a misplaced artist, and clearly, in *Romola*, the obscurity of Savonarola, the moral anomalies of his crusade and character, are accounted for by the corruption of religious impulse by the political medium in which it was forced to register. Plunged in an alien

Making Up Society

medium for the self, characters like Savonarola and Maggie are forced to swim in air. Improvising or distorting, accepting the caricatures of their impulses—as the gold is the caricature of Marner's, Casaubon of Dorothea's, Stephen Guest of Maggie's—they remain puzzles in the absence of a social reality adequate to the discriminations of their moral lives.

Index